Coast Lines Key Ancestors:
M Langlands & Sons

by

Nick Robins and Colin Tucker

FOREWORD

When I had the privilege of writing *The Kingdom of MacBrayne* with Dr Nick Robins in 2005-6, I became more than familiar with the name of M Langlands & Sons. Until then, I had scarcely noticed the company name. Langlands' ships were an integral part of the Liverpool-Glasgow trade of the nineteenth and early twentieth centuries. As I later learned, the company had been largely erased from popular memory by the passage of time, amalgamations (especially that with Coast Lines), and the increasing dominance of the larger or more immediate companies (such as David MacBrayne Ltd).

Having become aware of Langlands, thanks largely to Dr Robins, I began to notice their robustly-belted ships with their distinctive funnels, frequently in Oban, which was regarded as the Mecca of MacBrayne's. Their cleverly adaptable vessels, such as the **Princess Maud**, catered deftly for cargo, including cattle, or tourists intent on seeing the wonders of the Scottish coastline. 'Cattle class' on Langlands was not to be sniffed at!

I then discovered that Langlands was not merely a summer ornament in the West Highlands. It was also a company which could be considered as a potential operator of services, should David MacBrayne prove unwilling or unable to satisfy local wishes. It could provide back-up and replacement vessels for voyages as far west as St Kilda, the indisputable domain of Martin Orme and Captain John McCallum, founders of the amalgamated company known from 1929 as McCallum, Orme & Company, with its famous steamships, **Dunara Castle** and **Hebrides**.

Stornoway too was on the Langlands itinerary, and indeed one Langlands vessel was interchanged with the Stornoway Shipping Company. It is therefore singularly appropriate that, on this occasion, Nick Robins' co-author should be Colin Tucker, author of the splendid volume, *Steamers to Stornoway*. With Colin Tucker's particular interest in Hebridean services, and Nick Robins' unrivalled ability to set shipping companies in the context of 'the big picture', this is a book which illumines the life and times of an important operator whose achievements ought not to be forgotten.

From Leith to Oban, from Glasgow to Liverpool, and many stops in between, Langlands was a 'round-Britain' company, often running coastal liners 'in conference' with the biggest and the best.

I am delighted that this book has been written. I hoped that the elusive 'somebody' would write it, and two of our finest shipping historians – no mere 'somebodies'! – have done so. We stand greatly in their debt.

Another gap in our knowledge of British shipping services has been closed, with detailed information, broad contextualising, and a wealth of illustrations, brought together by Bernard McCall with characteristic precision and flair for the creation of an attractive volume.

Donald E Meek
Tiree and Falkirk
June, 2015

Published by Bernard McCall, 400 Nore Road, Portishead, Bristol, BS20 8EZ, England.
Telephone/fax: +44 (0)1275 846178 Email: bernard@coastalshipping.co.uk Web: www.coastalshipping.co.uk
All distribution enquiries should be addressed to the publisher.

Printed by Gomer Press Ltd, Llandysul Enterprise Park, Llandysul, Ceredigion, SA44 4JL.
Telephone: +44 (0)1559 362371 Fax: +44 (0)1559 363758 Web: www.gomer.co.uk

ISBN: 978-1-902953-71-7

FRONT COVER: The **Princess Irma** (1915).

(from a contemporary oil painting by A J Jansen)

BACK COVER: Langlands ephemera.

FRONTISPIECE: The first **Princess Royal** (1841).

(from an oil painting by contemporary artist J Beckett & reproduced with permission from the Steamship Historical Society of America, Posner Maritime Collection)

Coast Lines Key Ancestors: M Langlands & Sons

CONTENTS

PREFACE

A critical early acquisition by Alfred Read's newly-formed Coast Lines was M Langlands & Sons. Langlands gave Read the all-important access to the North Sea ports with its Liverpool to Leith and round-Britain services. It also empowered Coast Lines to run the famous summer season 'Langlands Yachting Cruises' to the Western Isles under its own name.

The Glasgow & Liverpool Royal Steam Packet Company was formed in 1839 to run crack iron-hulled steam paddle ships between its namesake ports. In due course the managing owners became M Langlands & Sons of Glasgow and Liverpool. The Langlands family originally came from Campbeltown. The family was close knit and was soon equally at home in Kelvinside and later also in Lancashire and Cheshire. The Langlands family championed the round-Scotland service from Liverpool to Dundee and Leith and subsequently the round-Britain service, in both cases offering passenger berths once the services were sufficiently established. Langlands is best remembered for the yachting cruises it operated in the Edwardian period offering value for money holidays to the west coast of Scotland from both Liverpool and Ardrossan, with ships such as the **Princess Alberta** and **Princess Royal** operating dedicated cruises. The company lost all but two of its major passenger units in the Great War and was taken over by Coast Lines in 1919, having operated in the highly competitive coastal shipping trades for 80 years.

The history of M Langlands & Sons has not previously been told, although anecdotal material has been published and republished, some of it incorrect. Virtually no company records survive; those that were deposited with Coast Lines were stored in a damp warehouse in Liverpool for many decades and eventually, soggy and beyond recovery, they were destroyed. The story has only now been possible to unravel using the British Newspaper Archive at the British Library which can be searched digitally. Numerous other sources, official and unofficial, published and unpublished, have also been consulted to reveal the story of the Langlands family's dedication to its various commercial ventures which included three transatlantic forays as well as its coasting interests. Langlands should be remembered for the various services it developed, each of which contributed to wealth creation in both Scotland and England. It was also a key component of the newly-formed Coast Lines, despite quickly losing its identity in favour of corporate Coast Lines branding.

The authors are grateful to the staff of a number of libraries and archives for helping with enquiries about M Langlands & Sons. In particular we are grateful to Linda Gowans for meticulously checking the manuscript for inconsistencies, errors as well as correcting poor use of English. Linda was also invaluable in uncovering the Langlands family history. We are also extremely grateful to Ian Ramsay, naval architect and marine engineer, for providing all-important technical edits to the manuscript. Both these editors have greatly added to the overall sense and readability of the book. We are also most grateful to Bernard McCall and his team at Portishead for yet again delivering a beautifully produced high quality book.

Nick Robins, Crowmarsh, Oxfordshire
and
Colin Tucker, Stornoway, Isle of Lewis

June 2015

CHAPTER 1

STEAM PACKETS BETWEEN THE CLYDE AND MERSEY

In the closing years of the eighteenth century, coastal shipping was strengthening its position as if in preparation for the changes, greater than it had ever known, which were to confront it in the new century. Prosperous though the industry was, ownership was vested in innumerable small units. Captains ran their own vessels, a merchant might possess half a dozen, many were chartered and fitted out for single voyages.

(From an article by Dr Ernest Reader, Publicity Officer for Coast Lines, first published in *Sea Breezes*, February 1949)

The Liverpool trade out of the Clyde had become very important by 1810. It was maintained summer and winter by fourteen small, but fast, brigantines and schooners known as 'rantapikes' literally meaning 'young rakish girls'. These halcyon days of the rantapikes were soon going to be dented by the sea-going wooden paddle steamer, at first only in the summer months but as engines and hulls became larger so competition from steam would extend all year round.

Glasgow and its harbour from an engraving produced in 1802.

(*Illustrated London News*)

The introduction of steamships on the west coast, beyond the confines of the Clyde estuary, was not long in taking place after the **Comet** first sailed down the river in 1812. Probably the first steamship to sail between Glasgow and Liverpool was the **Elizabeth**, owned by Colin Watson, which arrived at Liverpool from the Clyde in July 1815 to provide a ferry service on the Mersey. She was the second steamship to be built on the Clyde, having been constructed by John Wood, of Port Glasgow, the builder of the **Comet**. She was a 40 ton steam paddle ship, 57 feet in length and 12 feet breadth. A contemporary description tells of her having two cabins, one either end of the engine-house, furnished to a much higher standard than the **Comet**. The aft cabin of the **Elizabeth**, measuring 21 feet in length and about 10 feet in breadth, was carpeted, had seats all round, while a maroon sofa occupied one end. On each side were six sliding windows, each adorned with a maroon curtain with tasselled fringes, velvet cornices and gold ornamentation. Above the sofa was a large mirror, on either side of which were 'book-shelves for the amusement and edification of those who may avail themselves during the passage'. Other amusements, not specified, were also to be found on board. The smaller cabin was less luxuriously furnished, but was said to be a 'very comfortable place either on a cold day or a warm one,' having a lofty ceiling and the same type of windows as the larger cabin.

At the end of June 1815 'a vessel, worked by steam, on her passage from Greenock to Liverpool, came to anchor in Ramsey Bay'. This was the **Henry Bell**, named after the owner of the **Comet**. The **Henry Bell** eventually plied between Liverpool and Runcorn. On 7 May 1816, it was reported that 'great curiosity was exhibited at Douglas by the arrival at Douglas of the steam packet **Greenock** on the passage to Liverpool'. She sailed on a pleasure trip to Laxey, when she 'moved by apparent enchantment'. After the pleasure trip 'this curiously constructed vessel proceeded to Liverpool'.

It was really due to David Napier that a regular service between Glasgow and Liverpool was initiated. From the commencement of steam navigation in Great Britain in 1812, no great advance appears to have been made until the year 1818. The notion that hulls of sufficient size and strength could be made to carry the heavy and powerful machinery required to propel them safely and in all seasons through stormy seas was still regarded as visionary. Extending steam power to deep-sea navigation was reckoned a problem of difficulty and danger when Napier entered on the construction and improvement of steam navigation. In 1816, Napier fitted his first engine, of twenty horsepower, into the little steamer **Marion**; the following year he provided engines for two cargo boats, and then set his sights on sea-going traffic.

In 1818, Napier built a steamer, called **Rob Roy**, which he successfully sailed from Glasgow to Dublin, a notable 'deep-sea' voyage by a British steamship (American John Stevens had steamed the **Phoenix** from New York to Philadelphia in strong winds as early as 1808). In spite of encountering a gale from the south-west, the **Rob Roy** performed the voyage out and home successfully. Before the ship departed, Mr Charles MacIntosh, the celebrated chemist and inventor of waterproof cloth, stated that they 'should all be drowned'. Napier afterwards placed the **Rob Roy** on the station between Glasgow and Belfast, and commenced to build other steamers to run between various ports, including Greenock to Liverpool. His efforts, although on a relatively small scale, were sufficient to inspire confidence among commercial men, and led to the introduction and operation of a number of deep-sea steamships. In these further ventures Mr Napier appears to have borne a large share of the financial responsibility. In 1841, John Scott Russell wrote in his paper *Steam and Steam Navigation* that until about 1830 David Napier 'effected more for the improvement of steam navigation than any other man'.

David Napier established the earliest steamship company on the Glasgow to Liverpool route in 1819. Napier persuaded Provost Mills, a banker in Dennistoun, and other leading Glasgow citizens, to put steamers on for Liverpool. James Little was agent in Greenock, James Hamilton in Glasgow and John Richardson in Liverpool. Their first steamer was the **Robert Bruce**, built by John Scott & Sons in 1819. She measured 90 feet by 18 feet, had a tonnage of 155, and was powered by a two-cylinder engine of 60 horsepower. It was stated that, 'The passage between Greenock and Liverpool was accomplished in twenty-eight hours, an expedition that surpassed the London Mail'. The **Robert Bruce** plied between Liverpool, Douglas, Portpatrick and Greenock, but, like all her successors up to 1821, she operated only during the summer months. The Parliamentary Report of 1822 on Steam Navigation describes the conditions on the vessel:

I was exposed to a violent storm in the **Robert Bruce***, and was surprised at the ease with which she wrought in a very heavy sea, and the much less motion she had than a sailing vessel would have had in similar circumstances. Contrary to my expectation her decks were not inundated, we could walk tolerably on them, and even books in open shelves were not displaced, circumstances which also astonished Captain Scoresby junior who accompanied me. In the worst of the gale we made nearly half a mile per hour against a heavy head-sea and a violent gale at west, in approaching the Isle of Man from Liverpool.*

The **Robert Bruce** unfortunately did not have a long career, for on 28 August 1821, the wooden paddle steamer, with 38 passengers and crew on board, caught fire off Great Orme's Head and was scuttled. After passing the Great Orme's Head on passage for Dublin, the packet ship caught fire because the boilers were not properly attended, being described as 'from neglect in letting water out of the boiler'. Captain Carlyle chose to head for Cemaes Bay on Anglesey and scuttled her to put out the fire. Although much of the cabin and deck was burnt, it was hoped to salvage the ship. The passengers (16 cabin and 8 steerage) and 14 crew were all safe and much of the baggage was recovered. A letter written to the *Liverpool Mercury* suggested that, to avoid such disasters, steamships should be fitted with fire extinguishers.

The second steamer on the seasonal Glasgow to Liverpool route was the **Superb** (1820) – copied from an original painting at one time owned by David Dehane Napier.

In 1820 the **Superb** was built as consort to the **Robert Bruce**. Another product of John Scott & Sons, her dimensions were 120 feet by 20 feet, 246 tons, with two side-lever engines of 72 horsepower. She was the largest steamer on the Liverpool trade, and described in the *Steam Boat Companion* of 1820 as the 'finest, largest and most powerful steam vessel in Britain'. She was also reported to have had the first copper boiler ever put into a steamer. Her original owners were James Little, David Napier and others, although in 1824 she was listed as being owned by John Rowth, London, and James Tasker, Greenock. Later that year she was sold to Amministrazione Privilegiata dei Pacchetti a Vapore del Regno delle Due Sicilie (Pierre Andriel), Naples, although she remained under British registry until 1836. Under the name **Real Ferdinando**, she operated the first successful service between Naples and Messina in Sicily.

A third steamer was added in 1821. This was the *Majestic*, built by John Scott & Sons. Her dimensions were 135 feet by 22 feet 8 inches, 350 tons, powered by two-cylinder engines, 100 horsepower, and equipped with a copper boiler. She was reputed to have repeatedly made the voyage between Liverpool and Glasgow in twenty-two hours.

A handbill, issued by James Little, the agent in Greenock, shows a picture of the *Majestic* with three fully-rigged masts, a long slender funnel and a paddle-box, well forward, bearing the Royal Arms. The same handbill states that the *Majestic*, Captain Oman, and the *City of Glasgow*, Captain Carlyle, sail from Greenock and Liverpool every Monday, Wednesday, and Friday, 'calling off Port Patrick and at Douglas, Isle of Man, both in going and returning from Liverpool', and that 'the passage between Greenock and Liverpool is generally made within twenty-five hours'.

The *Majestic* (1921) was commissioned as a replacement for the *Robert Bruce* (1819) which was destroyed by fire in 1821.

These steamers took passengers only, with a cabin fare, with food, of 31/6 (31 shillings and 6 pence or in today's money £1.57), while steerage cost 10/- (50p). The ships did not ply further up the Clyde than Greenock because of the shallowness of the river and because of the lack of suitable berthing facilities at Glasgow. Around the start of the nineteenth century there was only about 5 feet of water at high tide and the larger ships had to offload their cargoes at Greenock and Port Glasgow to be ferried up to Glasgow in smaller vessels.

One of the steamers used for this purpose was the *Post Boy*, built by William Denny at Dumbarton in 1820. She was 74 feet long by 13 feet breadth, with a tonnage of 54 and powered by a side-lever engine of 24 horsepower built by David Napier. She had a clipper bow and figurehead, high square stern, and tall black funnel. She was significant in the development of steamships in two ways. Experiments with surface condensation were carried out in this vessel, while of greater importance in connection with the Liverpool service was the fact that she was constructed with a draught of only three feet. This enabled her to be independent of tidal conditions on the

The river steamer *Post Boy* (1820) from a sketch showing her arrival at Greenock.

(The Glasgow Looking Glass, Graham Lappin collection)

upper reaches of the river. She sailed from Glasgow every morning at 6 o'clock, taking four hours to reach Greenock where passengers connected with the Liverpool steamers.

The *City of Glasgow* was commissioned in 1822, her builder's certificate being dated 23 May 1822 and her first registration at Greenock dated 28 May 1822. She was another product of John Scott & Sons. The Greenock register shows that she was a single decked, three-masted vessel of 123 feet 6 inches by 22 feet by 12 feet 6 inches. Tonnage was given as 191 26/94ths. She was thus slightly smaller than the *Majestic* and was fitted with a figurehead of a woman. The *City of Glasgow* was reputed to be the finest steamer built at the time, and was arranged like the *Majestic*, the pair being considered the most important vessels in the Glasgow to Liverpool trade at that time.

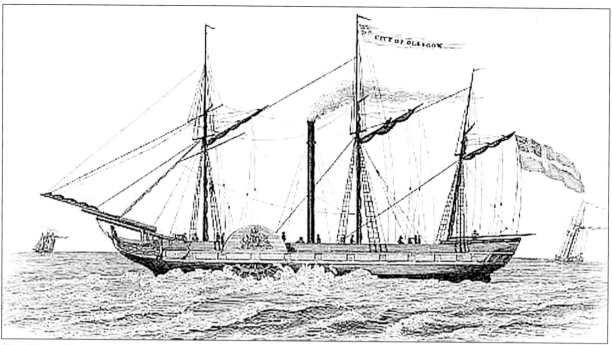

The *City of Glasgow* (1822) 'the finest steamer built at the time'.

In 1824 the ownership of the *City of Glasgow* was vested in the Glasgow & Liverpool Steam Packet Company of Glasgow. Like all the ships making the voyage between the Clyde and the Mersey, the *City of Glasgow* made occasional calls at Douglas; in 1825 she went on the rocks while entering Douglas harbour, but she was later refloated and repaired. In 1832 she was sold to the City of Glasgow Steam Packet Company and fitted for carrying goods as well as passengers. In 1836, after receiving new boilers, she was put on the Hull to London trade in the ownership of the British & Foreign Steam Navigation Company, London. She was finally scrapped in 1855 after a long and successful career under several owners.

ABOVE: City of Glasgow Steam Packet Company plate with Minton's lace border, circa 1831.

RIGHT: 1926 advertisement for the *Majestic* (1821) and *City of Glasgow* (1822).

There would appear to be some contradiction in how successful these first services were. David Dehane Napier wrote in *David Napier - Engineer - 1790 -1869, An Autobiographical Sketch with Notes*:

The shipping companies with the building up of which Napier was identified appear to have met with much success. His vessels attracted attention as being the largest and fastest of their time; and within a comparatively short period his reputation as a leading authority in steamship affairs had become well established.

An official report dated 1822 refers to 'Mr Napier, Engineer, Glasgow, whose skill in the construction of steamboats is allowed to be great.

Glasgow and Liverpool Steam Packet advert for 1834.

He has also been enterprising and successful, having established the Steam Packets between Glasgow, Greenock and Liverpool'. It was also stated at the time that the steamships constructed for David Napier 'were all vessels of a much stronger hull, a better form, and more correct proportion of parts than any others; and in these three years from 1818, the art of steam navigation had received in the Clyde an extension and perfection that rendered it an object of great national importance'. This was also reflected in the development of the Glasgow to Liverpool service. 'At the same time that Mr Napier was thus engaged in conferring on the public the benefits of the Post Office steam packet system, he also established the first line of commercial steamships on a station, which, ever since that time, has continued to be occupied by the finest, most powerful, expert and fastest steam packets in Europe – the station between Liverpool, Greenock and Glasgow'.

A further accolade appeared in Chapter Eight of the 1822 Parliamentary Report on Steam Navigation stating that '**Superb** and **Majestic** on the Greenock and Liverpool passage, will be found to be the first strong and powerful boats which were built, and they were the first that completely succeeded'. In May 1822 Napier himself wrote in a letter to Sir Henry Parnell, MP:

*I beg leave to state that I was the first that successfully established steam packets in the open sea... they are at present plying from Glasgow to Greenock and Liverpool... The **Superb** is now plying the third year between Greenock and Liverpool, and not a single article of her machinery has ever given way, although she has been out in the worst of weather; it would tire your patience enumerating the whole, several others being similarly circumstanced. I can say with certainty that the **Superb** and **Majestic**, presently plying between Greenock and Liverpool, are far superior in every respect to the **Sovereign** and **Meteor**, and will out-sail them in any kind of weather; as a proof of this, the **Sovereign** was at Liverpool the other day and sailed along with the **Superb**, when the latter out-sailed the former fully one mile in five.*

A completely opposite point of view was expressed in an account entitled, '*James Burns 1789 - 1871. The Early History of The Burns' Shipping Companies*', in *Memoirs and Portraits of One Hundred Glasgow Men* (1886):

This first Liverpool Company was a dead failure, and was given up, leaving the Manchester Company [the Huskisson Company] alone in the field. This company was established in 1823. It owned four ships; the **William Huskisson**, **Henry Bell**, **James Watt** *and* **Solway**. *Of the four, only the first was Clyde built, by J Scott & Sons, and engined by Scott, Sinclair & Company, both of Greenock. She was sold in 1833 to an unknown purchaser, and finally foundered in January 1840 on passage between Liverpool and Dublin. The other three were respectively built by Wilson of Liverpool, Sherriff & Company of Liverpool, and Grayson, Dawson, & Company of Holyhead, and engined by Fawcett & Company of Liverpool, Boulton & Watt, and Fawcett & Company. They carried both passengers and goods, and sailed from Greenock, to which passengers and the 'parcel-bag' were sent down on the day of sailing by river steamer, and goods the night before by lighter. They called at Port Patrick and the Isle of Man.*

A year before this, in 1822, a regular service was initiated between Liverpool and the Clyde via the Isle of Man by the Saint George Steam Packet Company, using two steam packets, the **Saint Patrick** and **Saint George**. The *Manks Advertiser* (sic) stated in May 1822, the steamer **Saint George**, of the St George Steam Packet Company, 27 Water Street, Liverpool, began to run in opposition to the **Superb** and the other vessels of James Little's Line. Their best steamer, the **Saint George**, is described 'as so fine a Vessel, so majestically beautiful in motion, so grand in her noble appearance, that she must afford additional gratifications (sic) to the gay concourse which are wont to crowd our Pier on the arrival of these beautiful aquatic accommodations'.

The number of steamships sailing between Liverpool and the Clyde gradually increased. In 1828 the minute books of the Port Glasgow Chamber of Commerce list five: the **Enterprise**, **William Huskisson**, **Henry Bell**, **James Watt** and **Solway**. Fowler's Directory of Renfrewshire later shows an increase to ten vessels, with the City of Glasgow Steam Packet Company (Liverpool agent, David McIver of Water Street) and the Glasgow and Liverpool Steam Packet Company (Liverpool agent, Matthie and Martin of 3 Drury Lane) each offering three sailings per week:

> **Ailsa Craig** (170 tons, 17 crew), Capt. Robert Crawford, 3 sailings per week
> **City of Glasgow** (183 tons, 14 crew), Capt. R Ewing, Friday sailing
> **Clyde** (195 tons, 20 crew), Capt. Thomas Wylie, 3 sailings per week
> **Eagle** (293 tons, 20 crew), Capt. R Crawford, 3 sailings per week
> **Glasgow** (214 tons, 20 crew), Capt. Alex M'Leod, Friday sailing
> **John Wood** (180 tons, 16 crew), Capt. Colin Ferguson, Saturday sailing
> **Liverpool** (200 tons, 20 crew), Capt. R Hepburn
> **Manchester** (219 tons, 20 crew), Capt. James M'Kellar, 3 sailings per week
> **Vulcan** (214 tons, 6 crew), Capt. John Boyd, Tuesday sailing
> **Unicorn** (300 tons, 20 crew), Capt. Hugh Main, 3 sailings per week.

Steam navigation had clearly come to dominate over the wind-powered schooners and rantapikes as hulls could now be built large enough to withstand the winter weather. Larger hulls meant more powerful engines and boilers with greater capacity to generate steam at higher pressures and larger volumes, but all this was yet to come. Fraser and Marer (1996) reported on the development of steam navigation between Liverpool and Glasgow:

Steamers soon gained status on the coast. The early ones lacked power, and were scarcely seaworthy. By the 1840s, they were taken on the ocean, or at least on the Irish Sea. In 1850-1851, 728,965 tons of Scottish steam trade entries were supplemented by 175,195 in the Irish trade and 101,063 in the English. By then Glasgow owned 81 steamers grossing 29,371 tons, and while this was only a sixth of the vessels registered in Glasgow and a fifth of their tonnage, it was 50% of the entire Scottish steam fleet and 58% of its tonnage. Their owning companies were chiefly organised and directed by men already experienced as shipping agents in the coasting sail trade, and most were developed as liner operations. The New Clyde Shipping Company, originating as its name suggests in the river trade, and running steamers there and to Liverpool, had David McIver as agents in Liverpool and A M Burrell in Glasgow; the Glasgow and Liverpool Steam Shipping Company had James and George Burns and James Martin of Glasgow and Thomas Martin of Liverpool as Trustees; the Glasgow & Liverpool Royal Steam Packet Company had as a Trustee John Tassie, a former manager of the New Clyde Shipping Company. These ships, it must be admitted, had as their first purpose, the support of the all-important connection between Glasgow and Lancashire, rather than the servicing of indirect foreign trade - between a consort of manufacturing districts which, it was said in 1847 'take their lead in the progress of civilization...' Manchester and Glasgow are the creations of machinery, and the centres of large districts which have grown great by the development of their means.

The development of railways must also be considered when looking at the growth of the Liverpool-Glasgow trade. Before their coming there were three ways of travelling direct from Glasgow to London. Those who could afford the cost of £40 could travel by post-chaise. For the rest there was the London Mail, which at the beginning of the century took sixty-three hours and was anything but pleasant. It was stated that 'stiff and sore were the inside passengers, and the unfortunates on the top had often to be lifted down half dead, sometimes caught their death outright'. The expense, including guards and coachmen, and not including two days' living, was about £10 inside and £7/10/- outside.

The Liverpool steamers immediately enhanced matters, and once a continuous railway was established from Liverpool to London, journey times, conditions of travel and costs all improved significantly. Growth in goods traffic was also accelerated by the Liverpool steamers.

David Napier's line did not carry goods, but the Manchester Company, which was established in 1823, advertised that goods by their steamers might reach London in four days 'by Mr Bretherton's coaches'.

Thus the stage was set for Messrs Langlands to enter the trade, a trade which they would dominate for the next 80 years, and their successor Coast Lines well into the twentieth century.

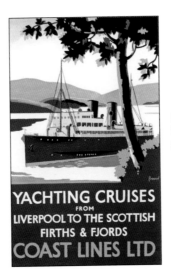

Cruise programme brochure for 1937 issued by Langlands successor Coast Lines.

From John Kennedy, *The History of Steam Navigation*, 1903

In the autumn of 1826 the New Clyde Shipping Company advertised that their steam packet **Enterprise** (Captain McFarlane) would sail weekly between Liverpool and Glasgow. She was a very small steamer, being only 210 tons burthen, and the owners announced that, in consequence of her light draught, she would proceed direct to Glasgow, and not transfer her passengers to river steamers at Greenock, as the larger steamers had to do. The first agents of the company were Messrs McNair & Brebner, 33 Water Street, but in January 1829 the agency was transferred to Mr David MacIver, 18 Water Street. A few months later the Glasgow and Liverpool Shipping Company was formed, and in 1831 that company acquired the Mersey and Clyde Steam Navigation Company's steam packets **Henry Bell**, **James Watt** and **William Huskisson**, as well as the **Enterprise**. The New Clyde Shipping Company ceased operations and Mr MacIver formed a new steamship line of his own, which he called the City of Glasgow Steam Packet Company. The **City of Glasgow** sailed on the first voyage from Liverpool on 25 April 1831.

Three other steamers were quickly added to the fleet, the **Solway**, **Vulcan**, and **John Wood**, the latter steamer being named after a celebrated shipbuilder at Port Glasgow. In 1835 the **City of Glasgow** (second) was put on the station, and the sailings were increased to three per week from each port. Mr Charles MacIver joined his brother this year, and the style of the firm was changed to D MacIver & Company.

In 1837 the celebrated steamship **Commodore** was built, followed in 1840 by her equally famous sistership, **Admiral**. All the steamers engaged in the Liverpool and Glasgow trade prior to 1839 were built of wood, but in that year a new steamship company entered into competition with the existing companies, and placed the **Royal Sovereign**, an iron steamer, on the station. The immediate result was a heavy drop in passenger and freight rates. Steerage passengers were carried for 1 shilling each, and boxes and bale goods for 1 penny per foot measurement. The following year [1840] a mail steamship service between Liverpool, Canada and America was established, the respective agents of the company being D & C MacIver, Liverpool; J & G Burns, Glasgow; and Samuel Cunard, Halifax. This service, which afterwards acquired a world wide reputation as the Cunard Line, was modestly inaugurated by the despatch of the Liverpool and Glasgow steam packet **Unicorn** (Captain Douglas). This vessel [the real pioneer of the Cunard Line] sailed from Liverpool for Halifax and Boston on Saturday morning, 16 May 1840. After she completed her outward voyage, she continued to ply between Pictou and Quebec in connection between the British and North American Royal Mail steamers.

CHAPTER 2

THE ROYAL LINE

In the 1820s the forerunners to the Langlands family became shipowners with shareholdings in five rantapikes. They were the **Mersey**, named after her home port, the **Onyx**, **Topaz**, **Sapphire** and **Garnet** and they were between 178 and 150 tons burthen. They maintained three sailings a week from both Greenock and Liverpool and it is reported that, with a favourable wind, voyages south could be made in as little as 13$\frac{1}{2}$ hours. While originally the seasonally operated, smoky paddle steamer was little match for the sailing ships, the steamers gradually assumed dominance.

The year 1829 was cold with continuous frost throughout January. Summer brought little respite and was characterised by wet and cool weather which ran into a cold autumn. Over an inch of snow fell in early October in south-east England and 6 inches fell in London and parts of the south of England in late November. Northerly and easterly gales caused snow to drift, while at sea the high winds made ships run for shelter in the lee of the west coast while others were wrecked on the east coast.

There was ice on the Thames from late December to late January. Further north snow lay on the higher ground in

Typical outline of one of the Royal Line's Glasgow/Liverpool rantapikes.

Cumberland, Northumberland and the southern uplands of Scotland from October onwards. The stage coach routes were maintained for the carriage of the mails as best as possible. Eventually even the stage coaches had to give up, essentially cutting Scotland off from the south by any overland route for a period of about six weeks.

The Liverpool to Glasgow rantapikes were enjoying rich pickings, with passengers diverted to the sea journey along with parcel traffic that might otherwise have gone by stage coach. The wooden-hulled paddle steamers, of course, were snugly laid up for the winter.

LEFT: The wooden paddle steamer – 'Passing the Cloch, a pleasant breeze!'

ABOVE: Night time on the Liverpool steamer in the 1820s.

(both The Glasgow Looking Glass, Graham Lappin collection)

Meanwhile, the English mail started to pile up in Glasgow while mails bound for Scotland were gathered in store at Liverpool awaiting the thaw. It was at this stage that the enterprising agent for the **Mersey** and her fleet mates made an offer to Government to carry the mails by sea to and from Glasgow and Liverpool. The offer was gladly accepted and in return for saving the mail crisis the name Royal Line was granted to the sailing packet fleet. Permission was also given for them to adopt the royal crown over the crossed flags of the city arms of both Glasgow and Liverpool as the new houseflag of the Royal Line. The winters between 1834 and 1838 were also very cold and snow lay in southern Scotland for long periods while the Royal Line reaped rich dividends.

A new steamer company was initiated in 1838 when the **Fire King** was advertised in conjunction with the Glasgow and Ayrshire Railway to run between Ardrossan and Liverpool. This unsuccessful venture was initiated by Thomas Assheton Smith, of Tedworth, then well-known as a hunter and a great yachtsman, latterly taking to steam yachts. The **Fire King** was built by Robert Napier, although it is thought that her hull was constructed at Troon, possibly by R Thomson. She was based on the designs for Smith's yachts, of which he had rapidly had eight constructed, and was built on the 'fine hollow water lines' of his own design. She was considered to be the fastest vessel then afloat, reaching a speed of 13 knots. However, Assheton Smith 'discarded her like the rest' of his yachts. Napier then got Mr McCall of Daldowie, Chairman of the Ayrshire Railway Company, and his co-directors to buy her, in reality for the Railway, and sail her from Ardrossan to Liverpool. The venture was a failure, for she only lasted on the service for the months of October and November before being withdrawn.

It was John Tassie at the Royal Line who was instrumental in creating the Glasgow & Liverpool Royal Steam Packet Company which overnight was to become the brand leader on the Glasgow and Liverpool coastal service. Tassie understood the trade as trustee for the Royal Line rantapike service but he could also see that the longer-term future lay with the steamers. But he was a visionary and was well aware that the wooden-hulled paddle steamers offered by the existing packet companies on the route had little in terms of creature comforts nor any real guarantee of adhering to their timetable, particular during inclement weather. His vision was of luxuriously appointed ships offering a fast and reliable service for which passengers and shippers would be willing to pay a premium fare. He was also aware of the serious tidal limitations at Glasgow and sought a design which gave him a shallow draft even when loaded; this required the lighter construction of the iron hull, but only a very few iron-hulled commercial ships had then been commissioned.

John Tassie knew that others were keen to break into the premium trade between Liverpool and Glasgow. In the late 1830s David McIver had paid a deposit on a wooden-hulled paddle steamer, the **Enterprise**, to inaugurate his own service between the two ports. At the last moment John Burns of Glasgow, cash in hand, took the vessel from under McIver's nose, keen also to acquire tonnage suitable for the service. As it happens, the **Enterprise** was put on Irish duties from the Clyde under the Burns' houseflag. Burns and McIver, of course, went on to develop the North American Steam Packet Company, later rebranded as the Cunard Line.

The royal crown over the crossed flags of the city arms of both Glasgow and Liverpool later became the crest of the Glasgow & Liverpool Royal Steam Packet Company, here preserved on a silver plated fork circa 1870.

John Tassie approached John Burns in Glasgow and David McIver in Liverpool with his proposal to develop a service between Glasgow and Liverpool with crack, state-of-the-art, iron-hulled ships offering luxurious first class passenger accommodation. It was quite common in those days for an individual to invest in and to promote rival interests, so neither Burns nor McIver were dissuaded from investing in a new company that would inevitably compete with their own existing business interests. The two men championed Tassie's idea and quickly gave him their backing, both financially and in name, with two provisos. The first was that John Tassie with his detailed knowledge of the trade developed from the sailing packets should be appointed as manager of the new company and the second was that the company should incorporate the Royal Line's rantapikes and be given the name the Glasgow & Liverpool ROYAL Steam Packet Company.

With a large part of the necessary finance in place, the three men approached shipbuilders, David Tod and John MacGregor at Glasgow to join the partnership. Tod and MacGregor had by then built some fourteen iron-hulled paddlers and were at the forefront of innovation with both hull design and engine design. In 1837, Messrs Tod and MacGregor built and engined the iron-hulled **Rothesay Castle** of 180 tons, with engines of 90 horsepower, to ply between Glasgow and Rothesay. She was acclaimed as the fastest steamer on the Clyde. Tod & MacGregor saw the Tassie/Burns/McIver proposal as an opportunity to showcase their engineering skills and gladly guaranteed the outstanding resources to build two new steamers. The steamers were to be large enough to work year round and powerful enough to complete the voyage in just 16 hours. The first vessel, launched in February 1839 from Tod & MacGregor's yard at Mavisbank, was named **Royal Sovereign**.

The **Royal Sovereign** started in service on 2 March with little fanfare but with much speculation as to which was now the fastest ship on the Liverpool run. The main competition was the wooden-hulled steamers of the City of Glasgow Company, the **Commodore**, **City of Glasgow** and **Vulcan**, whose owner proudly proclaimed:

The public will please note that the above are wooden vessels, and attention is directed to this fact that no accident to passengers or property has ever happened to this company's vessels.

The new Glasgow & Liverpool company responded with the statement under the title 'Improved Steam Conveyance to Liverpool':

*The Glasgow & Liverpool Royal Steam Packet Company have made every possible arrangement for speed, and comfort, and safety on board vessels [the **Royal George**, although not yet launched was also mentioned], which being divided into five sections by iron partitions air and water tight, are thus secured against accident from fire or water. Their vessels proceed with passengers and goods direct to Glasgow, thereby avoiding the inconvenience to passengers of transshipment at Greenock into river boats and delay in delivery of goods.'*

At 11.00am on 2 March the **Royal Sovereign** left the Broomielaw under the command of Captain McArthur to find the City of Glasgow Company's **Commodore** departing Greenock for Liverpool. The *Glasgow Herald* reported on 8 March 1839:

*The **Commodore** and **Royal Sovereign**: ...that betwixt the above vessels on their way to Liverpool the **Commodore** gained 2 hours and 32 minutes on her opponent – having arrived on Sunday morning at Clarence Dock at 6.40am Liverpool time, while the **Royal Sovereign** reached her destination at 9.25am to which there fails to be added the seven minutes the **Commodore** was behind the **Royal Sovereign** in starting from Greenock. The weather was delightful and the water perfectly smooth all the way. The above is one of the quickest voyages ever performed betwixt the Clyde and the Mersey. A contemporary says 'It would be unfair to state that there was anything like such a difference in their rate of sailing. The fact seems to have been, that during the first half of the voyage the **Commodore** gained from 25 to 30 minutes on the **Royal Sovereign**, that both vessels then encountered a thick fog, and that by steering to the westward the **Commodore** got quit of the fog and resumed the proper channel in the course of half an hour, while the **Royal Sovereign**, by steering to the eastward, lost two hours in the mist. But even this circumstance still leaves the **Commodore** the victor by about half an hour's sailing.' These rival vessels left Liverpool on Tuesday at the same hour, on their return voyage for the Clyde. They kept neck and neck to the Point of Corsewall, but from that to Greenock, the **Commodore** beat the **Royal Sovereign** by 19 minutes, and the **Royal Sovereign** came direct up to the Broomielaw.*

The **Royal Sovereign** soon proved to be both reliable and a comfortable sea boat and quickly developed the admiration of the travelling public and shippers alike. She was rostered to leave Glasgow on Saturdays and Wednesdays returning from Liverpool on Mondays and Thursdays. The single saloon fare was the same as her rivals at 20/- plus 2/- steward's fee, second class with sleeping berth 15/- plus 1/- steward's fee, and steerage or deck class 7/-. Her consort, the **Royal George**, was delivered by Tod & MacGregor later in the year and it was her arrival on the service on 24 August so allowing up to four round trips per week that attracted the media attention. The *Dumfries Courier* found that ship at the Broomielaw prior to her maiden commercial voyage:

*The **Royal George** has been for some time afloat, and as her engine and other gearing are well nigh complete, she will leave the Broomielaw on an experimental trip in a week or so from the present date... When loaded with 100 tons of goods the draught will not exceed seven feet of water. With the exception of the deck bulwarks, paddle boxes, rosewood [a dark timber that grows in South America and which smells of roses when freshly cut] lining of the principal cabins, the entire framework of the beautiful ship described is composed of* sheet iron, three eighths of an inch in thickness, and strongly riveted inside by bars or fastenings, which take the form diagonal, the strongest of all. With a view to safety in the case of a sunken rock or lee shore, the extreme length from stem to stern is divided into five compartments, and the largest is not so much the hold, which can be dealt with as is most expedient, as the gap filled with a double engine, furnaces, cylinders, and the other appurtenances that manufacture the propelling power. Should a hole, therefore, be stove in the vessel's side, by collision with a rock or other antagonistic body, water can only rush into one compartment, to the extent of a foot or probably less, and so long as the others remain perfectly dry, sufficient buoyancy remains behind for the crew to apply the pump and repair the leak.

Perhaps the writer was a little over optimistic about the damage stability of the **Royal George**! Equally admiring, however, was the report in the *Liverpool Standard* which acclaimed the new ship on her first arrival at Liverpool:

The Glasgow iron steam ship **Royal George**: This beautiful vessel, which belongs to the Glasgow & Liverpool Royal Steam Packet Company, is now on her second trip between this port and that from which she sails; and as another, and a new and splendid specimen of what can be accomplished by our Scottish competitors in steam navigation, she has attracted much and deserved attention. She is the second iron steam ship produced by the same proprietary, the **Royal Sovereign**, placed on the station a few months ago, being the first, and also a crack, we may say a twin, vessel ...

The **Royal George** is of about 500 tons burthen. She is 150 feet in length; 200 feet from the figurehead to the taffrail; 22 feet 6 inches in beam, or 46 feet over the paddle boxes. Her engines are of 120 horsepower. The diameter of the cylinder is 61 inches, length of stroke 5 feet. The engines are beautiful, highly finished pieces of machinery, and were manufactured by Messrs Tod & MacGregor, Glasgow. The saloon, or principal cabin, is a very spacious and magnificent apartment. The entrance from the deck is exceedingly well contrived, there being a door and flight of steps on either side of the vestibule or 'companion', leading to the landing at the top of the main stairs, so that in stormy weather, the windward door may be closed. The 'architectural' visitor on descending, may anticipate the general style of the whole. The panelling of the staircase is finely painted in rosewood. The banisters are of polished brass, the rails of polished rosewood, and all bespeak the old English or Elizabethan, in its massiest [heaviest] and purest fashion. The folding doors leading to the saloon are of rosewood; admirable specimens of the massive gothic; the styles are finely moulded, and the panel are projected into the alto releivo beyond them. The dark colour of the rosewood is relieved by massy floriated gilt hinge work and other ornaments of the same material.

On entering the cabin, the visitor cannot fail to be struck with admiration. The apartment is about 40 feet in length, and about 22 feet in width, occupying the whole breadth of the vessel. It is lightened by three windows of plate glass on either side, by the stern windows, and by the square dome or deck lights. The style is massy gothic; and the whole of the woodwork, including the walls and the furniture, is of choice dark and variegated rosewood, as a substitute or rather an improvement upon oak. Between the side windows there are inserted gothic panels of frames, with raised mouldings and interior gilded frames, for the reception of pictures in papier maché, in proportion, but now fitted up with crimson drapery. The mouldings and other decorations, including the trusses that form knees or brackets on the top of the pilasters, between the windows and the panels, in the angle formed by each pilaster and the roof beam that rests upon it, are beautifully carved in open work and richly gilded. Some idea may be formed of the very liberal expenditure bestowed on this apartment, when we state that the gilding alone of one of these trusses cost six guineas and a half. They are of two patterns, one of each being placed alternately, and have a fine effect. The corning and beading is also gilded. Across the stern windows there is a fine transparency, a view of Windsor castle, with the royal residents and their visitants in the foreground.

Sofas or ottomans surround the apartment, divided by massy carved rosewood arms or elbows. These are of great width, and the backs reach to half the height of the cabin, forming a semi-circle at the stern. They are cushioned in embossed crimson velvet of a peculiarly rich and appropriate fabric. The tables are also of rosewood, standing on massy single gothic pillars, and so contrived that though there is space between, they may be elongated and form a 'festive board', all around the room, in the form of a horseshoe. The chairs are in corresponding gothic style, of the choicest description. They are all solid rosewood, with cushioned seat and backs corresponding with the sofas. They probably weigh little short of 50lbs and cost upward of five guineas each.

The roof is one of the most attractive portions of this beautiful saloon; between the beams it is decorated with tracery and graining and most elaborately carved in alto. At the entrance there are two state rooms, one on *each side, which narrow the saloon for a short distance, from the doorway. The architect has rendered this arrangement highly decorative. The roof formed between the two state rooms is of a semi-circular form. The door is in the centre, and on each side there is a sideboard of gothic design, richly carved in rosewood. Over these are mirrors, each of their perpendicular plates placed in concave position, with the segment formed by the wall where they are placed. The frames of these are of fine, open gilded carved work. The doors of the two state rooms leading from the saloon, face the stern, and have been much admired. In the upper panel of each there is a mirror with antique framework, surrounded and surmounted by gilded ornaments of exquisite design and execution. The two skylights are glazed with stained glass; each pane, twenty in all, containing a separate portrait of a British monarch, surrounded by rich gothic decorations. These were executed by Mr Cooper of Edinburgh, who has discovered a new and admirable process by which to stain glass...*

On the whole we should say that this cabin is the most costly and magnificent we have yet seen, and that the whole, as well as the vessel, her engines, [by Messrs Tod & MacGregor] and her general equipments, are an honour to her proprietors, to the port from which she sails; indeed to the country to which she belongs.

The ladies' and gentlemans' state rooms are fitted up on a scale of corresponding elegance and comfort; but we have not room on this occasion, to notice them in detail.

*The **Royal George**, Captain Cook, is of a beautiful model. She is well put together [being 'as strong as iron can make her'] that no vibration is felt by the motion of her engines; and she has already proved herself the fastest boat on a station, second to none, in the beauty and swiftness of its steamers.*

The Glasgow & Liverpool Royal Steam Packet Company was here to stay. The Ardrossan Shipping Company had started running a service between Ardrossan and Liverpool with a rail connection to Glasgow in 1838, but this did not significantly impact the Glasgow to Liverpool services. In fact the **Royal George** returned to Glasgow on her maiden return voyage at 11.00am on 27 August having called at Ardrossan to discharge passengers and goods. Once the **Royal George** was in service, the Ardrossan company withdrew from the Liverpool route to focus on a new service to Belfast. In September, the **Royal Sovereign** and **Royal George** were advertised to make three departures from both Glasgow and Liverpool, on Tuesdays, Thursdays and Saturdays.

John Tassie appointed Mr Mathew Langlands as his Glasgow agent. Mr Langlands took up his post at 16 St Enoch Square, Glasgow, in late October 1839, while the service of James Brebner of 20 Water Street was retained as agent at Liverpool. Langlands was no newcomer to the scene and his reputation for aggressive but fair-handed business was well known both to John Tassie and to Messrs David Tod and John MacGregor. In 1836 Langlands had been appointed agent to the Glasgow & Stranraer Steam Packet Company. Tod & MacGregor had built the engine for the first **Maid of Galloway** that year and, as a result, became part-owners of the vessel under the title of the New Shipping Company, Stranraer. A close liaison developed between Mathew Langlands and the engine builder and, in due course, also shipbuilder, Tod & MacGregor. Indeed, at a later stage David Tod's nephew and namesake was appointed engineer for the Stranraer company and later still he became a trustee of the company. Mathew Langlands' link with Tod and MacGregor was to stand him in good stead for the next thirty years.

After only a few weeks of operating the two-ship service, the Glasgow & Liverpool Royal Steam Packet Company entered a vigorous price war with its competitors. On 20 September the passenger fares were reduced by half to saloon 10/-, second class with sleeping berth 5/- and deck class 2/6. Cargo in bales and boxes was carried for just 2d per cubic foot. By 22 November the advertised fares were halved again to 5/- saloon, 2/6 second class and 1/- deck class. Boxes and bales came down to 1d per cubic foot, and even a ton of cotton could be carried for as little as 10/-. The Burns interests were self-competing but the J Martin and J & G Burns sponsored Glasgow and Liverpool Steam Shipping Company service between its two namesake ports was then second fiddle to Burns' Irish services, although it had just put two new wooden ships on the run, the **Actæon** in 1838 and the **Achilles** in October 1839, while what later became G & J Burns focussed on the Irish and West Highlands routes. The City of Glasgow Company (Thomson & McConnell) and Burns both brought their fares down to match the Royal Steam Packet. However, the three companies eventually developed an informal sharing arrangement of the developing trade. To make it easy for the public, a set departure time, independent of tides, at 3.00pm was announced for Glasgow departures in November, although at Liverpool it was two hours before the high tide.

In September John Tassie and Hugh Tassie announced in the *Glasgow Herald* sailing advertisements:

*The company, in starting their new ship, the **Royal George**, have much pleasure in stating, that every person who has sailed in the **Royal Sovereign** bears the strongest testimony to the advantage from which iron vessels possess over wooden vessels, by being altogether free from the unpleasant effects of heat and bilge water, and considerably less liable to sickness.*

*The **Royal Sovereign** has now plied 25,000 miles, loading and discharging at the ports of Glasgow and Liverpool four times per week and never in one instance disappointed the public in her hour of sailing as advertised.*

The Interim Manager of the Glasgow & Liverpool Royal Steam Packet Company, Hugh Tassie, succeeded John Tassie in October. Within the month Mathew Langlands had risen from just Company Agent to Company Manager. He was the beneficiary of John Tassie being taken ill and Hugh Tassie, as Interim Manager, lacking the flair and business acumen of his agent. Langlands' first aggressive business ploy was to place the **Royal Sovereign** onto the Glasgow to Belfast run in order to 'test the water' with an iron-hulled paddler against the wooden-hulled vessels of Thomson & McConnell. David McNeill wrote in *Irish Passenger Steamships, Volume 1*:

*The Belfast-Glasgow trade was controlled by a monopoly shared by two companies, Thompson & McConnell, who worked in close cooperation with one another from the mid-30s until 1851. On 10 December 1839 the 'establishment' received a shortlived, but upsetting, challenge from Langlands' **Royal Sovereign** ... She ran twice a week and offered three classes of accommodation, at 7/-, 4/- and 1/-. Hitherto the fares had been 20/-, plus 2/- stewards' fee, for cabin class, and 3/- steerage.*

*The challenge was immediately taken up by the 'establishment' who offered the same cheap fares as those on the **Royal Sovereign**. Langlands reduced their steerage fare to 6d but made no reduction in the prices charged for superior accommodation; again the 'establishment' followed suit. The competition also extended to cargo: freights were reduced until a gallon of whiskey could be sent across the channel for a halfpenny.*

The **Royal Sovereign** completed five return voyages to Belfast in December leaving Glasgow on Mondays and Fridays. After just one week the fares were reduced to 5/- saloon, 3/6d second class and deck class 6d. The Belfast agent was Robert Henderson of Donegal Quay. The **Royal Sovereign** was advertised to maintain the service throughout January 1940, but in the event she stood down on Thursday 16 January having made few friends. The incursion into the Irish trade was not continued and the **Royal Sovereign** returned to her original route. In the meantime the **Royal George** had maintained Saturday, Tuesday and Thursday sailings from the Broomielaw for Liverpool and was again joined by the **Royal Sovereign** sailing to Liverpool on 18 January.

At the end of the year the **Royal Sovereign** and **Royal George** were running twice-weekly in collaboration with Thomson & McConnell's **Commodore** and **Admiral**, and Burns' **Achilles** and **Actæon**. By May 1840 the advertised fares to Liverpool were as low as 5/- saloon and 2/- deck class with bales and boxed freight at 1d per cubic foot. Fortunately agreement with the competitors was reached in June that both companies should maintain two sailings each way per week to provide a daily service save for Sunday. The fare rocketed to 20/- saloon and 5/- deck class and boxes and bales went up to 2$\frac{1}{2}$d per cubic foot. Mathew Langlands, now elevated to the rank of Manager, took a dim view of this inhibition, and quietly planned to take the others head on. As a warning shot in September he brought his saloon fare back down to 15/- and deck fare to 3/-, but raised the freight rate to 3$\frac{1}{2}$d per cubic foot.

After tenure of 80 years in the coasting trade the very last steamer to be ordered under the Langlands name was delivered as G & J Burns' **Lurcher** (1922). She later became Coast Lines **Scottish Coast** and was eventually wrecked off Newfoundland in 1960 under the Canadian Flag.

(B & A Feilden)

The Development of Iron Ships

With the exception of bolts and nails and other more minor fittings, it is thought that the first serious indication of iron being used as a substitute for timber components was about 1670 when the naval shipwright Sir Anthony Deane, a protege of Samuel Pepys, built the **Royal James** at Portsmouth using 'iron dogs', probably iron brackets similar to the simple iron clamps found on wrecks of Dutch colliers dating from about 1820. Pepys, then Clerk of the Acts, rebuked Deane for using materials not authorised by the Navy Board.

There is no further mention of iron fittings in British ships until 1719, although the French had begun experimenting with iron knees (courbes de fer) as early as 1707. At this time, most wrought iron was brittle and subject to fracture, mainly due to the impurities introduced from coke during the smelting proces. In addition, shipbuilders, traditionally conservative in attitude, still considered timber preferable to iron and were reluctant to adopt alternative materials irrespective of the advantage.

A major breakthrough in technology came in 1784 when Henry Cort, of Gosport, patented a new method for converting pig iron into malleable wrought iron. Taking advantage of this, Gabriel Snodgrass, the surveyor of the East India Company, introduced an innovative system using iron knees, riders, and braces to the new John Company ships being built in the 1780s. Soon shipbuilders incorporated iron framing fully, and completely eliminated wooden supports. The benefits of iron shipbuilding included reduced construction time, added strength, and an increase in internal volume by eliminating unnecessary supports.

There were a number of things that slowed the acceptance of iron ships. Magnetic deviation caused by the innate magnetic property of iron affected the accuracy of compasses. The construction process, involving repetitive hammering of iron, caused early iron ships to magnetise and create their own magnetic field. Another feature of iron ships is their susceptibility to corrosion. Iron oxidation quickly damaged iron hulls, often weakening them beyond repair. Iron ships also attracted lightning during storms. Most problems with iron ships were rectified with the production of higher quality iron and proper electrical grounding.

The earliest record of iron shipbuilding was an iron canal boat, which was taken to Birmingham in 1787. This boat was 70 feet long, made of riveted iron plates $3/_{16}$ths of an inch thick, but having the stem and stern post and the beams of wood. Iron boats began to be more generally used upon canals. In 1815 an iron pleasure boat was built by Joshua Horton, of Tipton, near Birmingham; it was looked upon as a curiosity because of its peculiar shape.

The first iron steam vessel and the first to put to sea was built by the Horsley ironworks of Staffordshire, in 1821. She was named the **Aaron Manby** after the ironworks' master. This vessel was built under the auspices of Captain (later Admiral Sir Charles) Napier, an eccentric but far-seeing naval officer. He had been interested in steam navigation since its beginnings, and began investing his considerable resources in a steam vessel service that would operate on the River Seine. She was prefabricated to a design of Napier, Manby and Manby's son Charles, and then assembled at Rotherhithe on the Thames. The ship was 120 feet long, of 116 tons, with a draught of only one foot. She had a flat-bottomed hull of $1/_4$ inch thick iron plate fastened to angle-iron ribs. She had a wooden deck, a bowsprit, and a single funnel 47 feet high. The engine was of the oscillating type, designed and patented by Aaron Manby, which achieved a speed of 9 knots.

After trials in May 1822, the **Aaron Manby** crossed the English Channel to Le Havre under Napier's command on 10 June 1822, and proceeded up the Seine to Paris. The ship was used on a service that took her up and down the Seine. She was later operated on the River Loire, until she was broken up in 1855. Napier had planned the ship as a first step towards an iron warship.

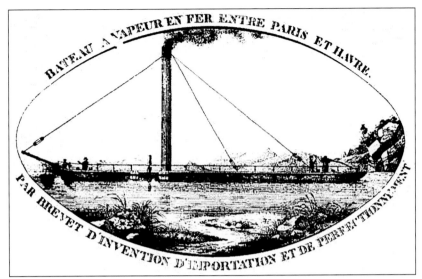
Advertisement for the **Aaron Manby** (1821) when in service on the River Seine.

The trials carried out on the Forth and Clyde Canal simultaneously with those of John and MacGregor Laird at Liverpool, led to a new era of shipbuilding in the early 1830s. Among the first sea-going iron vessels were two built at Manchester for the Forth and Clyde Canal Company. The first was the **Lord Dundas**. She was an experimental vessel, propelled by a locomotive engine of 16 horsepower, with 8 inch cylinders. Such was the lightness of her construction, that the plates were only $1/14$th of an inch thick, riveted to light T iron, which formed the ribs of the hulls. She was built in 1830, and was conveyed through the streets of Manchester on trucks and launched into the River Irwell. She then sailed to Liverpool, and from there to Glasgow via the Isle of Man. The second steamer was the **Manchester**, which for many years traded between Grangemouth and the coast of Fife, round to Dundee.

Some of the earliest iron steamships were built for service on the River Shannon. The first, the **Mountaineer**, owned by the Shannon Steam Navigation Company, was commissioned in 1826, followed the next month by the **Marquis of Wellesley**, a ship built with twin iron hulls with the paddle wheel placed between them. She was owned by John Grantham and was another product of the Horsely Iron Works.

Another significant early iron-built steamship was the **Alburkah**, built by Mr MacGregor Laird, about the year 1831. Under the personal direction of Laird, she ascended the Niger twice, having proved her seaworthiness during her voyage to Africa.

From its earliest days the Glasgow & Liverpool Royal Steam Packet Company was, without a doubt, innovative. In 1839 the first two ships they owned were constructed of iron rather than wood. They were named **Royal Sovereign** and **Royal George**, and were the largest iron vessels to have been built in the United Kingdom at the time.

In his book, *Iron Shipbuilding*, published in 1858, John Grantham describes the development of iron ships, concluding that he had 'watched with the greatest interest the progress of iron vessels, feeling convinced that they must ultimately supersede those built of timber'. He continues 'numerous iron steamers... of large tonnage are now afloat, or building. Great numbers of iron steamers are plying on the Thames, the Mersey, the Clyde, and on nearly all the continental rivers. Large fleets are to be seen navigating every sea, the property of every nation; the most satisfactory proof of their success.'

TWO PADDLE STEAMERS CALLED *PRINCESS ROYAL* – A ONE-SHIP FLEET

Having established his Glasgow-Liverpool service, Mathew Langlands determined to break the two-day a week sailing restriction that the Glasgow & Liverpool Royal Steam Packet Company had been obliged to sign in 1839. For this he needed something special and something even faster than the **Royal Sovereign** and **Royal George**. He entered discussion with the builders Tod & MacGregor and a contract was agreed against an advanced design for a new iron-hulled paddle steamer. Within weeks it was announced that Her Majesty Queen Victoria was expecting her first child and that 'he' would be born at about the time the ship was ready to be launched in November 1840. Dr Ernest Reader, in an article in *Sea Breezes*, February 1949, provides the oft-quoted choice of name for the ship:

*Having become fairly established in the trade, Langlands decided… to build a new ship that would place them [the company] in a position of superiority, and at the time this vessel was ready for launching the whole nation was awaiting with intense interest the birth of Queen Victoria's first child and the heir to the throne. In honour of the occasion the Directors had planned that the new ship should be called the **Prince of Wales** if the Royal Baby should be a boy. Work on the ship was slowed down, and eventually the launch was actually postponed for three days before the baby arrived. Then came the news that the heir to the Throne of England was a daughter, and the ship was named **Princess Royal**, the first of a long line of worthy Royal successors which were to reach the highest peak of efficiency in ship design and management.*

The name of the new paddle steamer, **Princess Royal**, was announced in the press in January 1841 following the birth of the royal baby on 11 November 1840. The master of the new ship was to be Captain J McArthur and as he stood by the construction of the vessel his place at sea was taken by Captain W Tassie aboard the **Royal Sovereign**, while Captain Cook was transferred to the **Royal George**.

The **Princess Royal**, with a tonnage of 747, was both larger and more powerful than her two predecessors. On her first round trip to Liverpool, starting from Glasgow on 18 June 1841, the **Princess Royal** established a record passage north

The first **Princess Royal** (1841) from a contemporary engraving reproduced in the Langlands Tour Guide for 1906.

to Greenock in just 15 hours and 40 minutes. Thereafter, the **Royal Sovereign** stood down and was laid up with problems relating to her boilers. Just prior to entering commercial service the new paddle steamer undertook a shakedown cruise as reported in the *Glasgow Herald*, 21 June 1841:

*On Thursday at 8.30am this fine new iron steam vessel [**Princess Royal**], commanded by Captain McArthur, which was built by Messrs Tod & MacGregor and belongs to the Glasgow & Liverpool Royal Steam Packet Company, sailed to Campbeltown on a pleasure and trial trip. There were about 150 gentlemen on board, who had been invited to take the sail, and we must say that every precaution was made by the Steam Company for their accommodation and comfort - the arrangements being under the management of, and most judiciously carried into effect by, Mr Langlands, the active manager of the company. The sail down the river, and indeed throughout the passage, was enlivened by the firing of guns in salute, the waving of flags, and the excellent band of the 17th Lancers - a member of which corps delighted the company during the day with many comic songs and mime performances.*

After breakfast, time was afforded for a glance at the vessel, which is exceedingly well fitted up in every respect. The main saloon is classily elegant – the chairs and sofas being covered with velvet, manufactured in Paris for the purpose, and they, as well as the doors, are of solid oak, finely polished. The walls are covered with painted glass and panelling, the subjects being illustrative of the history of the present Royals: the coronation of the Queen, her marriage and the christening with Her Majesty and Prince Albert visiting the royal baby in its cot. Each side of the entrance door to the saloon is decorated with a magnificent plate glass mirror, and everything to correspond. The ladies' cabin is also handsome and commodious, the door being real satin wood, and the sofas covered in richly figured silks from France, with views of Virginia Water and the Falls of Clyde.

An important feature in the **Princess'** is, that the berths are all ventilated by a very simple apparatus, the invention of Dr Fleming, in each berth there is a small aperture for the purpose which can be regulated at pleasure, or shut up altogether... The **Princess'** is 207 feet on deck, 28 feet betwixt the paddle boxes, 800 tons burthen and 400 horse power. The cabinet and upholstery workmanship of the **Princess'** was executed by Messrs J & J Campbell of Buchanan Street.

The *Glasgow Chronicle*, 1 June, 1842, alluded to the new ship's speed:

The **Princess Royal**: We feel much indebted to the agent [Mr M Langlands] of this splendid steamer for putting us in possession of the Morning Chronicle of yesterday morning three hours before the arrival of the 'London Mail' containing the details of the attempted assassination of Her Majesty. Copies of the 'Chronicle, Times, and other London journals were, the moment the train arrived from Greenock, forwarded to the different public reading rooms in town, and altogether the public are much indebted to the proprietors and agents of the vessel at Liverpool and Glasgow for their public spirit and enterprise. The passage from Liverpool to Greenock was made in the astonishing space of $15\frac{1}{2}$ hours.

Mathew Langlands clearly had an eye for every business opportunity, illustrated by the fact that he was agent to his very first cruise round the north of Scotland departing in mid-June, 1842. The ship used was the **Prince of Wales**, a newly-completed iron paddle steamer built by Tod & MacGregor and owned by Kemp & Company of Glasgow (although later to become an Irish Sea railway-owned ferry):

Pleasure trip from Glasgow to Leith (round the north of Scotland): The new and powerful steamship **Prince of Wales** (260 horsepower, 500 tons burthen) is intended to sail from Glasgow for Leith (with cabin passengers only) on Tuesday 14 July at 4.00pm. She will call (weather permitting) at Iona, Staffa, Stornoway, and the Orkney Islands and is expected to arrive at Leith on Friday morning. Passage money £3/3/-. The **Prince of Wales** will then sail (with passengers only) from Granton Pier to London on Saturday 18 June at 4.00pm.

Given the high reputation of the **Princess Royal** for speed, it was not surprising that she was chartered for experimental purposes by a Committee of the House of Commons (appointed in 1842) inquiring into the 'conveyance of the mails' between England and Ireland. The *Liverpool Mercury* reported:

The fine new iron steamboat called **Princess Royal**, at present on the station between this port and Glasgow, started from Clarence Dock on Sunday morning last [19 June] for Dublin. She arrived there in 9 hours 5 minutes, beating HM mail steam packet **Medusa** by 1 hour 45 minutes. On Monday morning she left Dublin for Holyhead, and arrived there in 4 hours 45 minutes, returning to Dublin the same day in 4 hours 28 minutes. In the evening she started for Liverpool, which she reached in 9 hours 35 minutes. The vessel had a head wind nearly all the way.

Clarence Dock, the Glasgow & Liverpool Royal Steam Packet Company's Liverpool terminal, seen in 1842. The dock was first opened to traffic in 1830 and was specifically designed for paddle steamships.

(Illustrated London News)

During the summer months of 1842 the **Royal George** was scheduled to call at Ramsey Bay, Isle of Man, weather permitting. The **Royal Sovereign** made one last voyage standing in for the **Royal George** on Tuesday 11 October while the latter received attention. On returning to Glasgow the **Royal Sovereign** was listed for sale and disposed of early in 1843. She was subsequently registered under the ownership of Henry F Denny of Liverpool who resold her a few years later for service on the Indian coastal trade.

Burns, meanwhile, had just the **Achilles** on the Liverpool service, and Thomson & McConnell had

Commodore and *Admiral* in service, although the *Admiral* was put on other duties from June onwards. In 1843 J & G Burns were running the *Aurora* and Thomson & McConnell the *Commodore* or the *Admiral* on their Liverpool services.

From January 1843 Mr Langlands advertised twice-weekly departures from Glasgow and Liverpool, on Tuesdays and Fridays. The service was provided by the *Royal George* and *Princess Royal*. At the end of January the *Royal George* stood down with boiler trouble and the *Princess Royal* carried on alone. She effectively maintained two and a half sailings each way per week for the rest of the year with a cabin class fare of 22/- inclusive of steward's fee and deck class at 5/-.

James Kennedy in *The History of Steam Navigation* described the sea-going qualities of the *Princess Royal*:

*The **Princess** had now established beyond dispute her claim to be one of the fastest Channel steamers leaving the port. The ensuing winter she proved herself to be also one of the best sea boats. The terrible gale of January 20th to 22nd, 1843, was one of the most severe that ever visited these coasts. The **Mona's Isle**, from Liverpool to Douglas, was 24 hours on the passage. At Cork the posts on the quays were carried away. The **Princess** was at sea during this storm, and fully proved her excellent qualities as a sea boat. She left Greenock at 11.30pm on Friday, and arrived at Liverpool at 5.00pm on Saturday without the slightest damage.*

Things did not always go smoothly, however, for a fatal accident was reported in the Glasgow press on Saturday 4 November 1843:

*Fatal accident, on Tuesday evening, about six o'clock, when the **Princess Royal** steamer was about to set sail from Broomielaw for Liverpool, the chief engineer of that vessel, Mr Hugh Marr, while going on board, was precipitated into the river in consequence of the steps upon which he was crossing from the quay to the ship sliding off the paddle-box.*

*The unfortunate man was got out of the water after being about ten minutes immersed and at this time he was quite extinct. Marr was a man in the prime of his life and has left a widow and several children to mourn his untimely fate. The accident, it is alleged, was occasioned by the arrival of another steamer in the harbour at the time which caused the **Princess Royal** to slightly diverge from her previous position. The unfortunate man who has been in service of the company since its commencement was highly and deservedly respected.*

The roster for the *Princess Royal* remained unchanged until May 1844 when the summertime calls at Ramsey Bay were reinstated on approximately three out of five voyages. Meanwhile the company had refurbished and reboilered the *Royal George* and were looking for gainful employment for their ship. She was advertised at the beginning of July by Mathew Langlands rather than the Glasgow & Liverpool Royal Steam Packet Company as follows:

*The splendid first class steamship **Royal George** (500 tons, 250 horsepower), Robert Cook Commander, is intended to sail from the Broomielaw for Cadiz and Gibraltar on Wednesday 17 July. The **Royal George** now fitted with new boilers and having undergone a general overhaul in hull and machinery, is greatly improved in speed and Captain Cook having had many years' experience on this line, this opportunity will be found equal to any other steam communication for expedition and comfort to passengers. Cabin fare £16 including provisions and wine.*

From January 1845 onwards the *Princess Royal* on the Liverpool service called at Greenock for passengers. At the end of January Captain McArthur retired and was succeeded by Captain Crawford. At this time the cabin fare was raised from 15/- to 17/-. Calls at Greenock were reduced in March and at the end of the month the *Princess Royal* stood down so that she could be reboilered and refurbished. Thomson & McConnell's wooden paddle steamer *Commodore* under Captain Hardie was taken on charter to maintain the core Liverpool service, the *Royal George* being occupied in the Mediterranean on charter work from April 1845 until she was finally sold in June 1847.

The *Princess Royal* was back on duty at the beginning of June and the *Commodore* stood down. The *Princess Royal* sailed from Glasgow on Mondays and Thursdays and returned on Wednesdays and Fridays. In July it was all change again when *Commodore* resumed on Glasgow to Liverpool duties with *Princess Royal* now based at Greenock with newspaper advertisements stating:

*The **Princess Royal**, having just undergone a thorough overhaul in every department including new boilers, is* *in first rate order, and as she will carry no cargo while on this station, it is expected her average passage will not exceed 15 to 16 hours.*

At the end of September the **Commodore** was returned to her owners to be rechartered, this time to J & G Burns for their Belfast station. **Princess Royal** reverted to her two and a half sailings per week roster from Glasgow via Greenock. During December some of the sailings were taken by Thomson & McConnell's **Fire King** while the **Princess Royal** received attention, but she was back in service by Hogmanay.

The rest of the decade was maintained with summer Greenock departures and winter Glasgow departures. In summer the **Princess Royal** sailed at 4.00pm from Greenock on Mondays and Thursdays and at the same time from Liverpool on Wednesdays and Fridays. Connecting train services were available at Liverpool to both Manchester and London. Occasional summer calls were made by the **Princess Royal** at Ramsey, Isle of Man, where passengers now embarked and disembarked by tender.

Some Liverpool sailings departed from Clarence Pier Head according to the tide. In 1846 the summer timetable was amalgamated with that of Burns and **Commodore** came under Langlands management for the three months of the summer timetable. In May 1847 the **Princess Royal** was out of service for seven weeks for overhaul and repairs, returning to the Greenock roster on 21 June. Her absence was covered by the new Burns steamer **Orion**. Fares fluctuated from 13/- in winter to 17/- in summer. The Liverpool agent, James Brebner, was replaced by Robert Lamont of 33 Water Street, later becoming Lamont, McLarty & Company. Good news at the end of the 1850 season was that Thomson & McConnell's City of Glasgow Steam Packet Company and its two wooden-hulled paddle steamers, **Commodore** and **Admiral**, were withdrawing from the Liverpool station leaving G & J Burns as the only competitor.

But it was not all plain sailing according to a rather disturbing report in the *Liverpool Albion*, Monday 6 October 1851:

*Accident to the **Princess Royal** steamer: On Sabbath, at noon, when about thirty-five miles from the Isle of Man, the Glasgow steamship **Princess Royal**, on her voyage to Liverpool, was struck by a heavy sea on the starboard quarter, which carried away the bulwark, mizzenmast, binnacle, and skylight, and deluged the cabin with water. The rudder was also rendered unmanageable for a short period. Captain Cumming and the mate were standing at the wheel when the disaster occurred, and 'we are sorry to say that the former was severely wounded on the scalp, and had three of his ribs fractured'. Notwithstanding the injury he received, the captain would not relinquish his post until he had to be carried below in a fainting state. The chief mate, Mr Clarke, and John Turner, the steersman, also suffered considerable injury. At this time Mr Hall, [first officer of the steamship **Asia**] volunteered, and, aided by the second mate, Mr Thomas, took temporary charge of the vessel, and soon managed to partially repair the damage done to the wheel, and brought her safely into the Mersey, where she arrived at half-past four in the afternoon. The passengers expressed their acknowledgements to the officers and crew of the **Princess Royal**, to Mr Hall... The **Princess Royal** had more than 200 passengers on board, including the officers and crew.*

The **Princess** was commanded by Captain Fraser from 1853 onwards, when the summer cabin fare was as low as 10/-. The **Princess Royal** continued her twice-weekly forays between Glasgow and Liverpool largely without incident. In 1856 she received new boilers and a thorough overhaul ready for the all-important summer season and was all set to continue her career. But on rejoining the service on returning to the Clyde on Wednesday 28 May she went aground 10 miles north of Portpatrick, as the *Glasgow Herald* reported in its next edition on 30 May:

*We regret to state that the **Princess Royal** steamship, Captain McChlery, which left Liverpool on Monday last at 5 o'clock, bound for Glasgow, with about 40 cabin and 80 steerage passengers on board, ran onto the rocks on Wednesday morning at 3.30am, at a spot called Point Laggan, about 10 miles to the north of Portpatrick, and near the entrance to Loch Ryan, and where she now lies hard and fast, with water in all her compartments saving one. The weather at the time was perfectly calm but densely foggy; and immediately after striking, Captain McChlery, who is reported to have behaved admirably and coolly on the unfortunate occasion, had all the passengers landed and conveyed to the house of Mr Kennedy, farmer at that quarter, who administered to their necessities with praiseworthy attention and kindness. The passengers at one time all proposed to leave with their baggage for Stranraer in Mr Kennedy's carts, when the **Herald**, Captain Stokes, from Dublin, made her appearance, and a boat having been sent off to her, that gentleman, with the consideration and goodwill of an honest sailor towards those in distress, immediately consented to delay his vessel and take the passengers of the **Princess Royal** on board his own vessel.*

*A difficulty however, here presented itself. The coast was dangerous, and its nooks such as to make it inadvisable that the **Herald** should come too near the rocks. Under these circumstances a clever farmer of the name of Cochran, undertook to pilot her to a safe bay not far off, and this he did with much skill. In this bay the **Herald** cast anchor in safety, and took all the passengers on board comfortably and quickly, which being accomplished, she started and brought them all to Glasgow where they were landed on Wednesday afternoon about 4 o'clock. The **Princess Royal** has evidently been much damaged, and should the wind come from the south – to which she is completely exposed – with any strength, she will be in a critical position. To endeavour to get her off before this happens, however, Mr Langlands, the manager, left Greenock yesterday with the **Albion** steamer, attended by a steam lighter, and with a gang of men, and it is to be hoped they will succeed in getting her off. This was the first return voyage of the **Princess Royal**, after receiving, towards the summer trade, a thorough overhaul with new boilers, at a cost of between £6,000 and £7,000.*

On 2 June the *Glasgow Herald* reported under the title '**Princess Royal** steamer':

It was with regret that we ascertain that the accident to this fine steamer proved serious. There is, it appears, no prospect of her being got off and the owners have, in consequence, been compelled to abandon her.

…and in the *Marine List*:

*Stranraer, 9th July. The **Princess Royal**, which went on Scaur Laggan [Craig Laggan] rocks 28 May, suffered severely.   7 July: her bow parted just before the paddle-wheels, and went down in deep water. Efforts are still being made to float off the after-part in hope of saving engines and boilers.*

The Return of Wrecks and Casualties on Coasts of the UK 1856 Session 1 recorded that:

*The **Princess Royal** steamship of Glasgow. Wrecked on Scaur Laggan in Daley Bay 3 miles west of Corsewall Light, weather being very thick. Master supposed he was 6 miles from land. Total loss.*

The enquiry took evidence that suggested the compasses were defective as they had been adjusted in unfavourable weather after the ship had been loaded with quantities of iron used as ballast, some of which was still lying on the quayside. Attempts to lighten the ship by removing cargo in order to salvage the engines failed, despite Mr Langlands directing the attempt from the **Albion** of the Glasgow & Stranraer Steam Packet Company. A terse article in the *Glasgow Herald* on 4 August drew a line under the incident with the following:

*Princess Royal** steamer: Monday last being the advertised period for selling off the wreck and remains of the **Princess Royal** steamer, the day proving singularly fine, a vast number of speculators and intending purchasers crowded to the coast at an early hour. After disposing of a few lots of rubbish, the auctioneer offered the remains of the hull and engines for sale, the upset price being £50. The competition continued extremely sluggish, and after considerable time, and some little altercation, the lot was knocked down to a Stranraer company for £300, which was by some judges, considered a great bargain. A great number of lots of wood was afterwards exposed, for which the competition continued extremely brisk, and quantities were sold above woodyard rates. The whole amount of the sale has not yet publically transpired, but it may be expected that it will fall short of a quarter of the expenses incurred since the vessel struck; in short a more complete destruction of property has never been witnessed upon the same coast.*

*Fortunately no lives were lost, it is frightful to contemplate what might have happened. With one foot more of water the vessel would have been propelled over the rock, with a rent resembling the furrow of a plough made in her bottom, and she would have initially sunk in deep water, when the **Orion** tragedy would have been re-enacted with many additional horrors…*

The Liverpool-Glasgow Burns steamer **Orion** had earlier been lost with great loss of life in June 1850 on the Galloway coast after coming too close inshore to save time on passage. Her master was none other than Captain Thomas Henderson who was resting below deck at the time of the accident, not as reported in the press at the time Captain McNeil (McNeil was the second mate). Captain Henderson, of course, after serving his gaol sentence, later went on to become a key promoter of the Anchor Line and two of his brothers later acquired the Tod & MacGregor shipbuilding and engineering business. At the Enquiry Captain Crawford, described as 'of the **Princess Royal**' was called to give supporting evidence and he basically corroborated what Captain John Boyd (retired, but formerly long-standing master of the **Admiral**) had said:

The captain was always on deck going down the Mersey, when off the Mull of Galloway, when off the Point of Ayr and generally when off the Cumbraes as also when going up the Clyde. Witness was in the habit of retiring occasionally for rest in good weather after passing the Mull, and generally gave instructions to be called in case of fog.

The Burns' Liverpool to Glasgow steamer **Orion** (1846).

(Illustrated London News)

The **Orion** (1846) sunk off the Galloway coast near Portpatrick on 17 June 1850 as seen at low tide.

(Illustrated London News)

Mathew Langlands was quickly able to place an order with Tod & MacGregor for a replacement paddle steamer of similar design to the **Princess Royal** save that there was to be no bowsprit and figurehead, just a plain almost vertical bow to facilitate berthing at Clarence Dock. In the meantime the company resolved to charter ships at least to try and maintain its business footing in the Glasgow and Liverpool trade. Langtry's iron-hulled paddle steamer **Waterloo** had previously been withdrawn from their Belfast station and she had earlier stood in for the **Princess Royal**. The **Waterloo** was hastily brought back on charter to maintain the Glasgow and Liverpool service again for Mr Langlands. In due course, the iron paddle steamer **Vanguard** was chartered for the service under the command of Captain Walker. The **Vanguard** had been built at Messrs Napier's yard on the Clyde in 1843 for the Dublin & Glasgow Sailing & Steam Packet Company.

In September 1856 the Liverpool agent Lamont, McLarty & Company was declared insolvent due to bad speculative investments in the Australian trade. In early 1857 the Liverpool agency for the company was vested in M Langlands & Son in addition to the agency at Glasgow. This was the first time that this title had been used and it recognises Mathew's son, John joining him in business at the Glasgow office. The new Liverpool office also acted for the Laird Line on their Liverpool to Westport and Garlieston (Galloway) services and the Galloway Steam Navigation Company's **Countess of Galloway** which was deployed on their Liverpool to Kirkcudbright service.

It is all credit to Mathew Langlands that he was able to rebuild as he was running a one-ship company with narrow margins and extremely competitive fares. The new paddle steamer was equipped with a steeple engine capable of generating 420 horsepower. She was 227 feet long, some 50 feet longer than her predecessor, though of the same beam, and was of 779 tons gross. The name given to the ship at her launch at Tod & MacGregor's yard on 13 April was, of course, **Princess Royal**. Her registered owner was none other than Mr M Langlands of Mathew Langlands & Son, 20 Dixon Street, Glasgow.

The second **Princess Royal** (1857).

(from an oil painting by Nick Robins)

Mathew Langlands & Son was now designated as the managing owners of the Liverpool & Glasgow Royal Steam Packet Company. The new paddler was, by all accounts, a fitting successor to her predecessors, with luxurious cabin class accommodation, a lady's state room and a gentleman's smoking room. Dining was in the main lounge on the traditional long table arrangement with sideboards strategically positioned to assist the stewards during their service. The *Greenock Advertiser* reported on 15 April 1857:

*The new Liverpool steamer **Princess Royal**, of 800 tons and 400 horsepower, built and engined by Messrs Tod & MacGregor, came down the river yesterday morning and proceeded to Gareloch to adjust compasses. On this being completed, she crossed to Greenock and took a number of gentlemen on board, after which she made a trial trip between the Cloch and Cumbrae lights. She ran the distance (about 12³/₄ miles) at slack water in 61¹/₂ minutes, the engines making 20 revolutions per minute under a pressure of 10lbs. Her draught of water, however, was too light to ensure a fair trial of her speed, and it is confidently anticipated that when she is fully loaded with goods and passengers, she will prove a very swift vessel. She is most satisfactorily built, has great breadth of beam, and will be an admirable sea boat, and she is fitted at both hatches with two of the largest size of Taylor's patent steam winches for loading and discharging cargo. The cabin accommodation is ample and handsomely fitted up. The saloon is panelled with bird's eye maple and rosewood, and adorned with beautiful glass paintings by Mr Laurie of Glasgow, and it is lighted by a fine cupola of stained glass. The **Princess Royal**, which is commanded by Captain McChlery, an experienced and cautious seaman, will be put at the Liverpool station on Thursday first, and will, we have no doubt, become as great a favourite as her predecessor of the same name.*

The **Vanguard** undertook her last sailing via Greenock on 11 May and was returned to her owners. The **Princess Royal**, under the command of Captain McChlery, made her maiden sailing to Liverpool on Thursday 16 May 1857 (not as predicted in the *Greenock Advertiser*, 1 May), leaving the Broomielaw at 2.00pm and arriving at Greenock at 4.00pm on passage for Liverpool. Thereafter, she settled into the old two and a half sailings a week routine from both ports in competition with Burns' steamer **Panther**. In December 1857 through to mid-February 1858 both the **Princess Royal** and the **Panther** reduced their services to one round trip a week, **Princess Royal** leaving Glasgow and **Panther** leaving Liverpool on Tuesdays with the respective return trips starting on Fridays. Burns replaced the **Panther** with their new paddle steamer **Leopard** in April. Thereafter passengers joined the ships at the Great Floating Stage at Liverpool, adjacent to Prince's Dock, the vessels having departed Clarence Dock earlier in the day. Summer freight rates went down to 10/- per ton but were back up to 17/6d by October when passenger departures from Liverpool reverted to Clarence Dock. The route saw its first screw steamer in October and November when the Burns' vessel **Harrier** deputised on some services for the **Leopard**.

In 1859 the **Princess Royal** and the **Leopard** together maintained the traditional two and a half departures a week service from both ports, calling at Greenock to uplift train passengers. In March, three of the **Leopard**'s trips were taken by the Burns' steamer **Harrier** and in April three of the **Princess Royal**'s trips were taken by the **Harrier**. This allowed both the **Leopard** and **Princess Royal** to be overhauled in time for the peak summer season. In June the service was increased to five sailings a week when the **Harrier** worked alongside the **Leopard** and **Princess Royal**, the three ships now leaving Liverpool from the Great Floating Stage again after having abandoned this facility during the winter months. At the end of September the **Harrier** stood down and the ships again sailed from Liverpool with passengers from Clarence Dock. The Great Floating Stage was not used the following summer when passengers continued to board at Clarence Dock.

There was a bit of an upset between July and the end of September when Cameron & Waterston, of Commerce Street, Glasgow, put their brand new screw steamer, the 650 ton **Thetis**, on Liverpool and Glasgow duties. Under Captain Kennor, she was scheduled to leave Glasgow on Saturdays in competition with Burns' **Leopard**, and return from Liverpool on Wednesdays in competition with their **Harrier**. Burns and Langlands, however, were too much for the newcomer and it gracefully withdrew, having picked up only a fraction of the summer trade.

During November and December the **Harrier** partnered the **Princess Royal** on the two and a half sailings a week roster. In January 1860 G & J Burns increased the level of competition by bringing the **Lynx** into service on the Liverpool run to work alongside the **Harrier**. The **Lynx** was replaced in March by the brand-new screw steamer **Heron**. She was joined by identical sister **Ostrich** in March 1860. This put considerable strain on the viability of the Glasgow & Liverpool Royal Steam Packet Company which was now up against two state-of-the-art and efficient screw steamers. In April the **Princess Royal** stood down for her spring time refit for two weeks while Laird's screw steamship, **Garland**, was chartered for three round trips. Mr Langlands was impressed by the performance of the screw ship. He quickly realised the benefits of screw propulsion on the coastal trade were considerable; not least because of the propulsive efficiency, related economy of fuel, and that the ship was no longer dependent upon the cargo loading condition and the associated immersion of the paddle floats.

The company's own paddler **Princess Royal** returned to duty at the end of April with Captain McChlery in charge, running against Burns' screw steamers **Heron** and **Ostrich**.

Given her finer hull and greater length compared to the first **Princess Royal**, speed was not a problem with the second **Princess Royal**. But because of her greater length over breadth ratio, she was found to be a tender ship needing careful handling in rough weather and Mathew Langlands resolved to replace her at the earliest opportunity with something at least as efficient as the Burns screw steamers. This must have been a difficult decision to make with the new paddle steamer not yet two and a half years old. However, it was clearly also a decision that Mathew Langlands knew must fall in favour of building his own screw steamer in order that his company remain competitive in the longer term.

Mathew Langlands was able to hold discussions with Messrs Tod & MacGregor about a replacement for the paddle steamer **Princess Royal** and together they hatched a design for an iron-hulled propeller-driven vessel that would be so fast that she would sweep the competition into oblivion. But this was to be an expensive project so at the end of November 1860 the almost new paddle steamer **Princess Royal** stood down, to be sold via a broker to the General Steam Navigation Company, London, who gave her the name **Berlin**. The monies released were much needed to pay instalments to Tod & MacGregor. The **Berlin** proved a reliable unit and remained in the GSN fleet until 1875 when she was sold for demolition.

For the moment the core service between Glasgow and Liverpool again depended on chartered vessels, but the hype was on the newcomer, a fine and handsome screw steamer. In the meantime Burns' **Leopard** was bare boat chartered from the beginning of December with Langlands' Captain McChlery in command. In March 1861 the **Leopard** was replaced with the Dublin & Glasgow Sailing & Steam Packet Company's iron paddle steamer **Vanguard** under Captain Ward, Captain McChlery now standing by the new-build at Tod & MacGregor's yard already identified as the third **Princess Royal**. Fares aboard the **Vanguard** were offered at 15/- cabin and 6/- steerage. The **Vanguard** stood down at the end of May and the **Leopard** was chartered back onto the service. Although by 20 June the new screw steamer should have been ready to take over from the **Leopard**, in the event she was not launched until that date and was only ready to take her maiden voyage from the Broomielaw on 11 July 1861. The **Vanguard** was hastily rechartered for three more round trips. And so should have ended the tenure of the paddle steamer on the Glasgow to Liverpool passenger and cargo services – but it was not quite yet to be (see Chapter 5).

From *Glasgow Past and Present* 1884

A journey to London then (in the early 1840s) was no trifling matter, especially on a winter or early spring night. No covered station, with fine waiting-room and orderly appointments, was provided to accommodate either the man of business or the member of a parliamentary deputation, who were left to scramble up the steps to the roof of the coach in Trongate in all weathers, amid a crowd of onlookers. The first stage to Carlisle was ten hours, and then there was an additional stage of six or seven hours to Lancaster, from whence the railway conveyed the weary traveller to London, in something like thirty-one hours after leaving Glasgow. Fortunately, the Liverpool steamers had at that period attained a high character for speed and comfort, no fewer than three companies being engaged in the trade: Messrs J & G Burns, Messrs Thomson & M'Connell, and the Messrs M Langlands and Son; and, when other arrangements permitted, this route was generally taken, avoiding the dreadful exposure encountered on the cold uplands of Lanark, and the fells of Cumberland. The recollection of these trips to and from Liverpool calls up many pleasant reminiscences of friends, both civic and social, who have long passed away. Another favourite route was via Fleetwood and Ardrossan, and it was thought a wonderful advance in rapid inter-communication with London, when by that route the journey from Glasgow could be accomplished in twenty-four hours.

CHAPTER 4

TRANSATLANTIC ADVENTURES AND WILLIAM INMAN

Mathew Langlands' interests were not confined to the coastal trade between Glasgow and Liverpool. The shipbuilders Tod & MacGregor, who had earlier built both the **Royal Sovereign** and **Royal George**, as well as the two second generation **Princess Royal** paddle steamers, had developed a good relationship between shipbuilder and shipowner and manager, through both the Liverpool & Glasgow Royal Steam Packet Company and the Glasgow & Stranraer Steam Packet Company for which Mathew Langlands was the Glasgow agent. As a consequence, when Tod & MacGregor found themselves the proud owners of a transatlantic liner they looked to Mathew Langlands, whom they respected greatly, as their manager and agent.

Tod & MacGregor were at the forefront of iron-hulled screw propulsion as the direct successor of the paddle steamer. N R P Bonsor describes the innovative evolution of the screw steamer on the Atlantic in an article that first appeared in *Sea Breezes*, November 1959:

*It is important to remember that the first ocean-going screw steamer, the 3,270 ton **Great Britain**, was not launched until 1843. Considerably larger than any paddle steamer then in existence, she was the first steamer of any size, paddle or screw to be built of iron; her maiden voyage from Liverpool to New York took place in July 1845...[She was followed by] the 1,400 ton iron screw **Sarah Sands**, which, surprisingly, was built for one of the sailing packet companies to compare the merits of the old and new means of propulsion.*

*Up to a point the **Sarah Sands** was a great success and in the summer of 1849 the Glasgow shipbuilders, Tod & MacGregor decided to lay down for their own account an iron screw steamer that was, in effect, a compromise between her and the **Great Britain**. The resulting ship, named the **City of Glasgow**, has been universally regarded as the prototype of the modern liner.*

The **City of Glasgow** (1850) on her first arrival at Philadelphia after having been purchased by the Inman Line. At the time she was commanded by Captain R B Mathews.

(Gleason's Pictorial)

Tod & MacGregor were keen to demonstrate the state of the art for the transatlantic trade and sought to develop their own steam packet company.

W H Flayhart takes up the story of the building and maiden voyage of **City of Glasgow** in a paper published in the *Northern Mariner* in 2002:

*The person primarily responsible for the use of iron in the construction of the **City of Glasgow** and for the use of screw propulsion was Mr David Tod, who was one of the outstanding and far-seeing geniuses among Clyde shipbuilders in the 1840s and 1850s. The engines were two-geared, one engine running at a slow rate while the screw, connected by spur wheels, ran at a faster rate, and capable of 380 horsepower. Furthermore, the liner was designed from the keel up to carry both cabin class passengers and steerage, while her contemporaries were fitted out only to accommodate the more expensive passenger traffic. In terms of design, propulsion and intended passenger distribution she was radically different from the wooden paddle-wheelers which dominated the first class trade. The **City of Glasgow** sailed from Scotland on 15 April 1850 with 52 first class passengers, 85 second class, and 'room' for 400 steerage when required. There was nearly a full passenger complement in her high priced cabins and should have pleased the owners greatly since she also carried a fairly substantial general cargo.*

The **City of Glasgow** was 227 feet long and 1,609 tons gross. She had a twin bladed screw of 13 feet in diameter and had geared beam engines of 350 horsepower with two cylinders 71 inches in diameter and a stroke of 60 inches. The working pressure was 10 pounds per square inch. She was fitted with five watertight bulkheads. There were six lifeboats. She had a clipper stem, one funnel, three masts (rigged for sail) and had a speed of 9 knots. She carried a crew of seventy, all hand-picked by the owners and by Captain Mathews, formerly master of the **Great Britain**. The crew included a baker, two stewardesses, a group of musicians and a ship's surgeon. The ship carried a stockman and a few livestock including a cow for the provision of fresh milk. She was launched on 28 February 1850 and started her maiden voyage on 15 April 1850 when she left Glasgow for New York. On her return to Glasgow, she berthed on the south side of the river and was visited by thousands of people. A report in the Glasgow press heralded the new service:

*It is an effort to combine a reasonable degree of speed with certainty and cheapness, and it is intended to link the west of Scotland with the principal seaport of the New World. We may expect in due course to see tourists taking advantage of the **City of Glasgow** for a pleasure trip to the United States, in the same way as they hereto made a voyage up the Rhine, or a run to the Highlands of Scotland; and there is little doubt that the same facilities, and moderate scale of charges, will induce our Yankee friends to extend their personal acquaintance with the land of their fathers.*

Tod & MacGregor (shipowners) appointed a board of five directors including Peter MacGregor, and Mathew Langlands, 'of M Langlands, Steam Packet Agent, Glasgow', who was appointed manager and agent. Tod & MacGregor (shipbuilders) did achieve a great deal with the new ship as she showcased the iron-hulled screw steam passenger ship for shipowners the world over to see. She was innovative in more ways than one as the **City of Glasgow** was designed to accommodate emigrants as well as the first and second class passenger. The Cunard paddle steamers of the day only carried first class passengers, the emigrants travelling the Atlantic in the sailing packets.

Tod & MacGregor was keen to commission a running mate for their steam ship, but in truth the one they had was too big for the Glasgow trade and a second ship would not have made economic sense. In spite of this they went ahead with the design and construction of a second ship, an improved and enlarged version of the **City of Glasgow**. The passenger hinterland was enhanced by Langlands' coastal steamer service supplying the big steamer with passengers from Liverpool who would otherwise have travelled by the Collins or British & North American paddlers to New York. But without repeated full passenger complements the ship just did not pay her way, and during her fourth voyage from the Clyde she was put on the market. In the meantime the larger consort to the **City of Glasgow**, the four-masted **City of New York**, was at an advanced stage of construction at Tod & MacGregor's yard.

As it happened, gentlemen by the names of Thomas Richardson and William Inman had been watching closely and both were convinced that the **City of Glasgow** was the way forward on the Atlantic. They arranged for her purchase and, in due course, also for the brand new **City of New York**, which was delivered to them with the new name **City of Manchester**, although at one time while still building she was referred to as the **City of Philadelphia**. R A Fletcher in his book *Steam-Ships* wrote of the consequent inception of the famous Inman Line:

*It was December 1850, that the Liverpool and Philadelphia Steamship Company was established. Their agents were Messrs Richardson Brothers & Company, who had already a number of packet ships of their own. They were the chief owners of the **City of Glasgow**, and the junior partner was Mr William Inman, who managed the shipping department business. This extract from the 'Official Guide' of the Inman & International Steamship Company, published about 1888, is of interest in view of the various accounts of the inception of* the company which have been made public. The first sailing of the **City of Glasgow** for her new owners took place on 17 December 1850, from Liverpool for Philadelphia. She was under the command of Captain Mathews, who formerly had charge of the **Great Western**.

In June 1851, the **City of Manchester**, by the same builder, and also of iron, was purchased by the Inman organisation. She was 2,125 tons and carried 'overhead' or steeple geared engines of 350 horsepower [see model of this type of engine in the Glasgow Riverside Museum]. Her cylinders and proportion of gearing, however, were identical with those of the **City of Glasgow**.

The **City of Glasgow** was lost at sea in 1854 but the **City of Manchester** became a key member of the embryo Inman fleet, being chartered for use as a transport for the French during the Crimean War in 1854, and for the British, departing London for Calcutta as a transport ship as a result of the Indian Mutiny in 1857. She was eventually sold and reduced to a barque in 1871.

The **City of New York** (1851) was to be the second transatlantic liner built by Tod & McGregor on their own account but was delivered to the Inman Line as the **City of Manchester**.

A number of reports covered the loss of the **City of Glasgow** but none was conclusive, as for example this article in the *New York Herald* under the title 'Missing Steamer **City of Glasgow**':

*At last, after months of painful suspense, indications of the probable fate of the steamship **City of Glasgow**, and of the hundreds of unfortunate beings who embarked in her, have come to light. Captain M'Leary, of the barque **Mary Morris** from Glasgow, arrived here yesterday, and reports that on 18 August, in latitude 53°26' longitude 16° 07', weather very thick at the time, and a heavy sea on, he fell in with the hull of a large iron vessel, apparently Clyde-built, painted black, with a bright red bottom. There were three or four compartments in the hull, and all the woodwork was entirely burnt out of her. Some of the men who were sent aloft to look into her, perceived she had machinery in her.*

*On the next day Captain M'Leary fell in with and took on board a full length female figurehead, about seven feet in height, with her hands extended, and a wreath upon her head, and green stripes in her dress. The figure can be seen on board the **Mary Morris**, at the foot of Pine-street. It was the impression of all on board the barque that the wreck was that of an iron propeller ship, supposed the **City of Glasgow**. From the circumstance that no other iron vessel has been reported lost, except the steamer **Helen Sloman**, some three years back, appearances favour the belief that the wreck was that of the **City of Glasgow**, and that the fate of the poor souls on board, though different from that hitherto supposed, was the most awful that can occur among the many disasters incidental to the ocean. Though the proofs are but small to identify the wreck as that of the **City of Glasgow**, the weather being too unfavourable to make a more thorough examination, still enough may have been seen to guide those to a decision who were acquainted with the unfortunate vessel.*

*Our Philadelphia correspondent telegraphs that the **City of Glasgow** had no such figurehead as that picked up by the **Mary Morris**. We think he is mistaken. She had such an ornament when she left this port, but it may have been taken off. She had, however, a red bottom. The figurehead may have belonged to some other vessel.*

A separate transatlantic initiative, though also with Peter MacGregor as a Director, The Glasgow & New York Steamship Company was founded by a group of Glasgow businessmen in 1851 when the **Glasgow** was delivered by Tod & MacGregor. She was a substantial vessel of 1,574 tons gross and a length overall of 262 feet. Her engine generated 400 horsepower. The new company was slowly built up to a three-ship service with departures by the **Glasgow** eventually supplemented by the **New York** (300 feet long, and launched in August 1854) and then also by the **Edinburgh** (300 feet long and launched in November 1855). With three ships in service, departures were approximately every two to three weeks. All three ships were built by Tod & MacGregor, indeed the **Edinburgh** was first registered under the ownership of David Tod & Company. Mathew Langlands was appointed General Manager and agent for the company at its inception. An advert dated 2 February 1852 announced the delayed sailing from January and read:

*Repairs of damage done to the **Glasgow** steamship will be completed on Friday 6 February and she will sail from Greenock for New York on Saturday 7 February at 3 o'clock afternoon. Passage 20 Guineas First Cabin, 12 Guineas Second Cabin. M Langlands, 32 St Enoch Square.*

Iconic image of the launch of the **Glasgow** (1851) from Meadowside on 16 August 1851.

(Illustrated London News)

Similar adverts appeared throughout the decade. For example, the three-ship service was first advertised on 10 March 1856:

*Steamer from Glasgow to New York: **Edinburgh** 2,400 tons, Commander William Cumming, **New York** 2,050 tons, Commander Robert Craig, **Glasgow** 1,962 tons, Commander John Duncan.*

*The Ghlasgow & New York Steam-Ship Company new and powerful steam-ship **Edinburgh**, will sail direct from Glasgow to New York on Saturday 19 April with goods and passengers. Cabin passage 15 guineas, steerage 8 guineas. Freight of bale and box goods £5 per ton measurement and 5% primage. Coarse goods per arrangement. Apply to M Langlands, 20 Dixon Street.*

The **Edinburgh** (1855) was the third and last ship commissioned by the Glasgow & New York Steamship Company and was sold to the Inman Line in 1859.

The **Edinburgh** returned to the Clyde on her maiden return crossing on 31 May 1856 in a voyage from New York that took just 12 days and 22 hours. The next voyage of the **Glasgow** took place on 22 July and of the **New York** on 2 September. The log of the **Edinburgh** on a return trip from New York in November 1856, which took 14 days and 7 hours, shows just how much these ships depended on wind energy to cross the Atlantic:

November 15: At New York. At noon cast off and parted; at 2.00pm anchored inside the Hook to wait for sufficiency of water to cross the bar; at 7.30pm weighed anchor, started, and at 8.30pm passed Sandy Hook.

November 16: Wind SW, 142 miles run. Fine steady breeze, all sail set, pleasant weather.

November 17: Wind SW, 242 miles run. Winds and weather same as yesterday, passed ship **Ellen Austine** at 10.00am.

November 18: Wind NW to NE, 251 miles run. First part wind at NW, all sail set; latter part wind at NE, fore and aft sail only.

November 19: Wind NNE and variable, 209 miles run. Dark cloudy weather, squally, under single reefed fore and main topsails.

November 20: Wind N and NNE and variable, 226 miles run. Weather as yesterday. First part under top sails, latter part fore and aft sails only.

November 21: Wind NE, 207 miles run. Strong gales, severe snow storms; under double reefed topsails. At noon passed a large iceberg.

November 22: Wind NE, 190 miles run. Light baffling airs; steaming only.

November 23: Wind E, 174 miles run. Strong gales; ship rolling and labouring heavily in heavy head seas.

November 24: Wind E to SW, 170 miles run. Strong breezes; first part steaming only, latter part under all sail.

November 25: Wind W, 230 miles run. Fine weather; steady breeze; all sail set.

November 26: Wind NW by W, 230 miles run. Winds and weather same as yesterday; all sail set.

November 27: Wind variable, 228 miles run. Variable easterly winds, most part steaming only.

November 28: Wind ESE, 140 miles run. Strong gales and cloudy; steaming only.

November 29: Wind NE by E, 180 miles run. Strong gales, snow squalls; at 2.45am abreast Tory Island; at 1.15pm Mull of Kintyre; at 7.30pm Cumbrae; at 1.15am Cloch.

November 30: Wind NE by E. At Greenock.

Disaster struck the company around midnight on the night of 13/14 June 1858, as reported in the *Glasgow Herald* the following Wednesday:

We much regret to state that the noble screw steamship **New York** ... has met with disaster which it is feared will result in her total destruction. She left the Tail of the Bank about 6 o'clock on the evening of Saturday last on her outward trip to New York; with a crew of 80 men, 223 passengers, a valuable cargo, consisting principally of cotton manufactured goods, and about 12 o'clock in the following morning she went on the rocks at the outer end of the Mull of Kintyre, three miles east of the lighthouse. It appears that she went on with great force, the concussion shaking the ship from stem to stern and rousing passengers in their berths, who rushed upon deck in their night clothes in a state of indescribable alarm. Though foggy, however, the weather was fortunately calm; and all the passengers, with their luggage, were safely landed in the boats on the rocks which gird this wild and dangerous shore.

Information was, as soon as possible, dispatched overland to Campbeltown, where the news reached about 8 o'clock on Sunday morning. The steamer **Celt**, which was then in the harbour, was put under weigh, and left about two hours afterwards, reaching the **New York** about 12 o'clock noon - the distance being about 12 miles. Lloyd's agent in Campbeltown drove overland. At this time the passengers were all onshore with their luggage, and had been there since 3 o'clock in the morning. The crew were on board, and the vessel was lying on her starboard side, with about 11 feet of water in the hold - her starboard quarter, exclusive of the poop, being *almost under water. Preparations were then made to bring the passengers from shore on board the **Celt**, by means of small boats; and by 5 o'clock upwards of 130, with their luggage, had reached the steamer; but the seas getting rough, those still ashore got afraid, and remained. When the **Celt** arrived at Campbeltown, the greatest sympathy prevailed on behalf of the passengers and the crew, and there was the greatest anxiety to provide lodgings for those who had safely reached them.*

*The owners of the **Celt**, and the Lloyd's agent, praiseworthily busied themselves towards securing for the night, lodgings for the unfortunate passengers, which we understand, were given gratuitously in every case. The **Celt** reached Glasgow on Monday afternoon with the passengers on board. The remaining will, it is supposed, make for Campbeltown overland, and arrive in Glasgow on Wednesday by the next steamer.*

*Meanwhile, as soon as the **Celt** arrived at Greenock, intimation of the disaster was telegraphed to the Underwriter's Association in Glasgow, and two tugs were accordingly dispatched to the spot the same evening with the view of assisting the ship and saving the cargo. The tugs carried a body of carpenters and a quantity of spars. We are afraid that any chance of saving the ship is hopeless. She lies upon the rocks on the wildest coast in the south of Scotland, on which the tide runs with great force, and on Sunday night the wind got up, and continued to blow pretty fresh throughout Monday. On that evening when the steamer from Derry passed, the **New York** still held together; but looking to the place in which she lay, and the state of the weather, little doubt was entertained that she must go to pieces; but it is hoped that meanwhile much of her valuable cargo will be saved.*

*It is necessary to say a word regarding the loss of the magnificent, well found ship, a few hours from port, and in the calm of a summer night, within a week of the longest day of the year. And we are afraid that we must attribute the disaster to the lack of requisite caution in the desire, laudable in itself, to make a quick passage. Notwithstanding that a pretty dense fog prevailed, the **New York**, we are informed, went on at full steam, and when we have mentioned this, we have said enough to account for the whole calamity...*

By January 1859 the company was offering cabin class at 15 guineas and steerage at 8 guineas against the Liverpool to New York service of the British & North American Royal Mail Steam Packet Company at £26 chief cabin and £18 second cabin. The final sailings from Glasgow under the Glasgow & New York house flag were **Glasgow** on 14 September and **Edinburgh** on 29 September from Glasgow. The two 'sailing screw steamships' then raised the flag of the Inman Line. The company never quite recovered from the loss of the **New York**, and the margins on the Glasgow route were small compared with the much larger catchment of the British & North American at Liverpool. Flayhart again:

*When possible Inman was more than willing to remove competition by purchasing a faltering rival. The Glasgow & New York Steam Ship Company (1851-1859) had struggled to maintain a Glasgow-New York service in the face of keen competition from the Anchor Line. In 1859 William Inman bought the Glasgow & New York Steamship Company, at least in part to gain control of their two ships, **Edinburgh** and **Glasgow**. Both vessels had proven quite satisfactory and, while it was announced that they would continue to maintain the Glasgow-New York sailings, the opportunity to have a weekly sailing from Liverpool to New York was so great that in 1860 the two ships moved south to Mersey.*

By January 1860 William Inman had opened his own agency in Glasgow. It was offering the new **City of Manchester**, built as **City of New York** by and for Tod & MacGregor, with a departure from Glasgow and Greenock for New York on 11 January 'And each month in winter and each alternate Wednesday in summer, making together with Liverpool a regular weekly communication with New York'. That being said and advertised in the press, there were no further sailings from Glasgow and all vessels transferred to Liverpool 'departing every Wednesday'.

The Edinburgh Gazette, dated 20 April 1860, carried the following short notice:

The joint stock company carrying on the business of trading and carrying goods, merchandise and passengers, between the port of Clyde and New York by means of steam vessels, under the firm of the Glasgow & New York Steam Shipping Company, has this day dissolved, in terms of Resolutions of General Meetings, and of a Minute of Agreement Between the Partners of the Company, all in conformity with the provisions of the Contract of Copartnery. Signed: Archibald Russell, Thomas Brounlie, James Reid, Peter MacGregor, Andrew Small, Hector Dove, and Alexander Miller, Directors and Mathew Langlands, General Manager.

Thus, for the time being, this brought an end to Landlands' interests in Atlantic shipping.

CHAPTER 5

AMERICAN MONEY

The new screw steamship **Princess Royal** was launched on 20 June 1861 and was ready for service in July. She had a gross tonnage of 652 and her iron hull was 198 feet 9 inches x 27 feet 3 inches x 16 feet depth. She had a single propeller and a two-cylinder engine with 49 inch diameter cylinders and a 3 feet 3 inch stroke geared up to an increased speed on the propeller shaft. Steam was generated in two horizontal tubular boilers. Her design speed was 11 knots. All in all, the first screw steamer in the fleet was highly successful and very popular with passengers and shippers alike. However, like all screw steamers she would be difficult to steer in a head wind if she was badly trimmed. Captain McChlery would quickly have adjusted to the new screw steamship despite having previously spent his entire career in charge of paddle steamers.

Following her maiden voyage from Glasgow on 11 July 1861, the new **Princess Royal** quickly settled into the two and a half sailings a week routine from Glasgow and Liverpool with calls at Greenock for rail passengers. The fares remained unchanged with 15/- single and 25/- return cabin class (servants in cabin at full fare!) and 6/- steerage, with 'splendid accommodation for cabin and steerage passengers'.

In March 1862, G & J Burns' steamer **Ostrich** and then the **Heron** were taken off service for overhaul while the steamer **Ariel** stood in for them. Collectively, the Langlands' and Burns' ships still provided a service most nights of the week from both ports. The **Ariel** took her last sailing on 2 April when the **Heron** returned to service. There was no downtime for the **Princess Royal** which continued in service.

From January the agency in Liverpool for the Glasgow and Liverpool company was awarded to John McMillan and in April he was joined by Mathew Langlands' son, William to form McMillan and Langlands. William left the co-partnership with his father at Glasgow in January in order to move south to Liverpool to work alongside McMillan. Meanwhile the Glasgow agent was changed from Langlands & Son to Langlands & Sons in recognition of both John and William now working in the interests of the company. Sadly, Mathew Langlands was diagnosed with pneumonia in mid-April and died ten days later on 28 April 1862; he was 64 years old. His son John now assumed the leadership of the company.

The Burns and Glasgow & Liverpool service remained unchanged throughout the summer and into the early winter. Towards the end of November, without any prior warning, the **Princess Royal** was withdrawn from the service and the steamship **Times** stood in for her. The **Times** was a small iron-hulled steamship built in 1851 and used on the Dublin & Liverpool Screw Steam Packet Company's Ardrossan to Dundalk and Drogheda service. She took two return trips from Glasgow and was succeeded on 6 December by the **Montagu** sailing from Liverpool to Glasgow with Captain McChlery in command, with a first sailing from Glasgow on 9 December.

The **Montagu** was an altogether more suitable steamer than the **Times**. She had been built for John Bacon of Liverpool in 1851 and was used on his Liverpool to Wexford service along with the **Troubadour**. John Bacon, of course, was eventually taken over by F H Powell & Company in 1912, which then merged with Samuel Hough in 1913, to be rebranded Coast Lines in 1917.

But what had become of the late Mathew Langlands' pride and joy, his steamship **Princess Royal**? She was nowhere to be seen. The British media had been following the cut and thrust of the American Civil War since it began in April 1861. But in 1862 the Federals (Northerners) had established a strict blockade of all the southern ports on the Atlantic seaboard preventing the cotton crop from being exported and munitions and other essentials from being brought in. Fast shallow draught steamers were in great demand for blockade running, bringing in goods from Europe paid for by the cotton crop. Amongst many steamers purchased for this purpose was the new **Princess Royal**, the price offered being far greater than her book price in a market that had escalated with the demands of the American Civil War. John Langlands clearly could not resist the financial carrot that he was offered and he knew he could cover the Liverpool service using chartered steamers whilst he went back to Tod & MacGregor for a repeat build. He sold the **Princess Royal** along with her 'splendid accommodation' in November 1862 to J F Sichel, London, who immediately prepared her as a blockade runner under contract to Fraser, Trenholm and Company for the Confederacy. One or two successful runs would more than cover Mr Sichel's financial outlay.

The US Consul at Liverpool reported to the Federal Government, 8 November 1862:

*The persons here engaged in aiding the rebels have purchased three more steamers to run the blockade. They are at Glasgow and are called the **Havelock**, **Princess Royal** and **Sultan**. I understand they are to have telescopic funnels or chimneys, so they can approach the Charleston port without showing anything but masts.*

Eric Heyl describes what happened next in *Early American Steamers Volume 1*:

On January 29, 1863 she tried to slip through the Federal fleet off Charleston, South Carolina. She came from London via Newfoundland, Nova Scotia and Bermuda with a very valuable cargo of marine engines for some rams that were being built at Charleston, rifled Whitworth guns, armour plates, small arms, shoes, hospital provisions and other contraband all consigned to the Confederate States and nearly worth their weight in gold.

*The USS **Unadilla** headed off the **Princess Royal** and forced her ashore where she was seized by a prize crew of her captor. Though the Confederates made the most desperate efforts either to recapture the blockade runner and her precious cargo, or failing that to destroy her, they did not succeed and she was finally floated off by the successful Federals and anchored alongside the USS **Housatonic**. Later she was taken north and condemned in prize court at Philadelphia, bringing $342,000 for distribution to the officers and crew of the USS **Unadilla**.*

*Bought March 18, 1863 by the US Navy Department for $112,000, she was given a battery of two 30-pound Parrott rifles, one 11-inch Dahlgren gun and four 24-pound howitzers, being commissioned USS **Princess Royal** shortly afterwards.*

*On June 28, 1863 she had a sharp engagement with some Confederate forces at Donaldsonville, Louisiana, in which USS **Kineo** and USS **Winona** also participated, driving the enemy forces off the field. On August 10 1863, USS **Princess Royal** captured the small schooner **Atlantic** loaded with cotton off Rio Orande, Texas. She continued on active blockading duty during the rest of 1863 and 1864, capturing several small brigs and schooners. On December 7 1864, assisted by USS **Chocura**, she captured the schooner **Alabama** from Havana and on February 7 1865, USS **Princess Royal** and USS **Bienville** nabbed several small schooners off Galveston, Texas.*

*In the summer of 1865 USS **Princess Royal** was brought to Philadelphia and decommissioned, being sold at auction on August 17, 1865 to Samuel C Cook for $54,175.*

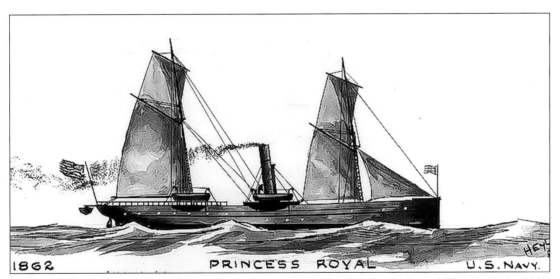

The third **Princess Royal** (1861) from a drawing by Erik Hayle dated 1950 and first published in Hayle, 1960, *Early American Steamers, Volume 1*.

The *Register of Ships in the US Navy, 1775-1990, major combatants*, sums up the career of the USS **Princess Royal** with the entry:

USS **PRINCESS ROYAL** (ex-**Princess Royal**). *Screw steamer, 3rd rate. 828 tons. 196 feet 9 inches x 27 feet 3 inches x 11 feet. Armament: one 9-inch, two 30-pounders. Machinery: horizontal geared engine, 1 screw. Speed: 11 knots. Complement: 90. Built by Tod & MacGregor, Glasgow. Launched: 20 June 1861. Captured by **Unadilla** off Charleston, 29 January, 1863 while running blockade. Purchased from Philadelphia Prize Court 18 March, 1863. Commissioned: 29 May, 1863. Sold: Philadelphia 17 August, 1865.*

Samuel Cook renamed his new acquisition *General Sherman*. Erik Heyl, with great political correctness, states that nothing is known about her until early in 1868... What is now widely known is that her adventures were only just beginning.

It would appear that Cook sent his ship to China with the hope of developing trade with America. Her crew, it appears, had other ideas and the ship started to be used as a base for raiding coastal villages. She was captured by the Chinese and sold to Meadows & Company, a British company registered in Tientsin. Meadows & Company resold her to W B Preston, an American who was keen to trade with Korea, the 'Hermit Kingdom'. Preston loaded her with merchandise of cotton goods, tin sheets, glass, and other tradable items.

The *General Sherman* (1861) depicted on fire in the Daidong River on a stamp issued by North Korea in 2006.

Seemingly the *General Sherman* left Tientsin on 9 August 1866 and reached the mouth of the Daedong River ten days later. On 5 September *General Sherman*, having disobeyed instructions from the Koreans not to sail up river, was beached near Pyongyang during a battle in which all 21 crew members were killed, some while fleeing from the ship which had been set alight by Korean fire boats. *General Sherman* was later refloated and moved to a shipyard near Seoul where she was refurbished and commissioned into the Korean Navy. However, under intense pressure from China, the ship was returned in 1867 to her original American owner, Samuel Cook, who resold her to William F Weld Company of Boston for its Merchants of Boston Steamship Company. For many years the Korean incident was kept quiet and the role that the former *Princess Royal* had played in the affair remained unknown.

Erik Heyl concludes the story of the ship:

*On January 4, 1874, the **General Sherman** left New York on her usual run with four passengers and a crew of forty-two men. Her cargo consisted of general merchandise consigned to New Orleans. The weather began to worsen and on January 7, 1874 at 2.00am the **General Sherman** sprung a bad leak, so that her pumps could not take care of the water pouring into her. The steamer was headed for the nearest shore.*

In the morning of January 8, 1874, the rising water had put out the fires, and the wind had now shifted and was blowing her back to sea. She anchored and sent a boat to Little River, about twelve miles off.

*The schooner **Spray**, followed by the schooner **Florence**, went to the assistance of the **General Sherman**, taking off six men, some baggage and a few lots of the cargo; the **Florence** removed the rest of the people on the **General Sherman**, also the passengers: one woman, two children and a man, as well as most of the baggage.*

*The **Spray** left about 4.00pm, the **Florence** staying behind until everything possible had been salvaged. Both of the schooners sailed to Wilmington, North Carolina, from where the steam tug **Brandt** was despatched about noon, January 10, 1874. She managed to put a hawser to the **General Sherman** and towed her as far as Tub's Inlet, 27 miles from Cape Fear, when she sank.*

But apart from the excitement of the *General Sherman* incident, the Glasgow & Liverpool Royal Steam Packet Company was again without a steamer to run its namesake service once the *Princess Royal* had been sold in November 1862. A new screw steamer was ordered immediately from Tod & MacGregor, and with the proceeds of the sale of the earlier screw steamer money was at last no problem. She was to be of broadly similar dimensions and design to her earlier namesake with a two-cylinder engine geared up to the propeller shaft and a speed of 11 knots. In the meantime the Liverpool service was left in charge of the chartered screw steamer *Montagu* under Captain McChlery.

In March 1863 the iron paddle steamer *Clansman* relieved the *Ostrich* on the G & J Burns service, then, in April, also the *Heron*. The *Clansman* dated from 1855 was delivered by J & G Thomson to David Hutcheson & Company. She was designed for their Glasgow to Stornoway service and as such had ample passenger berths for the Glasgow to Liverpool route. But she was not quite the last paddler to serve between Glasgow and Liverpool. Langlands' *Montagu* stood down at Liverpool after the departure from Glasgow on 2 April, the ship being needed by its owners back on the Liverpool to Wexford service. The next sailing was from Glasgow on Wednesday 8 April when Captain McChlery took charge of the venerable paddle steamer *Blenheim*, chartered from William Tod of Tod & MacGregor who had agreed to accept the steamer from the Belfast Steamship Company as part payment for a new vessel.

The *Blenheim* had been built for Messrs Langtry and Herdman by Tod & MacGregor in 1848. Fortunately this throwback to the past only lasted until mid-September when the new screw steamer *Princess Royal* (fourth of the name) came into service, again under the command of Captain McChlery. This allowed the *Blenheim* to return to William Tod for a new charter to the Great Eastern Railway starting in October 1863. In the following year William Tod sold the *Blenheim* for use as yet another blockade runner.

The former Belfast Steamship Company's *Blenheim* (1848) was chartered from William Tod to maintain the Liverpool service between April and September 1863.

(from an oil painting by Joseph Semple)

The new *Princess Royal* was launched in August and was essentially similar to her predecessor with a gross tonnage of 566 tons.

The Glasgow & Liverpool Royal Steam Packet Company was again back on track with its one-ship fleet, only this time it had money in the bank. The Glasgow & Liverpool was ultimately set to expand beyond its core service, but for the moment stability was what the company wanted most of all.

In February 1862 William Sloan & Company, jointly with Hermann Leo Seligmann, both of Glasgow, inaugurated a new cargo service between Glasgow and Dunkirk with the steamer *Auguste Louise*. She was to be joined by the newly-built screw steamship *Blanche* later in the year. The *Blanche* was noteworthy as the first ship to be built by A & J Inglis at Pointhouse. She was just 121 feet by 20 feet by 12 feet deep and was designed much as a contemporary collier. She was equipped with a twin single-expansion engine and had a boiler pressure of just 27 pounds per square inch. The Dunkirk service was not a success and Langlands & Sons was able to buy the newly-completed *Blanche* in January 1864 to inaugurate a new service between Glasgow and Havre commencing 6 February and sailing every fortnight thereafter. Her master was Captain Moir and the agent at Havre was A Lenormand Fils. The new route was in direct competition with Hutchison & Brown's existing service operated by the steamers *William Connal* and *Excelsior*. The *Excelsior* was withdrawn in March and the *William Connal* and *Blanche* then offered a weekly departure from both ports. The *Blanche* was withdrawn with a final sailing from Glasgow on 20 August leaving the service in the hands of the *William Connal*. This had been a valiant effort to break into the continental trade, but one which was not to succeed.

During the summer of 1864 John Langlands held discussions with James Cuthbert of the Clyde Shipping Company about inaugurating a service between Glasgow and Plymouth with the intention of developing it from cargo only to passenger and cargo once it was established. Henry J Waring & Company was appointed agent at Plymouth and on 21 November 1864 the *Blanche* inaugurated the new cargo service with onward transhipment available to London. Departures from Glasgow and Plymouth were scheduled at approximately fortnightly intervals. The Clyde Shipping Company maintained an interest in the service although it had not committed money towards the venture.

Some more American money was taken from the bank for the purchase of the Glasgow & Stranraer Steam Packet Company. The Langlands family had long been associated with this company and its predecessors, with Alexander Langlands, from Mathew's family in Campbeltown, appointed its agent in Stranraer back in

1851. Mathew Langlands & Sons was then also the company's agent in Glasgow. The Stranraer company's services at various times included the core route between Glasgow and Stranraer via Ayr, to Belfast, Campbeltown and seasonally also to the West Highlands to bring livestock south for wintering and to Liverpool to carry livestock to market (see Duckworth and Langmuir, *Clyde and other coastal steamers*, Chapter 4, for details of the company's activities). At the time of the Langlands takeover the company operated one ship out of Stranraer, the iron-hulled paddle steamer **Albion** built for them by Tod & MacGregor in 1860. She worked variously between Ayr, Campbeltown and Glasgow with calls that were served by tenders at Arran, Girvan and Ballantrae.

Meanwhile, the G & J Burns Liverpool and Glasgow service received the new steamer **Penguin** in April, replacing the **Heron**, and for a while she ran alongside the **Blenheim**, while the **Ostrich** was overhauled. The **Ostrich** was replaced in November by the new steamer **Beagle**, a smaller version of the **Penguin**. The **Ostrich** was back in December while the **Penguin** received attention.

The year 1865 started with the **Ostrich** and **Beagle** running for Burns and the **Princess Royal** for Langlands on the Liverpool service. In March the **Penguin** replaced the **Beagle** and the two companies collaboratively announced that 25/- return tickets were valid by these steamers or by **Princess Royal**. The new cargo only service to the south coast of England was expanding with the **Blanche** sailing from Glasgow for Shoreham on 3 April and the chartered screw steamer **Windermere** leaving Glasgow on 11 April for Plymouth. The **Windermere** was a 498 ton iron-hulled screw steamer built in 1851 for H W Schneider of London.

Also in April 1865 the paddle steamer **Albion** was sold by the wholly-owned Glasgow & Stranraer Steam Packet Company to Peter Lindsay Henderson, a Liverpool shipbroker, who chartered her to the Somerset & Dorset Railway Company for a short-lived ferry service between Poole and Cherbourg. Henderson then sold her to John Pool of Hayle to work between Hayle and Bristol via Ilfracombe with a weekly trip also to Swansea. Her place at Stranraer was taken by chartered vessels, initially by David Hutcheson's screw steamship **Staffa**, completed only in 1861, and from 20 May by the Belfast Steamship Company's screw steamship **Electric**, completed in 1862. The **Electric** earlier had stood in for the **Princess Royal** on the core Glasgow to Liverpool service between 3 and 18 May while the **Princess**, received her spring overhaul. The **Electric** stood down at Stranraer when the new screw steamship **Albion** was delivered by Tod & MacGregor in July. Her registered owner was John Reid. She was an attractive looking vessel with a length of 160 feet and a breadth of 20 feet,

RETURN TICKETS between GLASGOW & LIVERPOOL
Cabin, 25s. (available for a Month),
By PRINCESS ROYAL, PENGUIN, OSTRICH, or BEAGLE.

STEAM COMMUNICATION
BETWEEN
GLASGOW AND LIVERPOOL,
Calling at GREENOCK.

Unless prevented by any unforeseen occurrence, the under-noted or other Steamers are intended to Sail (with or without Pilots) between GLASGOW and LIVERPOOL, with Goods and Passengers, as under.

THE GLASGOW AND LIVERPOOL ROYAL STEAM-PACKET COMPANY'S STEAMSHIP
PRINCESS ROYAL....New Steamer.... Capt. M'CHLERY,
FROM GLASGOW—

March, 1865.		From Broomielaw, Glasgow, at	By Rail to Greenock.
Princess......Wednesday,	1........	1 P.M........	3 P.M.
Princess......Tuesday,	7........	6 P.M........	7 P.M.
Princess......Saturday,	11........	11 A.M........	1 P.M.
Princess......Thursday,	16........	1 P.M........	3 P.M.
Princess......Wednesday,	22........	5 P.M........	7 P.M.
Princess......Tuesday,	28........	11 A.M........	1 P.M.

FROM LIVERPOOL—

March, 1865.		From Clarence Dock.
Princess......Saturday,	4.....................	3 P.M.
Princess......Thursday,	9.....................	8 P.M.
Princess......Tuesday,	14.....................	11 A.M.
Princess......Monday,	20.....................	3 P.M.
Princess......Saturday,	25.....................	8 P.M.
Princess......Thursday,	30.....................	12 Noon.

Passengers leaving Glasgow by the Railway Train at the hours noted above will be in time to join the Vessel at Greenock.
Goods for shipment at Glasgow or Liverpool must be along-side the Vessel One Hour before the appointed time of sailing.
*** Box and Bale Goods conveyed between GLASGOW and MANCHESTER, including Lifting and Delivery, 20s. per Ton. Other Goods per agreement.
☞ Passengers are requested to take charge of their own Luggage, as the Ship is not responsible in any way for its safety
FARES:—Cabin (including Steward's Fee), 15s. ; Return, 25s Steerage, 6s. Servants in Cabin full fare.
Apply to M'Millan & Langlands, 1 India Buildings, Water Street, Liverpool; D. M'Larty & Co., Excise Buildings, Greenock ; or to
MATHEW LANGLANDS & SONS,
20 Dixon Street, St. Enoch Square, Glasgow.

"ANCHOR" LINE
OF
PENINSULAR & MEDITERRA-

Advertisement for the Glasgow and Liverpool service in the *Glasgow Herald*, 1 March 1865.

(Linda Gowans collection)

and offered day accommodation for her passengers on the run from Glasgow down the coast to Stranraer under the command of Captain Douglas. The **Albion** sailed from Glasgow and Stranraer on alternate days with a rest day at Stranraer on Sundays.

The **Windermere** was replaced on charter by the **Northumberland**, which was advertised to sail from Glasgow on 6 June for Plymouth. The **Northumberland** was transferred to a new service to London, and, for example, was scheduled to sail from London on 8 July and back from Glasgow five days later. Another screw steamer was taken on charter in July, the **Clyde** under Captain Murphy, and she sailed from Glasgow for Plymouth on

11 July. Both ships were chartered from Cram, Powell & Company, later F H Powell, of Liverpool; the **Clyde** built in 1851 and originally owned by the Carron Company and the **Northumberland** built in 1853 for the General Iron Screw Steam Collier Company but now also owned by Cram, Powell & Company. By August both the **Clyde** and **Northumberland** were on the London run and the **Blanche** was looking after Plymouth, now with an additional call at Penzance, although the ships did interchange as the **Clyde** was on Plymouth duties in November, while it was back to **Blanche** for Plymouth in December. The **Northumberland** was returned to her owners during the autumn. Meanwhile the only change by the end of the year on the Liverpool core service was that advertisements now proclaimed a new steamer for the route: '**Princess Alice** now building'; the remaining revenue from the Americans was being invested so that the company, with its new and diverse interests, would prosper.

The year 1866 saw the arrival of the new steamers **Snipe** for G & J Burns and **Princess Alice** for the Glasgow & Liverpool Company. In the early part of the year the **Clyde** terminated at Dunkirk and the **Blanche** was on the Penzance and Plymouth run, the London service having earlier been abandoned in favour of transhipment at Plymouth. In the spring the service to Dunkirk was discontinued and the **Clyde** was taken off charter. The big news in April was a sharing agreement between G & J Burns and the Glasgow & Liverpool Royal Steam Packet Company (M Langlands & Sons, managing owners) to provide steamers to maintain a daily departure from both Glasgow via Greenock and from Liverpool other than on Sundays. The Liverpool terminal now became either Clarence Dock as before or Trafalgar Dock. This schedule required two ships from Glasgow and Liverpool and the almost new iron screw steamship **Liverpool** (Captain Walker) was chartered, starting at Liverpool on 13 April and returning from Glasgow on 16 April, to run alongside the **Princess Royal** until the new steamer could be commissioned. Burns' **Ostrich** was sold at the end of January so they too chartered-in tonnage. Last of the paddle steamers on the service was Burns' new Glasgow to Belfast steamer **Buffalo** which ran prior to the arrival in service of the **Snipe** in mid-August.

On 19 April the **Princess Alice** was launched at Tod & MacGregor's Meadowside yard as described in the *Glasgow Herald*, 20 April 1866, presumably with a second paragraph provided by Mr Langlands' PR spin doctor:

There was a launch yesterday from the building yard of Messrs Tod & MacGregor, a fine screw steamer which was named **Princess Alice***. The vessel is built for Messrs M Langlands & Sons, for the Glasgow and Liverpool trade, and is intended to be consort to the* **Princess Royal***, already plying on that station. With this addition to their fleet of steamers, the firm just mentioned, in conjunction with Messrs G & J Burns, will accomplish daily sailings between the two ports with regularity [no Sunday sailings]. The* **Princess Alice** *is 780 tons burthen, being 200 feet by 28 feet by 15³/₄ feet, with a pair of direct-acting inverted cylinder engines of 150 horsepower, surface condenser, expansion valves, and all recent improvements, and will be fitted up in a style of completeness and efficiency similar to the* **Princess Royal***, and has elegant accommodation for 40 to 50 first class passengers.*

The service thus served between the two ports for the conveyance of both goods and passengers by daily sailings of such superior class of powerful and swift steamers must thoroughly meet the requirements of the trade, and place shippers and passengers in a position of advantage that can leave nothing to be desired.

The chartered steamer **Liverpool** stayed on service until she stood down at Liverpool in mid-July. In the meantime the new **Princess Alice** took her maiden voyage south on 1 June under Captain Scott and the **Princess Royal** went away for six weeks for a thorough overhaul. The registered owners of the **Princess Alice** were John Langlands, Mathew Langlands (junior) and John Reid, jointly. As it happened, she was to become one of the most successful steamers ever to be commissioned into the Langlands fleet.

The day that the **Princess Alice** was launched was also the day of another less fortunate launch, that of the whaler **Lion** from the yard of Messrs Robert Steel & Son at Greenock, and involving the steamer **Albion**. The *Glasgow Herald* again:

…While the **Lion** *was being launched, an accident of a somewhat alarming character occurred. Just as she began to move on the ways, the Stranraer and Glasgow steamship* **Albion***, Captain Douglas, approached the spot opposite the course the* **Lion** *would take when she entered the water. Captain Douglas seeing the imminent danger in which his vessel was placed, at once ordered the engines to be reversed, in order, if possible, to get the* **Albion** *out of the vicinity. Under these circumstances, however, a collision was unavoidable, so that when the* **Lion** *entered the water, and before the impetus of launching could be checked by the attendant tug steamer, she ran with great force against the* **Albion***, striking her abaft the luff of the port*

bow, carrying away her bulwark stanchions, foremast rigging, main rail, part of the hurricane deck, funnel stays, stoving in a lifeboat, and doing other serious damage. Fortunately the protective belting at the water's edge of the **Albion** saved any of that steamer's plates being started, at least as far as could be ascertained, but part of the belting was considerably bent in consequence of the shock. Of course, the alarm amongst the passengers and crew on board the **Albion** was for a time very great, and several narrow escapes from injury are detailed amongst the passengers forward. Fortunately no passenger was injured...

The **Albion** was temporarily repaired last night, and was expected to proceed on her passage. She was all tight below while lying at Greenock quay. We may state that a red flag was hoisted in the builder's yard as a signal of danger, but not having been observed by Captain Douglas, the result is as stated above.

No doubt Captain Douglas was instructed to report to Mr Langlands' office when the **Albion** next returned to Glasgow!

The new joint daily service between Glasgow and Liverpool settled in with the paddle steamer **Buffalo** finally standing down in September leaving Burns' **Snipe** and **Penguin** running with the **Princess Royal** and **Princess Alice**. The Burns steamer **Weasel** replaced the **Penguin** in October. Meanwhile the **Blanche** had settled on a new roster sailing from Glasgow roughly every two weeks to Plymouth calling at Wexford (eg departing Glasgow on 10 and 24 November and 6 and 19 December 1866). The services to Shoreham and elsewhere had ceased earlier in the year when the **Clyde** had been returned to her owners.

MacIver's Liverpool and Glasgow Steamers
From John Kennedy, *The History of Steam Navigation,* 1903

*Although there were three perfectly distinct steamship companies trading between Liverpool and Glasgow, yet so friendly were the respective owners towards each other that in 1846 they issued a joint sailing bill, which included the whole of the sailings for all the companies. This arrangement continued unchanged for seven years (1853), at the end of which period the **Princess Royal** was advertised separately. At this date the quickest, cheapest (although the fares were double what they now are), and most comfortable mode of travelling between Liverpool and Glasgow was by steamer. The steamers were large, swift, and luxuriously furnished, and so numerous were the passengers that the joint companies maintained a daily service. From the year 1853 the two services, the MacIver and the Burns, were amalgamated, the joint line being represented in Liverpool by Charles MacIver & Company, and in Glasgow by G & J Burns.*

*In 1850 Messrs Charles MacIver & Company instituted the steamship service between Liverpool and Havre, the pioneer steamer being the **Commodore**, the well-known Liverpool and Glasgow steam packet. About the same date the steamship services to the Mediterranean were begun by Messrs MacIver, under the style of Messrs Burns and MacIver. Until the year 1853 no distinctive class of name had been adopted for the coasting steamers of the MacIver line, but in that year the **Elk** and **Stag** were built, followed by the **Lynx**. These were the last of the paddle steamers built to run between Liverpool and Glasgow. In 1855 the owners decided to place screw steamers on this station, and accordingly built the screw steamers **Otter**, **Beaver**, and **Zebra**. The **Zebra** was a large and powerful vessel, and was amongst the earliest of the steamers taken up by government for transport duty during the Crimean War. All the succeeding steamers have been of the same type, and have been named after animals or birds. The joint service remained in force for nearly half a century, until [in 1895] Messrs G & J Burns opened an office in Liverpool, and placed the steamers **Mastiff**, **Pointer** and **Spaniel** on the station. The elder of the two brothers [the founders of the MacIver steamship business], Mr David MacIver, died unmarried in 1845. His brother, the late Mr Charles MacIver, of Calderstone, then became the head of the firm, which position he held until his death in 1885.*

CONSOLIDATION 1867-1875

The year 1867 began as a period of stability. The joint core service of the Glasgow & Liverpool Royal Steam Packet Company and G & J Burns continued to offer a daily departure from either port with the steamers *Princess Royal*, *Princess Alice* and the *Snipe* and *Weasel* from the Burns fleet. The Liverpool terminal had now reverted to Clarence Dock, South Side while Glasgow sailings were still from the Broomielaw via Greenock. The *Princess Royal* went for her springtime refit in mid-April, followed by the *Princess Alice*, while Burns' *Penguin* stood in for them. The Langlands cargo steamer *Blanche* sailed early each month for Plymouth only, occasionally as demand required calling at Penzance, and in the middle of the month she left Glasgow for a round trip to Wexford and Plymouth. This pattern was repeated until September. The chartered brand new, 482 ton, iron-hulled steamship *Osaca*, owned by E M de Bussche of London, restarted the London sailings at the beginning of July. At 2.00pm on 4 September the chartered steamer *Tuskar* was advertised to take the Plymouth sailing.

The *Tuskar* was chartered from the Clyde Shipping Company. She was an altogether more substantial vessel than the *Blanche*, being 172 feet by 2 feet 7 inches by 14 feet depth and she measured 456 tons gross. Typical of the day, and like the *Princess Alice* and *Princess Royal*, she had a whaleback bridge deck designed to shed water. She had a two-cylinder side lever engine and an iron hull. She had been one of four modern passenger and cargo ships maintaining the regular three times a week service between Glasgow and Cork, via Waterford, in partnership with the Clyde Shipping Company's steamers *Kinsale*, *Saltee* and *Sanda*. The attraction of the *Tuskar* was that, unlike the *Blanche*, she offered 'good accommodation for passengers' and was an ideal ship to develop the Plymouth service which now required greater cargo capacity and facilities to carry passengers. She was, however, too deep in draught to cross the bar at Wexford, except during the brief high tide period, and the Wexford call was left to the London steamer or served by occasional visits from the *Blanche*. The *Tuskar* maintained the same schedule as before, with sailings from Glasgow and Plymouth roughly every two weeks. The *Tuskar* was returned to her owners and replaced by the steamer *Arbutus* in November. The *Arbutus* was then owned by the Belfast Steamship Company but was previously in the Laird fleet at Glasgow and was originally built for William Wellan of London in 1854.

Langlands did not consider it worthwhile maintaining the *Blanche* just for occasional London trips from Glasgow. Passengers preferred the faster east coast route via Leith and through cargo rates via Leith were favourable as well. Consequently, the little *Blanche* was put on the 'for sale' list. She was bought during August by Joseph Weatherly of Glasgow for further service.

On 6 November 1867 the *Princess Alice* left the Liverpool service on arrival at Glasgow and then stood in for the *Weasel* on the Glasgow to Londonderry service at the start of a charter to G & J Burns. The *Princess Alice* finished on Londonderry duties at the end of January 1868 when the *Weasel* returned to duty.

The *Princess Alice* (1866) clearly showing her whale-back midships structure.

The core Glasgow to Liverpool service was then maintained on a four to five sailings a week basis; clearly the daily service had been hard to maintain particularly with the downturn in the passenger trade in the winter months. The *Princess Alice* came back on the Liverpool service on 21 March 1868 running for Burns as relief for the *Penguin* which was sent away for refit. She was then returned to Langlands and stood in for the *Princess Royal* at Glasgow from 10 May. Following her own refit the *Princess Alice* was then put on an extended time charter to Burns, Langlands' Captain Scott handed the ship over to Captain Archibald in Glasgow and she was sent down to Liverpool to become the main unit on the Burns & MacIver service between Liverpool and Havre. Captain Scott, however, remained with the ship as Deputy Master and, in due course, resumed command when he had learnt the peculiarities of the new trade. There was, of course, also an established regular passenger and cargo service between Glasgow and Havre operated by John and Peter Hutchison.

The Plymouth service received improved chartered tonnage when McConnell & Laird's new steamer *Rose* replaced the *Arbutus*. The first sailing by the *Rose* was on 21 January 1868 to Plymouth only, followed on 4 February with a sailing to Penzance, Plymouth and Teignmouth. Meanwhile, negotiations were taking place between Mathew Langlands and James Cuthbert over a purchase price for the Plymouth and Wexford services and the goodwill of the developed trade passing to the Clyde Shipping Company. Negotiations were completed during March and the Clyde Shipping Company put its own ships on the service to Plymouth with an inaugural sailing from Glasgow on 31 March. Initially the passenger and cargo service was monthly (from Glasgow on 31 March, 28 April and 24 May), but thereafter it was fortnightly (from Glasgow 9 June, 23 June, 7 July and so on). The four ships previously employed solely on the Clyde Shipping Company's Glasgow, Waterford and Cork service, *Saltee*, *Sanda*, *Tuskar* and *Kinsale*, now had to pick up the Glasgow to Plymouth roster as well. *Tuskar*, of course, had previously been trialled on the route during the early winter period. Calls at Wexford ceased and goods were instead forwarded from Waterford. Passenger fares on the Plymouth service were cabin 20/-, return 30/-, and steerage 10/-.

Once again the Glasgow & Liverpool Royal Steam Packet Company was effectively a one-ship, one-service fleet with the *Princess Royal* on charter to Burns. The sale of the Plymouth service indicated the low economic margins that Langlands had been coping with; it had never been financially sensible to build a new ship or charter a passenger and cargo steamer for the service. However, the Clyde Shipping Company, with its fleet of four steamers on the Waterford and Cork route, were able to fit the Plymouth roster into their existing schedule and thus make a profit.

At the start of 1869 the situation had not changed. The *Princess Royal* was running between Liverpool and Glasgow on the core service, with the *Snipe* and *Penguin*, and the *Princess Alice* was chartered-out to Burns & MacIver. At the beginning of March, the new Burns steamer *Raven* replaced the *Snipe* on the Liverpool service. Ominously at the beginning of May, the following advertisement appeared in the *Glasgow Herald*; it also served to remind shippers that the old sailing rantapikes were still available and that they offered far cheaper rates than the Burns and Langlands steamers:

Glasgow & Liverpool Screw Steamship Company: The new, 20-year first class, steamship Sardonyx, specially built for the trade, John Campbell Commander, will commence sailing regularly between Glasgow, Greenock and Liverpool, carrying goods at moderate rates, leaving Glasgow on Tuesday 4 May and every succeeding Tuesday at 4.00pm and from Canning Dock Liverpool every Friday evening. The steamer will sail in conjunction with the celebrated clipper schooners Jasper, Onyx, Sapphire and Topaz intended to be dispatched from each port twice a week. McArthur Brothers, Glasgow.

The *Sardonyx* hardly dented the Burns and Langlands monopoly on the Liverpool service but she was there to stay. The 'celebrated clipper schooners', which were still owned and operated by Robert Gilchrist, remained in the trade for a few further years but the reliability of the steamer schedules ultimately saw the demise of sail on the coast.

John Langlands bought the former Stranraer paddle steamer *Albion* back from John Bickford of Hayle, Cornwall, in time for the 1869 summer season. Her role was to assist with the Stranraer duties performed until then by the screw steamship *Albion*. The latter was chartered to Martin Orme in September while his new steamer *Dunvegan Castle* attended her guarantee refit. The *Dunvegan Castle* was back on duty on 27 September scheduled to sail from Glasgow for: Iona, Bunessan, Tiree, Coll, Dunvegan, Uig, Tarbert, Rodel, Lochmaddy, Kallin and Lochboisdale. Thereafter, the two *Albions* provided the services of the Glasgow & Stranraer Steam Packet Company; surely a cause for confusion by one and all – this *Albion* for Larne, that *Albion* for Ayr and Glasgow, or is it the other way around!

One of the hazards of the Irish Channel, and more so of the English Channel, was, and is still, that of cross-channel ferries cutting across the main through-channel traffic at right angles. A report in the *Glasgow Herald*, Monday 19 July 1869, described a ferry collision that could so easily have been a tragedy:

*On Friday morning a collision occurred between the Morecambe steamship **Roe**, (Captain Donnan), while on passage from Barrow-in-Furness to Belfast, and the steamer **Princess Royal**, bound from the Clyde to Liverpool, and belonging to M Langlands & Sons, of this city. The collision took place in the Irish Channel, off the Mull of Galloway, and the weather at the time was thick and hazy. 'On board the **Roe**', says the Belfast Whig of Saturday, 'the other vessel was not sighted till within a very short time of the collision. Every effort, we understand, was made on board both vessels to prevent the serious disaster which seemed impending. The **Princess Royal**, however, struck the **Roe** about two feet from the bowsprit, and cut her side down to near the water's edge, but the collision, fortunately, was not accompanied by great force, and the vessels soon got clear of each other. On examination it was found that the injury to the **Roe** was confined to the apartment over which she was struck, which is watertight. This portion of the steamer, of course, soon filled with water, but she was not otherwise injured. She arrived here yesterday about mid-day – some six or seven hours late. It is fortunate that the **Roe** was not struck three or four feet nearer the centre, as if she had, she would have gone down immediately. The people on board were, of course, greatly alarmed when the collision took place, but the excitement was considerably quieted when the extent of the injury was fully ascertained. The steamer was placed in dock last evening for repairs.'*

*The Belfast Newsletter states that one man, who was in his berth in the **Roe**, 'at the opposite side to that which the steamers collided, sustained some slight injuries to his head; but fortunately, the men who occupied the berths on the side where the injury took place were on duty, and they escaped almost certain death. The forecastle immediately began to fill with water, and in a few minutes it was filled up to the bulkhead which separates the forecastle from the forward hold. However, the bulkhead kept 'out of the water', and thus the cargo was preserved intact. Immediately before the collision, the engine of the **Roe** was being reversed, owing to the Captain having heard a whistle, and, doubtless, it is to this that the vessel's not sinking may be attributed. As soon as the **Princess Royal** struck... the vessel lay alongside the **Roe** so as to render assistance, if necessary, but there was no need of it and, it was found that the latter could proceed with safety to her destination. Some of the passengers of the **Roe**, however, were rather distrustful, and preferred going on board the **Princess Royal**. In about an hour and a quarter after the collision took place, both vessels proceeded on their respective courses...'*

This report was followed two days later by another article in the *Glasgow Herald* under the headline 'Collision between the **Roe** and **Princess Royal**':

*With reference to the collision between the Barrow steamship **Roe**, bound for Belfast, and the steamer **Princess Royal**, bound for Liverpool, which took place in the Irish Channel on Friday morning, Captain McChlery, of the **Princess Royal**, has furnished to his employers, Messrs Langlands & Sons, Glasgow, a report on the collision, substantially similar to the account published in Monday's Herald. He explains that he made every exertion, by sounding a whistle and reversing the engine, to prevent the collision, or at least to make the shock less severe, and states that when fears were entertained for the safety of the **Roe**, he sent his first mate and engineer on board her, to make minute examination of her, and they found her perfectly able to proceed on her voyage.*

*When the collision occurred, Captain McChlery sent a boat for the relief of a number of the passengers on board the **Roe**, who seemed to have considered that the damage the **Roe** had sustained was greater than it really was; and when on board the **Princess Royal**, these passengers, fourteen in all, presented the following address to Captain McChlery: 'We the undersigned passengers, on board the steamer **Roe**, from Barrow to Belfast, beg to offer our best thanks to Captain McChlery of the **Princess Royal** for sending his boat to our rescue after the collision of the two steamers at two o'clock this morning, and for his kindness and attention to us during the remainder of our voyage to Liverpool...'*

Burns' former Liverpool steamer, the **Snipe**, was also chartered-out. During the summer and early autumn she was running from Glasgow to the Highlands for David Hutcheson following the loss of his steamer the **Clansman** on Sheep Island, off the Mull of Kintyre, at the entrance to the Firth of Clyde on 21 July 1869. The **Clansman** had run ashore in thick fog but all personnel (about 100) and a good few sheep were brought ashore safely.

In the autumn came relief to the rather overstretched duties of the Clyde Shipping Company's four-ship services to Cork and Waterford and to Plymouth. The oldest vessel, the *Tuskar* stood down and was replaced by the new steamers *Eddystone* and *Cumbrae*, providing a five-ship service with much greater operational security.

The joint Glasgow to Liverpool route continued to be served by the *Penguin*, *Raven* and *Princess Royal*, the fares unchanged. There were five departures from each port so that there was one absent mid-week sailing, and, of course, no departures scheduled for the Sabbath. *Princess Alice* remained on charter to Burns. Langlands had adopted a berth in Trafalgar Dock, north side at Liverpool, during the year although the Burns steamers still used Clarence Dock.

The year 1870 was an exciting year for Langlands. The *Princess Alice* was due back from her charter to Burns and the *Princess Royal* was scheduled for lengthening and reboilering. There was yet another flirtatious attempt to break into the transatlantic business, this time with South America. In February, John Langlands (rather than M Langlands & Sons) announced in the press:

The Glasgow and South American Steamship Company will dispatch their new full-powered screw steamship Andes, *1,440 tons register Aa1 at Lloyd's, from Glasgow in June 1870 for Bahia, Rio de Janeiro, Monte Video and Buenos Ayres. To be followed by their new screw steamship* Alps, *1,500 tons register, Aa1 at Lloyd's. These vessels are being built expressly for the trade, and present an unrivalled opportunity to ship fine goods. They have also magnificent accommodation for first class cabin passengers. John Langlands, 28 Great Clyde Street.*

As it happened the *Andes* was not ready to take her maiden voyage until Saturday 3 September having only been launched on 11 August. She was registered in the name of James Reid Stewart. The two sisters were built by John Key & Sons at Kinghorn. The *Andes* was 272 feet long by 32 feet by 25 feet depth and measured 1,505 tons gross whereas the *Alps* was 281 by 33 by 25 feet depth. The *Alps* was launched at Kinghorn on 9 January 1871. The sisters had iron hulls and were equipped with two compound direct-acting engines with cylinders of 35 and 60 inch diameter and a stroke of 83 inches that gave them a service speed of 10 knots. They had three masts and accommodation was amidships. They were very square looking vessels and in no way could they be described as attractive. The *Andes* left Rio de Janeiro on her return voyage to Glasgow on 11 December.

The *Andes* sailed for South America under the command of Captain W Smith on her second voyage on 26 January and the *Alps* took her maiden voyage under Captain Webster six weeks later on 9 March. The *Andes* sailed again on 18 May, and the *Alps* on 18 July, having arrived back in the Clyde on 1 July via Liverpool. The service was now advertised at Glasgow by Wilson & Langlands rather than by John Langlands as initially had been the case. So far loadings had been less than expected and the economics of the new company were unlikely to pay the creditors much return. The other operator on the South American trade was Donaldson Brothers and they also found that the margins on the South American trade were unattractive, choosing to concentrate principally on the North Atlantic trades from 1874 onwards.

Further sailings from Glasgow were the *Andes* on 16 September, this time via Bordeaux but without the call at Bahia, followed on the same route by the *Alps* on 25 November. Each ship made one more trip, the *Andes* leaving Glasgow on 25 January and the *Alps* on 16 March 1872, before they were rerouted to call at London with some voyages continuing north to Leith. From then on John Langlands no longer represented the Scottish interests of the company. The *Alps* was withdrawn in 1873 and sold to the White Cross Line of Antwerp for their service to New York. The *Andes* stayed under the ownership of The Glasgow & South American Steamship Company until 1877, working partly under charter to other operators, when she too was sold to the White Cross Line, her sister having been destroyed by fire the previous year. The business of the Glasgow and South American Steamship Company was then wound up and with it the Langlands' family interests in the Atlantic trades.

An arrangement such as Langlands and the Glasgow & South American Steamship Company, whereby a coasting packet company was involved with and acting on behalf of a deep sea company, was not unusual. Another example, of course, is Burns and British and North American (later Cunard). The converse arrangement was also true; Handyside and Henderson's Anchor Line ran a weekly coastal passenger and cargo service between Glasgow and Barrow at this time with the steamer *Dom Pedro*, increased to twice-weekly in 1871 when the *Dido* and *Despatch* joined the route. This provided a link between the parent company's services at Glasgow with the Barrow Steamship Company's base in Furness, the latter part-owned by Henderson and operational from 1872.

On 11 February 1870 the *Princess Alice* passed the Mersey Bar and instead of turning south for Havre sailed north to Glasgow with a full load of cargo and the normal passenger complement. She remained on the service to allow the *Raven* to go for overhaul then, in April, the *Penguin*. In April Captain Scott and the *Princess Alice* deputised for the *Princess Royal*, although the *Princess Royal* returned to service for two weeks in June, taking the Liverpool departures on 19, 24 and 28 May. The *Princess Alice* remained in service with the *Raven* and *Penguin* for the remainder of the year. Meanwhile, the *Princess Royal* underwent a thorough overhaul, had new compound engines installed and received a 29 feet new hull section aft of the forward hold and before the bridge. This increased her gross tonnage from 566 to 712 providing considerably more cargo capacity and also providing a slightly increased speed. The lengthened and re-engined *Princess Royal* underwent acceptance trials and was put on the Liverpool service starting at the end of the year, releasing the *Princess Alice* once again for charter work, this time heading south to Spain under the command of Captain McDougall.

In October 1870 a stronger attempt to break into the Liverpool steamer trade was made by rantapike owner, Robert Gilchrist when he put the brand new steamer *Fire King* on the route with departures from Glasgow on Fridays and from Liverpool on Tuesdays. This was a more serious threat than that from the steamer *Sardonyx*.

Langlands started up a new route to the West Highlands and through the Caledonian Canal to Aberdeen and Dundee in 1871. James Kennedy later reviewed the new service, writing in 1903:

...the Royal Company opened up a new steamship service from Liverpool to the West Highlands, North of Scotland, and east coast ports. Owing, in large measure, to the natural attractions of the route, and the excellence of the accommodation and cuisine provided on the steamers, this is every year becoming a more popular and favourite trip. The first steamer employed on the West Highland and east coast route was a small cargo steamer, but in a very short time it was found necessary to place the **Princess Alice,** *a much larger steamer, carrying passengers as well as cargo, on the route.*

It was not actually the Royal Company that was behind the new initiative but a new partnership formed by John and Mathew Langlands, J & M Langlands, which also became the registered owners of the *Princess Alice* during the year. The first sailing took place in the spring of 1871 following detailed investigation of the viability of their proposal throughout much of 1870 and a prolonged, but abortive, search for a suitable vessel on the second-hand market. A new ship would have been too much of a risk for such a speculative venture.

Despite prophecies that the new service would not last more than two or three trips, the new J & M Langlands venture commenced in a modest way with chartered tonnage. The service was based at Liverpool and ran via the Caledonian Canal to Inverness, Aberdeen and Dundee and was operated by the chartered cargo steamer *Hayle*, sailing from both Liverpool and Dundee approximately every fortnight. The *Hayle* was a collier-type steamer owned by John Birnie Adam of Aberdeen. She had been built in 1867 for the Ton Mawr Colliery in Neath but within the year was re-registered under her Aberdeen owners. She was equipped with the new and novel water ballast system and was just 147 feet long by 25 feet breadth.

By June 1871 the Liverpool service was advertised in the *Dundee Courier*:

SS **Hayle**, *353 tons, via Caledonian Canal, via Aberdeen and Inverness. Departs Liverpool 8 and 20 June and 4 July and returns from Dundee 14 and 28 June. M Langlands & Sons, 17 Water Street, Liverpool; James Crombie, 17 Market Street, Aberdeen; J T Inglis, 33 Dock Street, Dundee.*

It had quickly been found that J & M Langlands did not have the resources to run the blossoming new service and its management reverted to M Langlands & Sons almost as soon as the project had begun. Initially the economic margins of the route were slim but as a client base developed in Aberdeen and Dundee the service slowly became more viable.

On 30 June 1871 the *Princess Royal* was chartered to Messrs Valéry Frère et Fils of Marseilles, to run between there and Algiers for six months, with an option for an extension. In the Mediterranean the *Princess Royal* was given a French captain and crew, but Langlands retained a British certificated master and an engineer on board to look after the ship. Although she was registered at Glasgow the French government insisted that she should occasionally hoist the French flag, and they had given her a special licence to do so. Thus on 21 July the *Princess Royal* sailed from Marseilles under the French flag to the consternation of the British Consul who duly complained to the Admiralty. The Consul was even more upset in September when the *Malvina* of Leith, owned by the London & Edinburgh Shipping Company, arrived on charter also to convey the mails from Marseilles to Algiers. Her contract stated emphatically that she should wear the French flag. The British Consul suggested that an Admiralty warrant could be the solution to the contravention.

The Admiralty response to the Consul was basically that they neither had any objection to the ships flying the French flag nor had they any power to issue a warrant for British ships to fly a foreign flag. In October the Admiralty wrote to the Board of Trade regarding the **Princess Royal** and **Malvina** advising that it had no power to authorise wearing of any other national colour than those sanctioned and required by Act of Parliament. The Board of Trade added that the Merchant Shipping Act forbade the use of any national colour other than the Red Ensign for any ship registered in Britain… and so the debate went on until the two ships were returned to their owners.

Thereafter, the **Princess Royal** remained the mainstay of the Liverpool service. The **Raven** and **Penguin** continued for Burns with the new steamer **Bear** standing in during the springtime refit period. The **Hayle** continued to develop the West Highland and Dundee trade.

The new Burns steamer **Bear** (1870) which deputised on J & G Burns' Liverpool to Glasgow service in 1871.

Early in 1872 the **Hayle** stood down on the Liverpool to Dundee service and was replaced by the steamer **Yarrow**. She was owned by William Gunn of Granton and had been built in 1850 at Renfrew as **Louise**. She had slightly larger capacity than the **Hayle** at 450 tons gross reflecting the increased volume of traffic that was now being attracted to the service. The **Yarrow** was too long to use the Caledonian Canal but was still able to maintain a fortnightly service by calling only at Aberdeen on the outward trip to Dundee and returning direct for Liverpool, mostly with fine export goods destined for transhipment to America. In mid-May 1872 the **Yarrow** was replaced by an even larger steamer, and for the first time on the route providing some passenger accommodation for cabin class passengers. This was the former Clyde Shipping Company's steamer **Tuskar**, originally chartered by Langlands in autumn 1867 when the Glasgow to Plymouth service was being developed, and now purchased specifically for the Dundee service. The Clyde Shipping Company had sold her in 1869 to owners in Dundee and she had been resold to a Montrose-based company in 1870. Under Langlands ownership her black funnel quickly received the two white bands originally used for the ships of the Liverpool & Glasgow Royal Steam Packet Company. On her second round trip, having started her first voyage for Langlands at Dundee in May, and now including a call at Stornoway, the **Tuskar** very nearly came to grief, as reported in the *Dundee Courier* on Tuesday 18 June 1872:

*A central news telegram announces that on Sunday evening a large steamer said to be the **Tuskar** of Glasgow, went ashore in the fog at Swansa Island, one of the Orkneys. The vessel which has thus gone ashore is supposed to be engaged in trading between Dundee and Liverpool calling at Aberdeen and Stornoway. She arrived in Dundee a number of days ago with a general cargo from Liverpool, and, after discharging, took on board a very full and valuable cargo of heavy bale goods, principally intended for shipment to America. The **Tuskar**, being also certified to carry passengers, had a few on board when she left Dundee on Saturday. She is a vessel of 317 tons register, and in every way admirably adapted for the trade in which she was employed.*

*The Pentland Firth, as one of the islands in which the vessel has gone ashore, is most dangerous to navigate as it is studded with islands, and the tide there runs very fast. The **Tuskar**, which took the place of the Yarrow about the middle of May, on the run between Dundee and Liverpool, belongs to Messrs M Langlands & Sons, Water Street, Liverpool.*

Happily, Langlands' new acquisition was released from her perch on a subsequent tide and was able to proceed on her way being watertight and seemingly little damaged. The impact had been quite gentle as she had been steaming at slow speed in slack water, despite the falling tide leaving her beached high and dry.

The **Tuskar** (1863) in full Langlands livery working cargo at Dundee. Originally built for the Clyde Shipping Company whose next ship to be named **Tuskar** is illustrated on page 79.

The **Princess Royal** shared duties at Liverpool with **Princess Alice**, the latter on charter for much of the year on the Havre service. When the **Princess Royal** stood down for attention in the early summer she was replaced by the steamer **Toward**, chartered from the Clyde Shipping Company. In January 1873 the **Princess Royal** made a single trip from Liverpool to Stornoway and round to Dundee allowing **Tuskar** to be overhauled. This pattern was repeated the following year when the **Princess Royal** again stood in for the **Tuskar**, sailing from Liverpool on 15 January. Late in the year an order was placed with David & William Henderson & Company at Partick for a new passenger and cargo steamer of suitable length and draught to traverse the Caledonian Canal. Tod & MacGregor, who had built all the company's previous ships, had been taken over in 1873 by the Hendersons who were brothers of the Anchor Line Hendersons; so to all intents and purposes the order was again placed with Tod & MacGregor.

At the end of the 1873 season the Glasgow & Stranraer Steam Packet Company's screw steamer **Albion** was sold to the London & Edinburgh Shipping Company for use on their service between Leith and Berwick. The main duties at Stranraer were left to the paddle steamer **Albion**. This seemingly retrograde step reflected the downturn in business on the short coastal routes and was almost certainly a shrewd business move by the owners, M Langlands & Sons. Besides, the service to Belfast was discontinued in June and only one ship was needed to maintain the Glasgow to Stranraer run departing alternate weekdays from either port.

In June 1874, during the peak summer season, the **Tuskar** was joined by the newly-acquired steamer **Fairy Queen** to provide a weekly service to Dundee. She had been completed in 1860 by Gourlay brothers for R W Jackson of West Hartlepool. She was a substantial cargo steamer of 345 tons gross with limited cabin accommodation for passengers. During the 1860s and early 1870s her owners changed almost yearly, passing to Newcastle-based William Scott in 1866 and London owners Louis Merton in 1871.

A report in *An Gaidheal (The Gael)*, June 1874, under the title 'Island of Lewis emigration to Canada' stated:

*On Saturday, 23rd ultimo, the steamer **Fairy Queen** called at Ness, near the Butt of Lewis, and took on board about thirteen families of emigrants bound for Canada. They came into Stornoway in the afternoon, where they were joined by several more, making in all about eighty. The men were all of the labouring class, and presented a very good appearance. They left in the afternoon for Liverpool, in charge of Mr Angus Nicholson, Emigration Agent of the Canadian Dominion. Mr Nicholson has been very successful in this district, having sent away a large number within the last three years. A number more are expected to follow this year. Those* *who have already gone are reported as doing well, and sending home very favourable reports. We have seen several of their letters from the provinces of Quebec, Ontario, and Manitoba, and all were very encouraging.*

The **Fairy Queen** otherwise stayed on the Dundee service until the end of September and was brought to the Clyde for extensive refit. Once the work was completed she was chartered to Martin Orme for use on the Glasgow to the West Highlands services starting with a first sailing from Glasgow on 9 November 1874. The **Fairy Queen** replaced the **Talisman** which Orme had sold and worked in tandem with the **Dunvegan Castle**. This provided the **Fairy Queen** with gainful employment throughout the winter.

The *Dundee Courier* (Tuesday 20 October 1874) reported on the launch of the new and rather special steamer ordered by M Langlands & Sons:

*Launch of a new steamer for the Dundee and Liverpool trade: Last week a new screw steamer of 400 tons, and named **Princess Beatrice**, intended for the trade between Dundee and Aberdeen and Liverpool, was launched from the builders yard at Messrs Henderson, Partick. The **Princess Beatrice** is built in a special manner in order to be enabled to go through the Caledonian Canal, thus shortening the passage very materially between Dundee and Liverpool. The steamers on the passage at present are not, however, to be withdrawn, but are to sail at stated periods on their present route, in order to undertake the traffic at the different ports on the passage. The building of the **Princess Beatrice** has been a necessity, owing to the great and still growing increase of the Liverpool trade. At one time a steamer of 100 tons was dispatched only once a fortnight, but now steamers of 300 tons, sailing weekly, have to leave out goods here [Dundee] for want of room.*

The **Princess Beatrice** was just 150 feet long by 25 feet 5 inches breadth with a depth to main deck of 14 feet. Her gross tonnage, modest by today's standards, was 371 tons. She was equipped with an inverted compound engine constructed by her builders, David & William Henderson, at Partick, that provided 91 horsepower. The cylinders were 24 inch and 41 inch diameter respectively and the stroke was 28 inches. The *Glasgow Herald* reported that she was fitted with 'every facility for loading and discharging cargo rapidly'. She was launched on 14 October 1874 and was named by Mrs McNair. Her role ultimately was to provide a new service from Liverpool to Leith via the Caledonian Canal, although her first duties were to add Inverness to the ports of call prior to extending the route to Leith.

The **Princess Beatrice** (1874), affectionately known as the 'Wee Beatrice', seen lying alongside another vessel at Stornoway.

Langlands had retained its position on the Glasgow and Liverpool coastal liner service alongside G & J Burns' **Raven**, **Penguin** and **Owl**, with an upgraded **Princess Royal** or the **Princess Alice**. The **Fire King** was now a serious competitor for trade with scheduled departures from Glasgow on Fridays and Liverpool on Tuesdays. But Messrs Langlands & Sons was now set to move into the Liverpool to the North of Scotland, Dundee and Leith service with dedicated and specially-built tonnage. It also had the **Tuskar** operating from Liverpool via Stornoway and now also Stromness to Aberdeen and Dundee, supplemented by the **Fairy Queen** in summer. Both ships called elsewhere by inducement. Otherwise the **Fairy Queen** was busy earning valuable charter fees alongside the **Princess Alice** which also spent much of her time out on charter, while the **Princess Royal** had also undertaken the valuable work between Marseilles and Algiers in 1874.

CHAPTER 7

THE GREAT VICTORIAN DEPRESSION

In 1875 the **Princess Royal** again did one round trip to Dundee sailing from Liverpool on 22 March to relieve the **Tuskar** for overhaul. The **Fairy Queen** was put on the Dundee run for the summer, starting in July and working until the end of September when she was again needed by Martin Orme to deputise, this time, for the **Dunvegan Castle** which had been beached, ironically, in sight of the Castle at Dunvegan, and badly damaged. The new **Princess Beatrice** meanwhile was running through the Caledonian Canal from Liverpool to Inverness, Dundee and Leith and calling at Aberdeen on the return leg of the journey.

The company tour guide describes the first part of the journey through the Caledonian Canal on board the **Princess Beatrice**:

While the steamer is ascending Neptune's Staircase, a series of eight locks leading up to the western extremity of the Caledonian Canal, a visit, if time permits, should be paid to Glen Nevis, famed for its romantic scenery, its waterfalls, and the remains of Dunhairdghall Castle, a vitrified fort on the summit of a green hill about 1,200 feet in height. Before leaving Corpach a view may be had of Prince Charlie's monument, on the side of Lochiel... Loch Lochy is ten miles in length and one mile in breadth. On the cutting between Loch Lochy and Loch Oich is the village of Laggan... Entering the last named Loch we pass, on our left, the picturesque ruins of Invergarry Castle... At Aberchalder the steamer leaves Loch Oich, enters the canal and descends to Loch Ness, after passing through seven lochs – one at Aberchalder, one at Kytra, and five at Fort Augustus... Passing through the locks at Fort Augustus necessitates some delay and affords time to view the buildings... Reaching the head of Loch Ness, here called Loch Dochfour, we again enter the canal and shortly arrive at Inverness... At Inverness the steamer remains several hours discharging cargo before again entering the sea, giving passengers time to visit several places of interest in the neighbourhood. After leaving Inverness the steamer usually goes to Aberdeen and Dundee, stopping generally 12 hours at each of these places.

A new Liverpool steamer was ordered from the London & Glasgow Engineering and Iron Shipbuilding Company on the Clyde during 1875. Whether it was cost considerations or speed of construction that persuaded the Langlands Board to part with its longstanding relationship with Tod & MaGregor / D & W Henderson is not recorded, but there will inevitably have been sound commercial judgement behind the move. The London & Glasgow Company occupied the Middleton Yard that used to belong to Smith & Rodgers until it was bought out in 1863 and was, in turn, acquired by Harland & Wolff of Belfast in 1912.

On Wednesday 16 June 1875 the *Liverpool Mercury* carried an intriguing story:

*The Liverpool and Glasgow steamer **Princess Alice**, belonging to M Langlands & Sons, left Greenock on Monday evening shortly after 7 o'clock and during the night encountered a severe gale from the south west, with a heavy head sea, on her passage to Liverpool. At 8 o'clock in the morning, when 12 miles south of Maughold Head, Isle of Man, she fell in with the barque **Perseverance**, Captain Davey, of Bristol, which left the Mersey on Monday, with a cargo of salt bound for Archangel. On the previous evening the barque was completely disabled in a storm, and when seen by the **Princess Alice**, had flags of distress flying from her mizenmast. Her fore and main topmasts and yards had been carried away, and her rigging and sails were flying in tatters. As viewed from the **Princess Alice**, the disabled vessel presented a novel spectacle to those passengers on board the steamer unaccustomed to seeing wrecks at sea. Captain Scott, the commander of the **Princess Alice**, promptly proceeded to the assistance of the barque. Notwithstanding a heavy sea, a small boat was lowered and a crew of four, under the command of Mr Clarke, the Chief Officer of the steamer, bravely made their way to the disabled vessel...*

*To pass a cable from the **Perseverance** to the **Princess Alice** was, however, a work of great difficulty and required considerable skill, owing to the high state of the wind and the heavy sea. ...unfortunately the line parted, but Captain Scott and his brave crew set to work and, after two more fruitless attempts, succeeded in getting the hawser attached from the steamer to the **Perseverance**, which was taken in tow into Ramsey Bay where she dropped anchor and rode safely. On board the **Princess Alice** there was a considerable number of passengers who were warm in their commendations of the humane conduct of Captain Scott, and the bravery of Mr Clarke, the mate... The **Princess Alice** would have reached Liverpool about 12 to 1 o'clock yesterday, but owing to the delay... it was nearly 8 o'clock last night when she arrived in the Mersey.*

The *Liverpool Mercury* for 17 July 1875 advises sailings to the north of Scotland as:

Princess Beatrice, **Fairy Queen**, **Tuskar** or **Sanda** *from Liverpool Trafalgar Dock: to Stornoway, Thurso and Aberdeen, 17 July, 10.00pm; to Inverness (via Caledonian Canal), Aberdeen, Leith and Dundee, 20 July, 11.00pm; to Stornoway, Aberdeen and Dundee, 27 July 4.00pm.*

The **Princess Beatrice**, affectionately known throughout the company as the 'Wee Beatrice', had a fortnightly departure via the Caledonian Canal and Inverness to Leith. The **Tuskar** maintained the Stornoway, Stromness, Thurso to Aberdeen route from June onwards having been moved south for some of the early part of the year to work the Stranraer to Glasgow service. Her replacement for the duration was the chartered Clyde Shipping Company's **Sanda**. **Fairy Queen** came off West Highland duties for the summer service to Dundee between July and September.

The **Princess Royal** was away for much of the time on charter but she did rejoin the Liverpool service in 1876 to deputise for the **Princess Alice** and made one call at Stornoway on 10 February on a voyage to Dundee. She was then advertised for sale going to owners in Cuba who renamed her **Juan G Meiks**.

The highlight of the year was the launch of the new Liverpool steamer **Princess Royal** on 9 June 1876 from the Middleton Yard of the London & Glasgow Engineering and Iron Shipbuilding Company. The ship had an inverted compound engine to provide 220 horsepower, engines aft, had a gross tonnage of 648, and measured 227 feet by 29 feet by 15 feet 6 inches. This was the fifth **Princess Royal** to be commissioned by the company. She was rather a curiously constructed ship. Her boilers were amidships by the bridge, but her compound engines were right aft, and consequently there was no shaft tunnel, but a steam pipe some 60 feet in length between boilers and engines. The wheelhouse at the stern was very high, and signalling from the bridge was operated by a 5 feet long beam pivoted on its base and connected to the wheelhouse telegraph by wires running between the masts. She was also novel in having her cabins amidships, the engine position allowing this.

The new **Princess Royal** (1876). Note the raised wheelhouse at the stern to facilitate communication with the bridge.

But for all her peculiarity the new **Princess Royal** was a welcome addition to the Glasgow and Liverpool service when she took up station later in the year allowing the **Princess Alice** to stand down to be modified for the Dundee service. The **Princess Alice** was tried on the Stornoway and Stromness route with one call at Stornoway on 14 September en route from Aberdeen to Liverpool but was otherwise employed running from Liverpool direct to Dundee via Aberdeen. The **Tuskar** maintained the service via Stornoway and Stromness and was again joined in the summer by the **Fairy Queen** between May and September.

Langlands decided to close the Galloway Steam Navigation Company's Solway ports cattle and sheep service to Liverpool in 1876 following the opening of the Wigtownshire Railway the previous year. Langlands had managed the company since 1843 and was able to buy the goodwill of the company and its one steamer, the livestock carrier **Countess of Galloway**, at a modest price to clear the debts of the Galloway company. The **Countess of Galloway** could carry 200 head of cattle and was a useful ship to have in the fleet. She was then put on a new scheduled cargo route running from Glasgow via Stranraer to Liverpool, a composite of the old Galloway company's service to Liverpool from Wigtown, Garlieston and Kirkcudbright and the Glasgow & Stranraer company's commitment to the Stranraer to Glasgow service. It was, at best, a thinly disguised attempt to gain an increased share of the available freight on the Liverpool to Glasgow route restricted to Langlands by existing sailing agreements with G & J Burns.

The **Fairy Queen** hit the headlines inbound from Stornoway as the *Inverness Advertiser* reported on Tuesday 25 July 1876:

*The grounding of the steamer **Fairy Queen**: The screw steamer **Fairy Queen**, which stranded in Machrihanish Bay, west coast of Kintyre, on Wednesday afternoon [19 July], was got off on Thursday night at half past eight. Two tug steamers arrived from the Clyde in the morning at nine, but little or no progress was made with the steamer until the afternoon, when she was gradually drawn off the bank, and was moved towards the Mull of Kintyre. The **Fairy Queen** was making very little water. Her cargo of limestone and salt was thrown overboard, and the sheep were also put into the sea. About 700 of them were saved, and 30 dead animals were washed ashore. It is believed 50 are still missing. The sheep were put on a neighbouring grazing farm.*

The luck of the little steamer held, though it was not quite such a happy story for the sheep! Some accounts of the **Fairy Queen** incorrectly maintain that she was abandoned at Machrihanish Bay; however, the **Fairy Queen** was back in service in a few weeks running again between Liverpool and Dundee.

The year 1877 saw changes in rosters of several ships on the Liverpool to Dundee service. The **Tuskar** made only one call at Stornoway on 10 February en route between Aberdeen and Liverpool and was otherwise engaged in the direct Liverpool to Aberdeen and Dundee service or occasionally used on Liverpool-Stranraer-Glasgow cargo-only duties alongside the **Countess of Galloway**.

The **Countess of Galloway** (1874) from a contemporary oil painting by local artist William MacMurray.

(Stewartry Museum)

The **Fairy Queen** maintained the Stornoway and Stromness calls between Liverpool and Dundee, some trips continued also to Leith, while the new **Princess Royal** made one call at Stornoway after leaving Liverpool on 3 February for Dundee while the **Princess Alice** stood in for her between Liverpool and Glasgow. Thereafter, the **Princess Alice** served the Liverpool to Aberdeen, Dundee and Leith route for the remainder of the year. The correspondent for the *Dundee Courier* was clearly impressed by the turn of speed of the **Princess Alice**, as he reported on Wednesday 28 November 1877:

*Rapid steaming of a Dundee trader: Last night the steamer **Princess Alice**, Captain Kerr, which trades between Dundee and Liverpool, arrived from Aberdeen. She passed Girdleness [a lighthouse outside the harbour at Aberdeen] at 3 o'clock yesterday afternoon, and arrived at Dundee at 8 o'clock in the evening, having sailed a distance of over 70 miles in the short time of five hours.*

The old fashioned side-lever engine was replaced aboard the **Tuskar** during the year with a modern compound engine considerably improving the coal efficiency of the vessel and improving the output to 80 horsepower.

The luck of the **Fairy Queen** finally ran out at the end of the year as *The Evening Telegraph* (Angus) reported on Monday 31 December 1877:

*The fatal loss of the **Fairy Queen**: Last night a portion of the crew of the **Fairy Queen**, of Glasgow, arrived at Leith on board the tug **Express**, and found accommodation at the Sailor's Home. They report the total loss of their vessel on the Carr Rock, at the entrance to the Firth of Forth, early on Saturday morning. The **Fairy Queen**, which traded between Leith and several northern ports, left Stromness at 4 o'clock on Friday morning with a small general cargo. Good progress was made until the evening when the weather became heavy, with much rain. The night was very dark, and about 12 o'clock the vessel was found to have struck a rock. Some of her compartments filled rapidly with water, and the crew, eighteen in number, prepared to leave with the boats. In the morning they succeeded in reaching Anstruther. Subsequent visits to the place showed that there was no chance of saving the vessel, and at noon yesterday, when the tug left, the **Fairy Queen** was entirely under water. The crew saved all their effects, and the ship's papers and other property were also taken off. The steamer was owned in Glasgow by Messrs Langlands & Sons, and is said to be valued at £6,000. The cargo was not a very large or valuable one. Captain Munro remains at the scene of the wreck. Twelve of the crew proceeded to Glasgow last night.*

Both the **Countess of Galloway** and the **Tuskar** ran on the Glasgow-Stranraer-Liverpool cargo service until inevitable complaints arose from G & J Burns regarding Langlands violating existing sailing agreements. Langlands argued that they had developed the trade themselves. After protracted negotiations between M Langlands & Sons and G & J Burns over the right to put a cargo-only ship on the direct Liverpool to Glasgow route, agreement was eventually reached in 1878 to share the Burns cargo steamer **Wasp**. The **Wasp** was to make one return voyage a week starting from Glasgow on 28 May between Liverpool and Glasgow and the takings pooled between the two companies. Langlands initially purchased a 50% stake in the vessel and undertook her management but in a short time she was wholly-owned and operated by Langlands. The announcement was made in the *Glasgow Herald* on 27 May 1878:

*Extra steamer Glasgow and Liverpool: The screw steamer **Wasp**, 550 tons, is to sail with cargo only from Glasgow Shed Number 17 South Side every Tuesday afternoon and from Liverpool Canning Dock every Saturday afternoon.*

Langlands also agreed to withdraw the **Countess of Galloway** and the **Tuskar** from the indirect cargo service between Glasgow and Liverpool. As a consequence the **Countess of Galloway** maintained the Stranraer-Glasgow link in place of the paddle steamer **Albion** which was withdrawn from service. The **Tuskar** meanwhile, was engaged on the cattle and sheep run between Stranraer and Liverpool, taking over from the **Countess of Galloway** in 1879. She too was withdrawn, closing the Glasgow service at the end of that year. An intermittent service to Liverpool continued into 1880 when that also ended.

With the **Wasp** in service in 1878 alongside the new **Princess Royal**, Langlands was assured a better return on its longstanding shared interests with G & J Burns in the Liverpool to Glasgow coastal liner route. The **Wasp**, a sister to the **Hornet**, was a cargo steamer with only limited accommodation for cabin and steerage passengers.

The Liverpool services via the Caledonian Canal to Dundee and Leith in 1878 are summarised in an advertisement in the *Inverness Advertiser* on Friday 7 June 1878:

*Steam Communication between Liverpool, Leith, Inverness, Aberdeen and Dundee. The screw steamer **Princess Beatrice**, or other steamer, is intended (weather and other circumstances permitted), to sail from Inverness to Liverpool Thursdays 6 and 20 June at 11.00am; From Liverpool to Inverness on Tuesday 28 May at 1.00pm, Wednesday 12 June at 8.00pm and Tuesday 25 June at 6 .00m; From Inverness to Leith, Aberdeen and Dundee on Fridays 31 May at 10.00am, 14 June at 8.00pm and 28 June at 10.00am; From Leith to Inverness calling at Dundee on Mondays 3 and 17 June at 8.00pm; From Aberdeen to Inverness on Wednesdays 5 and 19 June at 2.00pm.*

Fares: Inverness to Liverpool cabin 25/-, return £2 and steerage 10/-; Inverness to Aberdeen or Leith cabin 15/-, steerage 7/6.

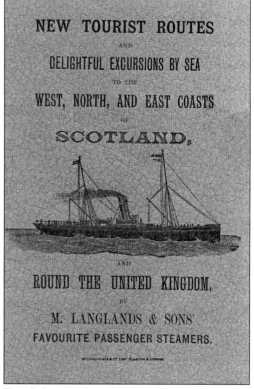

The **Princess Beatrice** (1874) depicted on the company passenger tour schedule pamphlet.

All goods are carried at through rates via Bridgwater Navigation Company to and from Manchester, Birmingham, Wolverhampton, Warrington etc. For particulars of freight or passage apply to M Langlands & Sons, Glasgow and Liverpool or D MacPherson, 9 Union Street, Inverness.

The **Princess Alice** had settled into her duties on the Dundee service north-about via Stornoway and Stromness, supported by **Tuskar**. Together they maintained a weekly departure for much of the year with **Princess Beatrice** offering fortnightly departures via Inverness to Leith.

John Langlands and Mathew Langlands jointly became owners of the small wooden steamer **Enterprise** in September 1878. She had been built at Cockenzie on the Forth in 1865 for John Barclay of Kirkcaldy and was re-registered at Alloa in 1876. She was a mere 63 feet 6 inches in length by 14 feet 8 inches breadth. Her role was to provide a feeder service from various Forth ports from Alloa down river to Grangemouth, Kirkcaldy in Fife and other small harbours as required, to transhipment at Leith for the company steamer to Liverpool. The little steamer plied her trade until May 1881 when she was withdrawn and the feeder links were outsourced.

The *Morning Post*, Thursday 1 May 1879, carried a curious, although delightful, story:

Strange elopement: About 8 o'clock on Tuesday night, as the steamer **Princess Alice**, *which trades between Dundee and Liverpool, was leaving Dundee, a young man and woman stepped on board and took berths for the voyage. Scarcely had they done so when another young man rushed on board and claimed the young woman as his wife. He in turn was followed by a woman who clambered over the* **Princess Alice** *and stoutly maintained that the young man first named was her husband. A violent altercation ensued, in the course of which blows were exchanged between the men. Meantime the ropes of the steamer had been cut loose, and as the tide was ebbing rapidly, the Captain saw he had no time to spare, and the vessel steamed ahead, taking with her the two men and two women.*

The **Princess Alice** *touched at Aberdeen at 6 o'clock yesterday morning, and from statements made it would seem that the scene between the eloping couple and the pursuers after the steamer left Dundee was extraordinary. So violent was the behaviour of the two men that the Captain of the* **Princess Alice** *had to place both men in irons, and it was only on the intercession of the runaway wife that her husband and the companion of her flight were released. In a subsequent struggle the injured husband violently took from his wife a purse containing £14, and on her companion attempting to recover it, the purse and its contents was thrown into the sea. On the arrival of the steamer at Aberdeen, the two couples were put ashore, and marched up the quay apparently on the best of terms.*

From 1879 there followed an important period of stability while the Langlands company traded with the assets it held while returning satisfactory dividends to its owners. The mid-1870s and much of the 1880s was a period of economic stagnation, sometimes referred to as the Great Victorian Depression, which was not helped in Scotland by the spectacular failure of the City of Glasgow Bank in 1878. Britain lost its economic lead over many of its near European neighbours and trading was at best flat-lining with little opportunity for growth.

Langlands found that it was able to maintain its existing services at a profitable level but saw no opportunity for growth or the development of new routes. It did, however, identify the need to extend its services down the east coast and yearned for improved economic conditions to start a service from Dundee to Newcastle and beyond. In the meantime the **Princess Royal** and the cargo steamer **Wasp** were the mainstay of the Liverpool to Glasgow route working alongside G & J Burns' steamers, principally the **Owl**, **Raven** and **Rook**, while the **Princess Beatrice** ran fortnightly to Leith via the Caledonian Canal and the **Tuskar** and the **Princess Alice** maintained a fortnightly service north-about to Dundee and Leith calling as required at Stornoway, Stromness and Aberdeen.

Advertisement in *The Scottish News*, 3 July 1886, showing both the passenger sailings and those of the new cargo service operated by the **Wasp**.

(L Gowans collection)

Additional tonnage was chartered-in as required, notably Davidson's small cargo steamer **Banchory**, which served the smaller ports on the east coast and in the Western Isles on passage between Liverpool and Dundee for much of 1882 and 1883.

The link that had been developed between Stornoway, Stromness and Aberdeen and with Inverness was in direct competition with existing, although erratic, services provided by the North of Scotland Orkney & Shetland Steam Navigation Company from Leith and Aberdeen, as described by Gordon Donaldson in his history of that company:

*The next step of expansion was the extension of Stornoway, at least as an occasional feature, of the programme of Wick and Thurso sailings. This is recorded for the first time in the summer of 1861, and it was to remain part of the programme, with varying frequency and regularity, for upwards of forty years. It is not clear how far it was the intention to try to establish a connection between the Western Isles and Aberdeen which could compete seriously with the well-established service to Glasgow, but we do find the **Queen** making an isolated trip (with cattle) to Lochboisdale in July 1879 and a special trip to Stornoway in November of that year. And it must have been realised that the distance from Stornoway to Aberdeen is actually rather less than that from Stornoway to Glasgow. Another sign of activity was the revival, in 1874, of a service to Inverness, after a lapse of fifteen years, but this was not maintained, and only an occasional isolated run to Inverness is to be found in later years, as by the **St Clair** in November 1884.*

Messrs Langlands & Sons rarely got into the news – an altogether good thing for a shipping company. Occasional reports were logged by the newspapers, such as that by the *Glasgow Herald*, Thursday 11 January 1883:

*Accident to an Aberdeen steamer: The **Banchory**, belonging to Messrs Davidson, Aberdeen, and at present chartered by Messrs M Langlands & Sons, 88 Great Clyde Street, Glasgow, on a voyage from Liverpool to Aberdeen and Leith, when coming through the Hoy Sound, was unable to cut the ebb tide, which was running very strong at the time, and sheered to starboard, stranding on the Cleat – a long and dangerous reef lying in the Sound, and within a few yards of the island of Graemsay. The vessel took the ground about two hours before low water. She was got off again yesterday evening, without sustaining any damage, with the assistance of some fishermen from Stromness and the adjacent island of Graemsay. After discharging what cargo she has to land at Stromness she will proceed on her voyage to Aberdeen and Leith.*

On Wednesday 26 September 1883, the *Aberdeen Journal* carried news of a collision off Aberdeen Harbour that had occurred sometime previously:

*The collision off the Girdleness, Claim for damages: The Kirkwall & Leith Shipping Company have lodged a claim against Messrs M Langlands & Sons, Liverpool and Glasgow, for the loss of its schooner **Paragon**, of Kirkwall, and the cargo, recently run down by their steamer **Tuskar** off the Girdleness, Aberdeen, during a thick fog. The precognition of the captain and crew of the **Paragon** have been taken at Kirkwall.*

Another news item in the *Glasgow Herald*, 7 March 1885, read:

*The **Tuskar** from Leith, when off the Bar Lightship on Thursday her engines became disabled, and the steamer was taken in tow by the **Albatross**, and brought into the Mersey and docked, supposed with either damage to screw or shaft.*

Happily, such incidents were few in number, and the reputation for safety and efficiency of the Langlands fleet was second to none. The ships were all maintained to a high standard with holy-stoned decks and varnished teak handrails; the deck officers were adorned in frock coats and full uniform. The ships were also well maintained with paintwork and brightwork regularly washed down by the deck crew under the direction of the bosun and the ship's carpenter. The engineering departments on all ships took pride in the operation and maintenance of the machinery they oversaw. Of course, the housekeeping of the passenger ships was all-important for passenger comfort and safety and the stewards were always dressed in company uniform and fully instructed in 'the passenger knows best' dictum.

THE RELATIONSHIP WITH THE RAILWAY COMPANIES

**From an essay by J Armstrong, 1991, in *Railways and Coastal Shipping in Britain
in the Late Nineteenth Century: Cooperation and Competition***

In the early 1870s the railways noted that the traffic between Liverpool and the east coast Scottish ports was 'unsatisfactory'. This was because of the direct steamer that had recently been put on the route. By 1872 the direct steamer was doing so well that in a four-month period it carried nearly 7,000 tons of goods between Liverpool, Dundee and Aberdeen, equivalent to more than 20,000 tons per annum. Armstrong wrote:

Throughout 1872 the Liverpool, Aberdeen and Dundee traffic by rail continued to show a decrease because of the competition by 'direct steamer' so that in the autumn the railway companies commenced negotiations with Messrs Langlands & Sons, who ran the direct steamer, to try to get the freight by both modes of transport raised.

*On this route the railway companies faced a double difficulty for they had competition from one of their number, the North British Railway, operating in conjunction with the steamboat between Liverpool and Silloth, as well as the direct steamer operated by Langlands. Hence, the all-rail share of the traffic was negligible. By the autumn of 1874 the railway conference was reporting 'a large fall in the goods traffic carried by the rail through route' and blaming it on 'the increased number of steamers between Liverpool and Aberdeen and Dundee'. In December of that year Langlands stole a march on the railways by having a steamer [the **Princess Beatrice**] built specially for this trade that could travel by the Caledonian Canal, cutting the mileage by sea drastically. As a result in the autumn of 1874 the coaster was carrying over 1,700 tons per month between Liverpool, Aberdeen and Dundee whereas the direct rail route was carrying about 200 tons per month. The coaster was not confined to low value, high-bulk commodities, carrying syrup, oils and rice as well as soda and jute from Liverpool and mostly bale goods, manufactured textiles, back.*

In order to compete, the railway conference recommended a reduction in the freight rates, as from January 1875, to flat rate of £1 per ton, station to station, for a whole range of commodities, as it would result in Messrs Langlands seeking an interview with the companies to arrange differential rates on a fair basis as between sea and railways. This proved of no avail and in January 1875 the flat rate was reduced to 15/- per ton. Even this drastic reduction did not benefit the railways, for they calculated that in the first quarter of 1875, the direct steamer increased the tonnage it carried from Dundee to Liverpool by about 400 tons per month, whereas the direct railway route carried 700 tons less per month.

Since outright price competition was not working in the railways' favour and since Langlands were now running their direct steamer to Leith as well as Aberdeen and Dundee, the railways felt their only option was to come to an arrangement with Langlands. Consequently in July 1875, a formal agreement was drawn up between Langlands and the English and Scotch Conference, whereby the former agreed virtually to abandon the trade with Leith, except where the quantities offered were in excess of 50 tons, for the coaster agreed to charge the same rate as the direct rail route. For lots of 50 tons or more of one article the steamboat charged a price lower than that by the direct rail route by 6/8d per ton. For the Liverpool to Dundee and Liverpool to Aberdeen routes the parties agreed a series of rates based on the Railway Clearing House classification, in which the steamers enjoyed a differential of between 10% and 32% below the railway rate. The differential in favour of the coastal ship was rather greater for some 'exceptional rates'. The differential was greatest on the lower rates and narrowed as the freight rate rose for higher value commodities. The railways then cancelled their special 15/- rate and the parallel £1 to Inverness.

Even this agreement seems to have benefited the railway companies very little. For in 1881 the Conference was complaining that the direct steamers were carrying about 2,000 tons of bale goods per month from Scotland to Liverpool, whereas the direct railway line was carrying only about 650 tons, a quarter of the total traffic. In part, they blamed this on the increased frequency of the steamboat service, now running twice per week. Having reached an agreement with Langlands on freight rates, they could not reduce these and considered ignoring the service. At the same time the English and Scotch Conference still had the problem of the rail-steamer route offered by the North British Railway via the steamboat service from Liverpool to Silloth.

CHAPTER 8

NEW SHIPS TO REPLACE THE OLD

It was well into the 1880s before any new tonnage was contemplated. In 1884 an order was finally placed with David J Dunlop & Company, at Inch Port Glasgow, for an iron-hulled passenger and cargo steamer to support both the Liverpool and Glasgow service and the Liverpool and Dundee and Leith services. The new steamer was intended to provide the company with an element of improved flexibility of operation. Launched on 5 March 1885, she was given the name ***Princess Maud***. She was equipped with a single compound engine with cylinder diameters of 28 and 56 inches with a stroke of 42 inches. Significantly, improvements in boiler design meant that the operational steam pressure for the cylinders was 80 pounds per square inch, providing energy rated at 140 nominal horsepower.

The ***Princess Maud*** measured 732 tons gross, being some 209 feet 4 inches long by 29 feet 8 inches breadth. As with all Langlands ships her accommodation was second to none with lavishly appointed public rooms and a dining saloon arranged around the long table which was designed to seat all her cabin passengers in one sitting. Much use was made of polished wood panelling, drapes and heavy upholstery, and careful positioning of mirrors and skylights provided natural light to the lounge. Steam winches and deck cranes supported rapid cargo handling to access the 'tween decks and lower holds while the forward well deck allowed cattle to be walked aboard from the quay through heavy steel cargo doors in the bulwarks to stalls on the well deck. The new ship presented the new face of technological improvement in the coastal liner, although it is interesting that Langlands still fought shy of the steel hull.

The ***Princess Maud*** (1885) on the Mersey.

(from an oil painting by Nick Robins)

The ***Princess Maud*** was designed both for the Liverpool and Glasgow route so that she could stand in for the ***Princess Royal***, but was primarily intended for the Liverpool to Dundee and Leith service. The *Aberdeen Evening Express*, Wednesday 13 May 1885, described the ***Princess Maud*** on her first arrival at Aberdeen:

*The new steamship **Princess Maud**: The new screw steamer, the property of M Langlands & Sons, Glasgow, arrived in Aberdeen last night, after making her first run between Liverpool and Aberdeen. She has a fine, substantial appearance, and is of very serviceable build. Her makers, David J Dunlop & Company, have fitted her with all the latest improvements, so that besides being strong and durable she will no doubt soon acquire an excellent reputation for comfort and convenience...*

From her construction she will be able to carry a considerable amount of cargo, for the loading and unloading of which two very powerful steam cranes are provided, one on the forepart of the vessel and the other nearly amidships. There are besides three steam winches. Her propelling engines are two in number, fitted with compound inverted cylinders, and Fox's patent corrugated flues [furnaces]. Her gross tonnage is 749 tons, and she carries 266 steerage passengers and 52 first class passengers. Her speed is 11 knots. She is supplied with Harrison's patent steering gear, and with Sir William Thompson's [later Lord Kelvin] patent compass, which claims to be the best, as it is the newest make. Her bulwarks are made higher than usual [either side of the forward deep well deck] in order to protect the livestock, which it is expected she will frequently carry. She is provided with four boats which are hoisted to the level of the upper deck, which leaves the spar deck quite free for passengers to promenade upon. The vessel is commanded by Captain Archibald Kerr, who has been promoted from the **Princess Alice**, belonging to the same firm. She [the **Princess Maud**] was launched about a month ago, and in all her trials has given the utmost satisfaction. It may be mentioned as an interesting fact that the **Princess Maud** has on board six seats, which in case of mishap, if thrown into the water, form rafts supported by air-tight cylinders, which are each capable of sustaining six persons.

This trade has wonderfully developed. Some years ago there was no such trade, and was begun under difficulties in the way of finding suitable steamers. The trade was started with one small chartered boat, and now there are four available: the **Tuskar**, **Princess Beatrice**, **Princess Alice** and **Princess Maud**.

The new **Princess Louise**, built three years after the **Princess Maud**, was also a magnificent ship, the first in the fleet with an all-steel hull, the first to be equipped with a modern triple expansion engine, and built to the larger dimensions of 226 feet length by 32 feet breadth and 14 feet depth. By now, thanks to the use of mild steel in place of wrought iron, steam pressures had increased even higher and the operational pressure of the boilers was 180 pounds per square inch. This allowed use to be made of the multiple, or triple, expansion steam engine. It is interesting that the Langlands' board returned to D & W Henderson to deliver this rather innovative ship. She was a passenger and cargo steamer with cabin accommodation of the usual high standard. She also had facilities for steerage passengers for the Glasgow to Liverpool route, when she stood

in for the **Princess Royal** when that ship was on annual overhaul. She was placed for a brief period on the Liverpool to Bristol route on delivery in April 1888, but soon transferred to Leith duties to make better use of her passenger facilities. Apparently on one return trip through the Pentland Firth the **Princess Louise** approached Cape Wrath in heavy westerly gales and snow flurries. The ship was not quite powerful enough to make much headway, and time after time the Cape Wrath light came abeam only for her to be forced back with the light creeping forward of the beam again. Eventually, with the coal stocks running low, the **Princess Louise** was brought into the shelter of Loch Eriboll to await a collier to replenish her bunkers so that she could resume her voyage to Liverpool.

An early photographic postcard of the **Princess Louise** (1888) approaching the pier at Stromness.

Unhappily the arrival on duty of the **Princess Louise** was followed by the loss of the Glasgow to Liverpool cargo steamer **Wasp** which sank in the Mersey on the southern bank of the Sloyne on 11 July, adjacent to the moorings used by the Cunard Line's transatlantic liners. The incident was one of several accidents in the Mersey caused by unseasonally severe weather; the **Wasp** having arrived in the Mersey in the late evening correctly hugged the southern side of the channel, until she attempted to swing to port into the wind and tide in the Sloyne ready to come head to wind to make her approach to the Canning Dock entrance. The *Evening Telegraph*, Thursday 12 July 1888, carried the small news item:

Large steamer sunk in the Mersey: The weather in Liverpool has been severe, and the ferry traffic during the night was interrupted at a late hour. The Glasgow steamer **Wasp** belonging to Mr Langlands, came into collision with the German barque **Hypatia**, and immediately sank in the river. The steamer was worth £30,000.

A more detailed account appeared in the *Glasgow Herald* the following day, Friday 13 July 1888:

Glasgow steamer sunk in the Mersey, Narrow escape of the crew: A collision of a serious nature occurred in the Mersey late on Wednesday night between the steamer **Wasp** *and the barque* **Hypatia**, *resulting in the sinking of the former and serious injury to the* **Hypatia**. *The* **Hypatia** *is a German barque of 806 tons, and was lying at anchor in the Sloyne Sound, from Parrsborough, United States, with a cargo of timber to Garston. About eleven o'clock at night, the steamer* **Wasp**, *bound from Glasgow, with a general cargo, was coming up the river, when she came into collision with the barque. The impact was very severe, and the* **Wasp** *had evidently a serious breach made in her hull, for she rapidly began to sink, and went down in ten minutes, a little to the south of the Cunard Shipping Company buoy which is moored in the Sloyne. The* **Wasp** *appears to have been carried by the strong current on to the bow of the* **Hypatia**. *The Captain and crew were rescued by the steam tug* **United States**. *The* **Hypatia**'s *bows are badly damaged. The* **Wasp** *had on board a general cargo, a portion of which was intended for transhipment to other steamers lying in Liverpool Docks. She was not a passenger steamer, though a regular trader between Liverpool and the Clyde. She was an iron screw steamer of 550 tons gross register, built at Port Glasgow in 1874, and was the property of Mr Langlands, of Glasgow. In the present position she will prove a serious impediment to the up-river traffic, and Lieut. Sweeney, the marine surveyor, has been cruising about with the intention of discovering the easiest means of removing the obstruction, and also to place a guide to other vessels while she remains there.*

She had left Glasgow under the command of Captain McNeill the previous day and was working on the route alongside the passenger and cargo steamer **Princess Royal** which was commanded then by Captain Read. On Saturday 14 July the Langlands advert in the *Glasgow Herald* proudly announced its Glasgow Fair special return to Liverpool of only 8/- by **Princess Royal** or **Princess Maud** and just below this announced: 'Liverpool cargo steamer: There will be no steamer sailing from No 5 South Side on Tuesday 17th inst'. Sailings resumed on 24 July with the Burns steamer **Mastiff** under the command of Captain Neill, the ship then spare from Burns' Londonderry to Glasgow service. The **Wasp** had successfully served the Liverpool to Glasgow cargo service, with a Tuesday departure from Glasgow and Saturday from Liverpool, for just over ten years. She had been relieved by the **Mastiff** in April when she went for annual overhaul resuming service only on 13 May. The cargo service was maintained by the **Mastiff** until February 1889 when it was suspended, although the **Mastiff** did some runs in June and September and was again rostered between Liverpool and Glasgow in February the following year.

For the last few years of the 1880s the passenger services comprised the **Princess Royal** serving Liverpool to Glasgow, occasionally relieved by the **Princess Maud**. The Liverpool to Leith route was maintained as a weekly departure from both ports by the **Princess Maud**, **Princess Louise** and **Princess Alice** supported by the **Tuskar**. The steamers called at Stornoway, Stromness and Aberdeen with an additional call at Dundee on the return voyage. They occasionally also called at Oban in the summer months. In addition the **Princess Beatrice** maintained a fortnightly departure to Dundee via the Caledonian Canal and Inverness. This was supplemented by a weekly service at Inverness from January 1889 onwards although the second ship did not use the Caledonian Canal.

Henry Lamont now had the **Fire King** and **Fire Queen** in service with departures from Glasgow every Tuesday and Saturday at 5.00pm and from Liverpool on Monday and Wednesday at 7.00pm. G & J Burns maintained the **Owl** and the **Bear** on the route.

As the country recovered from recession, Langlands strove to develop its international links by providing the feeder services to Liverpool's transatlantic routes from Dundee and Leith as well as Bristol and Swansea. It was a logical next step to link Leith with Newcastle and the vision was to complete the circuit to Bristol, although calls in the Thames were forbidden by a number of agreements made with competitors on the existing services, notably the Clyde Shipping Company, the Dundee, Perth and London Shipping Company and the Tyne Steam Shipping Company as well as various Liverpool-based companies including F H Powell & Company and Samuel Hough. But there were other south coast ports including the new railway port of Southampton, and the important regional ports of Plymouth and Falmouth. This then would be the next initiative when new tonnage could be sourced.

A new ship was urgently needed to support the longer term vision of the company, and this time Langlands looked at the second-hand market. The ship they found was the one-time Belfast Steamship Company's steamer **Galvanic**, which Langlands purchased and renamed the **Princess Helena**. Originally employed on the Belfast company's Liverpool to Londonderry service, the newly-renamed **Princess Helena** was something of a veteran when she arrived in the Langlands fleet in June 1889. Completed in 1867, she had been lengthened by 26 feet in 1877 and been given a new set of triple steam expansion engines in 1887 to replace her original twin cylinder non-compound engines. It was the new engines that attracted her to Langlands only two years later. Although she still had some cabin class passenger accommodation it was generally not used by Langlands, who viewed it as uncomfortable and out of date, and she was employed as a cargo-only steamer on the Bristol route.

The large steamer *Princess Louise*, serving on the Leith service, worked alongside the *Princess Maud* and the smaller *Princess Alice* and *Tuskar*. With four ships on the route the opportunity was taken to withdraw the smallest of all the passenger steamers, the *Princess Beatrice*, and with her passing came the suspension of the Caledonian Canal transit to Dundee via Inverness and Aberdeen. It also meant that all Liverpool sailings now terminated at Leith, calling at Dundee on the return journey only, but no longer including Inverness, unless by inducement. The *Princess Beatrice*, the 'Wee Beatrice' as she had always been known, was sold early in 1890 to W A Black of Glasgow. On passage from Halifax to Isaacs Harbour, both in Nova Scotia, still named *Princess Beatrice* and still registered at Glasgow, the 'Wee Beatrice' ran aground on New Harbour Ledge just outside Isaacs Harbour on 16 September 1890 and became a total loss.

M Langlands & Sons was one of 14 shipping companies and associations successfully to petition the Commissioners for the Northern Light Houses for a lighthouse and foghorn to be erected at Rattray Head. Langlands submitted reports from four of its masters, each report outlining the hazards of navigating around Rattray Head without a fixed light. Other petitioners included Lloyds of London, the Leith Shipowners' Association and the North of Scotland, Orkney & Shetland Shipping Company. Work eventually began on the project in 1892 and the light was finally commissioned in October 1895.

Langlands had every intention of reinstating the passenger service via the Caledonian Canal. Contemporary advertisements still included the service overprinted by the text 'The Caledonian Canal service is temporarily suspended'. As it happened the service was never reinstated although the smaller ships in the fleet, notably the *Tuskar*, then the *Princess Sophia*, and in later years the *Princess Mary*, dating from 1894, frequently called in at Inverness.

In the summer of 1891 the new cargo initiative was commenced using the *Princess Helena* running a service round Britain as an extension to the Leith and Bristol routes. The ship left Liverpool every alternate Tuesday bound for Oban, Stromness, Aberdeen, Leith, Dundee, Newcastle, Portsmouth, Plymouth and Swansea before returning to Liverpool. Passengers were accepted for the entire circuit or any segment they chose but Langlands played down the route for passenger use as they believed that the accommodation aboard the *Princess Helena* was not of the required standard and that passengers would want to visit London, a port of call prohibited to Langlands by agreement with other shipowners.

Consolidation took place at the end of the summer season when it was acknowledged that the cargo capacity of the elderly stalwart *Princess Alice* was no match for the *Princess Louise*, with her capacious holds, and that the *Princess Alice* was fast becoming inadequate for the trade on offer. The sale of the *Princess Alice* was also in anticipation of a new cargo steamer then building at Dundee. Having served both the core Liverpool to Glasgow route and latterly having been instrumental in developing the Liverpool to Dundee and then Liverpool to Leith routes there must have been many that were sad to see her go. But there was life in the old ship yet and the *Princess Alice* was sold quickly to Sociedad Isleña Maritima, Palma, and renamed *Isleño*. She served three subsequent Spanish owners and was eventually broken up in 1969 at the great age of 103, surely a record for any coastal passenger liner. The fact that she was an iron-hulled steamer, and not constructed in mild steel, certainly contributed to her longevity.

For the moment this left the Leith service in the charge of the *Princess Maud*, *Tuskar* and *Princess Louise*, with the *Princess Royal* on the Glasgow service and the *Princess Helena* on round-Britain duties, while the *Tuskar* was used also for relief duties round-Britain. During the annual refit in 1890, the *Tuskar* was converted to cargo-only with her passenger accommodation, including 60 berths, either converted for crew use or sealed off. The public rooms were locked. By doing this the gross tonnage fell considerably. She was also given a new funnel, the old one having become so corroded over the years that it was becoming unsound. The *Tuskar*, although the oldest and smallest ship in the fleet, remained an important unit as she could gain access to the smaller ports where cargo was available by inducement. Her deadweight capacity was about 480 tons. Southbound goods included whisky from various distilleries and consignments of Harris tweed, both for transhipment for the Americas via Liverpool, as well as livestock destined for slaughter at Liverpool.

The new cargo steamer was launched from the yard of W B Thompson & Company at Dundee on 13 December 1890 and given the name **Princess Irene**. She was equipped with the now customary triple steam expansion engine working at 165 pounds per square inch. The *Dundee Courier*, Thursday 1 January 1891, reported:

*The new steamer **Princess Irene**, lately launched from the yard of Messrs W B Thompson & Company, made her trial trip on the Tay yesterday. The engine worked smoothly, and the general behaviour of the steamer gave every satisfaction. The **Princess Irene** is to trade between Dundee and Liverpool.*

The **Princess Irene** (1891) started life on the Liverpool to Dundee and Leith service and later progressed onto the round-Britain service. She is seen here at Bristol.

The year that followed was the first with **Princess Maud** looking after the passenger service to Leith supported by the cargo-only **Tuskar** and the **Princess Irene**. Disaster struck when on 27 November 1891, the **Tuskar** ran aground on the Skernaghan Rocks, Islandmagee, near Larne, County Antrim, while on passage from Dundee to Liverpool. She subsequently became a constructive total loss. The ship had called at Glenarm in County Antrim to load limestone for Liverpool and had previously taken on board a consignment of whisky from the Islay Distillery bound for transhipment to the United States. The weather being fine, her master, Captain Duncan Kerr, had opted to sail through the narrow channel between the Hunter Rock and the mainland, a decision that was subsequently confounded when fog came to reduce visibility to only a few yards. The *Belfast Newsletter* for Monday 30 November 1891 reported:

*Wreck of the steamship **Tuskar** on Islandmagee: On Friday night last the steamer **Tuskar**, from the ports of Dundee, Wick, Islay and Glenarm bound for Liverpool, went ashore. The **Tuskar** left Glenarm, Captain Kerr in command, at about 7.20pm on Friday night last after having taken on board [about] 100 tons of limestone, at which time it was blowing a stiff breeze from the westward, so that in order to get the benefit of the smoothed water the vessel was kept up close along the land, the Marden Lights being on the vessel's left. The night was a fine clear one, up to the time the steamer was abreast of the Maidens when the steamer's course was changed in order to round the point of Islandmagee. At this time Larne Lough Light was visible. Immediately on getting south of the Maidens the steamer ran into a thick bank of fog. The Larne Light was at times sternwards seen, and the steamer... struck on the rocks at Skernaghan Point, which lies about one and a half miles west of Larne Lough entrance, at which time a course of east by north was being steered. The rocks at this point of the coast project a good distance into the sea.*

The Captain was on the bridge all the time from the steamer leaving Glenarm until she struck on the rocks at about 8.40pm, and a good look-out was being kept. Captain Kerr had the pumps [pump wells] sounded immediately after the vessel struck, and it was found that about 8 feet of water was in the forward hold, but the after part of the steamer was dry. As the tide ebbed away the steamer settled down onto the rocks, and the rugged points penetrated the ship's bottom and sides. Since the vessel settled down on the rocks the after part, which had previously been dry, owing to the vessel having strained herself, is now fast making water, and on Saturday night last there was found to be 12 to 14 feet of water in the after hold. At present the steamer lies in a very critical position with a list to port side. The stern portion of the vessel is hanging over the rocks, and from the opinion of those who have examined the steamer it is stated that the **Tuskar** is done for, and at any minute may become broken in two. The crew remained in the steamer for some time, and afterwards twelve of them left in two of the boats and made ashore. The four left were provided with another boat in case it was found necessary to leave the vessel, and during Saturday the remainder of the crew left, and are at present at Larne. On the deck of the steamer can be seen, braced fast, a piano, going to Liverpool, in order to prevent it tumbling into the sea.

...The following are the officers: Captain Duncan Kerr, First Officer Daniel McColl, and Chief Engineer Archibald McQuarry. There were 16 of crew all told on board at the time the steamer stranded. The crew have removed all their effects, and the Captain has taken possession of the ship's papers...

Mr J B Bennett, the Deputy Receiver of Wrecks, Larne, has been in attendance and took the usual depositions from the Captain and other officers. It is expected that a representative of the owners will arrive today (Monday), when arrangements will be made for discharging the cargo.

At the subsequent Board of Trade Enquiry it was decided that:

The Court, having carefully inquired into the circumstances attending the above-mentioned shipping casualty, finds, for the reasons stated in the annex hereto, that the loss of the said vessel was due to the negligent navigation of her by the master, Mr Duncan Kerr, and suspends his certificate for three months.

The report continued:

The **Tuskar**, official number 47817, was a British screw steamer of the port of Glasgow. She was built of iron at Glasgow in 1863. Her length was 181.5 feet, her breadth 24.6 feet, and her depth 13.7 feet. She was fitted with two direct-acting inverted engines of 80 horsepower combined. Her gross tonnage was 432.6 tons, and her registered tonnage was 215.28 tons. She was owned by Mr Mathew Langlands and others, Mr Mathew Langlands, of Liverpool, being her registered managing owner.

The **Tuskar** left Dundee for Liverpool, on 23 November, with a general cargo. She was commanded by Mr Duncan Kerr, who held a certificate of competency as master, numbered 101620, and had a crew of 16 hands all told. She called at Glenarm, County Antrim, on 27 November, and having taken in 120 tons of limestone, she left that place at about 7.00pm the same day, with a total cargo of about 240 tons. Her draught on leaving was 10 feet 6 inches forward, and 12 feet aft. At about 8.00pm, when, according to the master, Larne Light bore about SW, distant 1½ miles, she was put upon a SE by E course, with the intention of proceeding through the channel between the Hunter Rocks and Magee Island, the former of which the master expected to pass at a distance of about half a mile to the SW. At the time that her course was altered, the Maidens Lights, as well as Larne Light, were in sight, but the master took no cross-bearings, and did not verify the position of his vessel in any way.

The weather was fine, with a light breeze from the SW; the tide was flood, running about 2½ to 3 knots, and the vessel was making from 8 to 9 knots through the water. About 8.15pm the vessel ran into a dense fog, and the master ordered the engines to be put half speed, then slow, and then full speed astern. When the vessel's way was about stopped, the master ordered a cast of the lead, and this was taken by the chief mate who was stationed on the look-out on the forecastle head. A hand line of 20 fathoms was used, and the mate reported 'no bottom'. By that time, through the action of reversing, the head of the vessel had come round to the SW, and with the view of bringing it round to the eastward and to get more room to come round on a starboard helm, the master again ordered the engines astern for three minutes. A second cast of the lead was ordered to be taken, and the mate again reported 'no bottom'. The helm was then put hard-a-starboard, and while the vessel was slowly coming round, the mate, who saw something dark ahead, sung out 'hard-a-starboard'. By that time the helm was hard over, and the master, to make the vessel answer more rapidly, ordered one turn ahead full speed, which brought her head to E ½ N. The engines were then stopped, but in two or three minutes the vessel struck on the rock off Skeenaghan Point, her head at that time being about NE. A third sounding was said to have been taken before she struck, but without finding any bottom. These attempts to get soundings were all made with the hand line lead, the deep sea line and lead which were at hand not being used.

The vessel was sounded and 6 inches of water were found in the forehold, which in two or three minutes increased to 6 feet. As the water astern of the vessel was found to be from 4½ fathoms to 5 fathoms, the master made no endeavour to back the vessel off, as he feared she might sink in deep water. A boat was got out, and some of the crew sent on shore to seek assistance, which, however, they were unable to procure, as the wind at that time was blowing too hard. The next morning the master went ashore and proceeded to Larne, hoping to get a steam launch or lighter for the purpose of getting out some of the cargo, but was unable to obtain one. He, however, telegraphed to his owners, who placed the matter in the hands of the Salvage Association. All the crew were saved, but the vessel ultimately became a total wreck.

The Court came to the conclusion that had the master taken the ordinary precaution of ascertaining his exact position at 8.00pm, when he altered his course, he would have had far greater confidence as to the vessel's position when the fog came on, and by proceeding at a reduced speed and making frequent and careful casts of the lead, would have been able to avoid the great danger of manoeuvring as he did in a confined space, exposed to the effects of the tide.

The loss of the **Tuskar** was a serious blow to the company and the reprimand given to her Captain by the Board of Trade was hurtful not only to Captain Kerr, but to all concerned. Although the **Tuskar** had been the oldest and smallest ship in the fleet, her loss left the company's schedules without any flexibility and under considerable stress. Langlands was also without a steamer small enough to enter the various harbours where cargo was loaded and discharged by inducement, for example Wick, Islay and Glenarm. A search for a suitable steamer was made and a small engines aft bridge amidships coaster belonging to William Robertson's Gem Line was targeted for purchase, the deal going through in the early months of 1892. The ship was Robertson's **Topaz**, launched on 5 November 1891 from Scott's yard at Bowling, of 502 gross tons and equipped with a modern triple steam expansion engine. Robertson parted with his new ship for a premium price and at his next launch from Scott's on 25 May named his new ship the **Topaz**! To add to the confusion, the **Topaz** and the **Topaz** were identical sisters. Happily, before the launch of the second **Topaz** the first had hoisted the Langlands house flag under the new name **Princess Sophia** and had taken up the duties of the former **Tuskar**.

FROM ONE OF THE FIRST COMPANY TOUR GUIDES

The 1885-1889 company guide book:

Front cover

Back cover

LIVERPOOL TO EAST COAST,

Via Pentland Firth.

WE are about to start on the Royal Route among the Western and Northern Islands of Great Britain; the route taken by the triremes of the Roman Caesars; by the galleys of the Vikings of Scandinavia; and the war-ships of James V. of Scotland when he went forth to subdue the unruly men of the Isles; the route that inspired the rolling numbers of Scott's "Lord of the Isles," and the pictured pages of his "Pirate," and tuned the harp of Mendelssohn to the glorious music of the "Isles of Fingal."

We are off. Liverpool and the Mersey are far behind us, and if Manninan-beg-mac-y-Lear, the first King of Man, has not conjured up one of his mists (as was his custom when out of sorts) we are in sight of the Isle of Man, the Mona of past times. Coasting along its eastern shore, we round the **Point of Ayre**, with its lighthouse, and come in full view of the mountain ridge that stretches across the island, Snafield, the Snowy Hill, the highest, being two thousand feet above sea-level. When the peaks of **Man** are growing purple in the distance, the Mull of Galloway is on our right, with its rugged and almost perpendicular cliffs of from two to three hundred feet high. This rocky promontory was well known to Paul Jones, the reputed son of a Galloway gardener, who became the Commander of the American navy. Jones was the master of a trading vessel belonging to the port of Kirkcudbright. He was thrown into prison by the magistrates of that town, and on being liberated became pirate for a while. Before leaving the shores of Galloway behind us, we have a glimpse of Port Patrick, distant from Donaghadee, on the Irish mainland, 21½ miles. Steering up the North Channel, past the entrance to the Firth of Clyde, we are in sight of the island of Sanda (a favourite rendezvous for the galleys of the sea-kings), the Mull of Kintyre, and, if the weather be favour-

Mull of Galloway.

Mull of Kintyre.

Example of text

Steamer at Stornoway

The Glasgow & Liverpool Royal Steam Packet Company Steamers, M Langlands & Sons, tour guide, *Excursions by the West, North & East Coasts of Scotland*, was first issued in the 1880s (price six pence). This publication emulated that issued by David MacBrayne for their West Highland tours and was a final realisation by Langlands that passengers really were interested in the routine sailings of the company from a leisure point of view. The guide for the period 1885 to 1889 (the guide was revised every few years as ships and tours were changed) provides the following information on fares and routes:

	Cabin	Cabin return	Steerage
Liverpool and Greenock or Glasgow	12/6	20/-	6/-
Liverpool to Aberdeen, Dundee, or Leith	40/-	60/-	10/-
Liverpool to Inverness, Stornoway, Stromness, or Scapa	30/-	45/-	10/-
Liverpool to Oban	25/-	37/6	10/-
Dundee to Inverness	15/-	22/6	7/6
Dundee to Aberdeen	5/-	7/6	2/6
Leith or Dundee to Stornoway	25/-	37/6	10/-
Leith to Aberdeen	7/-	10/6	3/6
Leith to Dundee	5/-	7/6	2/6
Aberdeen to Inverness	12/-	18/-	6/-
Aberdeen to Stromness	15/-	22/6	6/-
Aberdeen to Stornoway	21/-	31/6	8/6
Oban to Stromness, Aberdeen or Leith	30/-	45/-	10/-
Stromness to Stornoway	10/-	15/-	5/-
Liverpool to Glasgow	12/6	20/-	6/-

An extra charge is made for deck cabins and two berthed state-rooms.

These fares do not include provisions, which can be had on board at the following rates, viz: Breakfast, 2/-; Dinner, 2/6; Tea, 2/-; or passengers may contract with the Steward.

Passengers have the option of disembarking at any Port of Call, and going on by any of the Company's succeeding steamers in which there may be room. Return tickets to and from East Coast are available either Pentland Firth or Caledonian Canal Route.

To prevent disappointment, intending passengers are invited to make early application for berths, which are allocated to and from any port according to priority of applications. Passengers wishing to retain the same berths for the return journey, should intimate their intention of returning by the same steamer when taking out their tickets, otherwise berths cannot be guaranteed.

The tour guide describes five basic excursions offered by Langlands in the late 1880s:

No 1 Between Liverpool and East Coast Scotland via Pentland Firth: This service is conducted by the favourite screw steamers **Princess Royal**, **Princess Maud** and **Princess Alice**, which leave Liverpool and Leith once a week. From Liverpool the course followed is generally through the inner Sounds; occasionally, when weather and time permit, calling at Staffa, Loch Scavaig, Loch Hourn, Gairloch, or other picturesque locality. The steamers call at Stornoway and Stromness, at each of which place passengers have some time on shore. From Stromness the steamers continue the voyage to Aberdeen, where a stoppage of 12 hours is made, thereby giving passengers an occasional opportunity of visiting Balmoral, Braemar, etc, besides the points of interest in the more immediate neighbourhood of Aberdeen. At intervals during the season, the steamers, instead of proceeding direct from Stromness to Aberdeen, go on to Shetland, for the purpose of giving tourists an opportunity of seeing the magnificent cliff scenery there. After Aberdeen, the next port is Leith, where the steamers remain for about 12 hours, giving passengers ample time to visit the principal places of interest in Edinburgh, which is only a mile and a half distant, and with which there is frequent cheap communication both by rail and tramway. From Leith the same course is taken on the return voyage, with exception that in addition to the other Ports of Call, the steamers stop 12 hours at Dundee, and occasionally call at Oban. The double voyage, Liverpool to Leith, and back to Liverpool, or vice versa, is accomplished in less than 12 days.

No 2 Between Liverpool and East Coast via Caledonian Canal: This service is performed by the fine screw steamer **Princess Beatrice**, which has been built expressly for this trade. The route from Liverpool is the same as No 1 till a little north of Oban, when the Caledonian Canal is entered at Corpach. The canal is 60 miles in length, only 23 of which have been artificially formed, the remainder being a chain of natural lakes; and as the passage is always made in daylight, tourists have an opportunity of seeing some of the finest loch and mountain scenery in Scotland.

No 3 Between Liverpool and Glasgow calling at Greenock: This service is presently performed by the splendid and fast screw steamers, **Princess Royal**, **Princess Maud**, or **Princess Alice**, all of which are great favourites with passengers. The voyage between Liverpool and Greenock usually occupies about 16 hours. Between Greenock and Glasgow there are numerous railway trains, making the run in about an hour, of which, at trivial expense, passengers can avail themselves, if they wish to avoid the delay of sailing up or down the River Clyde. Return tickets are good for two months from date of sale, and are available also for the steamers of Messrs G & J Burns.

No 4 Excursions via Oban: Passengers from Leith, Dundee, or Aberdeen, who wish to have the cruise round the North of Scotland, and at the same time visit Staffa, Iona, etc, should take the company's steamer on any trip when advertised to call at Oban, and leaving there, spend a few days making excursions in the neighbourhood, returning by any of the numerous routes open, viz by rail direct, via Dalmally and Callander, which passes through a magnificent country, and some of the finest scenery in the Highlands; by coach, via Loch Lomond or Loch Awe; or by MacBrayne's splendid steamers **Iona** and **Columba**, via Crinan, Ardrishaig, and Kyles of Bute, to Glasgow, and thence per rail. Passengers can land at Oban, and proceed, at their own expense, by either of the above routes, to Glasgow or Greenock, and join the Company's steamer there for Liverpool. Passengers from England can take the Company's steamer from Liverpool to Glasgow; thence by rail, or MacBrayne's swift steamers to Oban; and then return to Liverpool by the Company's steamer direct, or proceed by steamer from Oban to Leith, via Pentland Firth. The fares by the above routes from Oban, to Glasgow, Edinburgh, etc, can be ascertained by referring to the Railway Tourist Guides.

No 5 Steamer to Glasgow, thence rail to Leith, and then per steamer to Liverpool: Passengers can leave Liverpool per **Princess Royal**, **Princess Maud**, or **Princess Alice** for Glasgow; proceed to Edinburgh and Leith by train, and join the steamer at Leith for Liverpool, via Pentland Firth; or the route may be reversed, it being optional to begin the journey at either Glasgow, Liverpool or Leith.

CHAPTER 9

THREE CORE SERVICES FROM LIVERPOOL

In the early 1890s an interesting set of tour itineraries was advertised, some in conjunction with other shipping companies. The **Princess Louise** and **Princess Maud** were then the key units on the Liverpool to Leith service and a popular excursion was to travel on the Glasgow service aboard the **Princess Royal**, transferring to Leith by rail to join the homebound Liverpool steamer via the north of Scotland – all for 48/- . Another was advertised as Liverpool to Oban and Stornoway and back:

*The **Princess Louise** or **Princess Maud** leaves Liverpool every Saturday for Oban and Stornoway, reaching the last named port on Monday morning. Passengers have the whole day at Stornoway, and can leave again for Oban and Liverpool on Monday night, reaching Liverpool on Wednesday forenoon. Fare 45/-.*

But the most exciting tour was the newly-inaugurated service round the United Kingdom without change of steamers:

The steamer leaves Liverpool every alternate Tuesday, calling at Oban, Stromness, Aberdeen, Leith, Dundee, Newcastle, Portsmouth, Plymouth and Swansea; thence to Liverpool. It is optional to join the tour at Liverpool, Oban, Leith, or any other port of call. Fare 40/-, duration 12 to 13 days.

This new initiative had been commenced during 1890 by the **Princess Helena**. It was very much focussed on cargo-carrying but a small number of berths on board the elderly **Princess Helena** were sold during the summer months to a discerning clientele wishing to tour the entire coastline of the UK. The service was subsequently taken by the **Princess Irene** and from 1892 also by the new **Princess Sophia**, both steamers offering only a few passenger berths. However, Langlands made little effort to advertise their own round-Britain tour. The passenger tour around the UK that was advertised was run jointly with other companies rather than aboard the Langlands steamers, as the company firmly believed that accommodation aboard the **Princess Helena** was not to their own high standards and that passengers would prefer an itinerary that included time ashore at London. Langlands' advertising advised:

To those that wish a more extended tour this is one of the most enjoyable trips, and can be accomplished in a fortnight. Between London and Liverpool the steamers owned by Messrs Powell, or Hough, leave each port every Saturday, and call at Plymouth and Falmouth, cabin fare between London and Liverpool 25/-, average passage three days. On the east coast, tourists have the option of going between London and Aberdeen by the Aberdeen Steam Navigation Company's steamers, leaving each port every Wednesday and Saturday, average passage 36 hours, cabin fare 30/-, or they can go between London and Leith by the London & Edinburgh Steam Packet Company's steamers, leaving each port every Wednesday and Saturday - average passage 35 hours, cabin fare 22/6 and complete the round by M Langlands & Sons' steamers, either per itinerary 1 or 2 [Liverpool to east coast or to Glasgow]. The cabin fare between Liverpool and Aberdeen or Leith is 40/-; thus the whole trip can be made for 95/-, or 87/6 according to route chosen. This does not include provisions, which can be had aboard all the steamers at moderate rates. Passengers are allowed to sleep aboard all the steamers at all ports except where steamers are changed, say London, Liverpool, Aberdeen or Leith, where, if required, they must provide themselves with hotel accommodation.

The **Princess Helena** (1867) initiated the round-Britain sailings when they began in 1891. She is seen here at Bristol.

Both **Princess Sophia** and **Princess Irene** remained dedicated to the round-Britain service with an increased emphasis on marketing the tourist passenger potential for this service, 'around-Britain without changing steamers'.

The **Midnight Sun** (1874) was the first ship to popularise cruising by offering cheap trips to the Norwegian fjords from 1893 onward.

Until 1893 cruising had been largely marketed at middle and upper class clientele. A successful venture to popularise the cruising concept and widen the market was the dedicated cruise ship **Midnight Sun**. She operated from 1893 onwards largely from Newcastle and had been built originally as the German liner **General Werder** in 1874. Until then the North of Scotland, Orkney & Shetland Company had put the **St Rognvald** on cruise duties in the summer months, mainly serving the Norwegian fjords, with trips from £10 per head. Both initiatives served Langlands well by spreading the word to all comers that holidays afloat were both enjoyable and affordable.

As usual the **Princess Louise** stood in for the **Princess Royal** during her February refit at the beginning of 1893. Lamont's **Fire King** and **Fire Queen** then operated a cargo-only service to Liverpool and Birkenhead.

The new steamer **Princess Beatrice** was launched as reported in the *Dundee Courier*, Thursday 9 March 1893:

The **Princess Beatrice** (1893) at Dartmouth. Note the passenger's observation platform above the bridge and the protective awning aft.

(National Maritime Museum)

There was launched yesterday afternoon from the shipbuilding yard of Messrs D & W Henderson & Company, Meadowside, the **Princess Beatrice**, a steel screw steamer of about 1,000 tons, for Messrs M Langlands & Sons, Glasgow. The vessel, which is intended for the firm's north of Scotland service, is 250 feet long, 34 feet broad and 16 feet deep. She is designed especially for this tourist trade, and when the Ship Canal is opened will be able to sail from Manchester. Dundee will be one of the ports called by the vessel, and it will be remembered that a representation was recently made by the Dundee agents (Messrs Inglis & Christie) to have the dock suitably altered for her reception.

The new **Princess Beatrice** was shown off at various ports in a public relations exercise to endear shippers to the Liverpool to Leith service.

The *Aberdeen Journal*, Monday 15 May 1893 reported on one such event:

*Inspection of the **Princess Beatrice**: On Saturday a number of ladies and gentlemen were, at the invitation of Mr James Crombie, agent for the Glasgow & Liverpool Royal Steam Packet Company, conducted over the new* steamer **Princess Beatrice** at present lying at Provost Jamieson's Quay. At the closure of the inspection the company were entertained to dinner in the saloon of the steamer. Mr Ralph Langlands, of Messrs Langlands & Sons, presided, and Captain McNeill, commander of the **Princess Beatrice**, was croupier. Among the company were Lord Provost Stewart; Mr James Crombie; Mr David Littlejohn, sheriff clerk; Mr Spencer, National Bank and ex-Baillie Pyper.

After dinner, Mr Crombie, in proposing the toast of the commerce and trade of Aberdeen, remarked that they had with them that day Mr Ralph Langlands, a worthy son of a worthy father, and he was sure they were all pleased to see him. He [Mr Crombie] was very pleased to see them all present, and he trusted they were all satisfied with the new vessel which would not have been in dock had it not been for the patronage of Aberdeen traders. He ventured to say that she was some credit to the Port of Aberdeen.

Their present trade was begun some 22 years ago under very inauspicious circumstances. It was a very dear time in shipbuilding, and there were no vessels at the time by means of which the trade could be developed. There was, therefore, no help but to go in for chartered ships, and though some prophets said they might only run three times between Aberdeen and Liverpool, he was glad to say that that prophecy had not been fulfilled, for they had now five steamers, of which the **Princess Beatrice** was the best example. With regard to the development of the trade, Mr Crombie remarked that it was not an uncommon thing in the earlier days for shippers to complain that the boats were behind time, but he used to remind them that they had the worst passage almost in the world, for there was no worse passage to make than round Cape Wrath in the winter. And he thought it was not too much to say now, that the steamers did it with very great regularity.

Lord Provost Stewart, in responding, said that he was one of the first of Mr Langlands' customers, and the enterprise with which the firm had conducted the business, assisted by the great energy of Mr Crombie, had made it a complete success. There was a great necessity at one time for such a firm. There were two things in existence - a traffic and a waterway - but they wanted a firm to carry on the business of shippers and at last Messrs Langlands supplied the need. For that the traders of Aberdeen were greatly indebted to the firm, and although he was a railway director, there was no temptation to induce him to pass by the Liverpool and any other steamship company. He was very much pleased with his visit to the ship that day, and there was only one mistake about it - it was not built in Aberdeen - but he hoped Aberdeen builders would get a chance the next time a ship was required. His Lordship concluded by proposing 'Success to the firm of Messrs Langlands & Sons'.

Mr Ralph Langlands, in reply, expressed his pleasure at meeting those present, this firm has received many kindnesses from the traders of Aberdeen, and this was one of the few ways in which they could be repaid. The health of Mr Crombie was proposed by Mr W C Good, and Mr Shepherd proposed 'Prosperity to the **Princess Beatrice**' to which Captain McNeil responded. Mr Spencer, National Bank, and Mr Wilson of Messrs, Sheed & Company having spoken, in complimentary terms of the services rendered by the line of steamers, Mr Langlands gave the statement of 'Bon-Accord', and the proceedings terminated.

The commissioning of the **Princess Beatrice** allowed the now rather dated **Princess Maud** to stand down, preparatory to being sold. Despite her iron hull and inefficient compound engine she was quickly bought for further service under the Spanish flag, operating for the next seven years as the **Sitges Hermanos**. In 1900 she was acquired by Maritime Isleña and given the name **Balear** and she then served on the mail run to the Balearics for the next thirty years. Her spacious open deck area was ideal for the Mediterranean and she operated tourist trips to Mallorca and Cabrera in between ferry duties. Her last voyage was from Palma to Mahon, where she was finally broken up early in 1932.

The older consort to the former **Princess Maud**, the **Princess Royal** remained on service on the Liverpool to Glasgow route for several more years; this was partly because a rate war ensued with consequent very low economic margins on this route (Chapter 10).

Almost immediately after the **Princess Beatrice** had entered service an announcement was made of an order for an even bigger passenger and cargo steamer. The *Dundee Courier*, Friday 21 July 1893 reported:

...Messrs W B Thompson & Company have contracted with the Glasgow & Liverpool Royal Steam Packet Company, the managing owners of which are M Langlands & Sons of Glasgow and Liverpool, and whose agents in Dundee are Messrs Inglis & Christie, to build for them a steel screw passenger steamer to be employed on the passenger and cargo trade between Liverpool and Dundee. She will be larger than the latest addition to the fleet, **Princess Beatrice**, her dimensions being length 245 feet, breadth 35 feet and *depth 16 feet. She will be fitted with triple expansion engines having cylinders 22 inch, 35 inch and 57 inch in diameter, by 39 inch stroke, and be designed for a high rate of speed. She will have sumptuous accommodation for a large number of passengers, and will be a decided acquisition to this already popular fleet.*

Maritime Isleña's **Balear** (1885), was originally commissioned as Langlands' **Princess Maud**. As the **Balear**, she served on the mail run to the Balearics for more than thirty years.

(From a contemporary painting by Ramón Sempel Isern)

This latest addition to the fleet was to be the magnificent **Princess Victoria**, and her launch was subsequently reported in the *Dundee Courier*, Friday 26 January 1894:

*Launch of steamer at Dundee: Yesterday afternoon the steamer **Princess Victoria**, built by Messrs W B Thompson & Company for the Glasgow & Liverpool Royal Steam Packet Company, Glasgow, was launched from the Caledon Shipyard, Dundee, in presence of a number of invited guests. The christening ceremony was performed by Mrs M P Lamb, Broughty Ferry, and the launching was undertaken by Miss Gilroy, Craigie House. The vessel entered the water gracefully, and she was subsequently towed into Victoria Dock with the object of having her engines and boilers put on board.*

*After the launch the guests assembled in the office of Messrs W B Thompson & Company, and partook of cake and wine. Mr W B Thompson presided, and Mr William Moir acted as croupier. The others present included Mr R E Langlands, Glasgow, and Mr Nicoll, Glasgow, both partners in the firm of Messrs, Langlands & Sons, owners of the **Princess Victoria**; Mr Lamb, Broughty Ferry; Mr A Bowie, superintending engineer for the owners; Mr A Watt, Board of Trade surveyor, Dundee; Mr C E Gilroy; Mr F Sandeman Jnr.; Mr W Nixon; Mr R K Christie, Dundee; Captain Howing of the London & Edinburgh Shipping Company; Captain Turnbull of the steamship **Glasgow**; Mr A W Anderson, Secretary of Messrs W B Thompson & Company; and others.*

The **Princess Victoria** (1894) loading passengers alongside the Prince's Landing Stage at Liverpool.

After the loyal toasts had been duly honoured, Mr Thompson proposed 'Success to the good ship *Princess Victoria*'. He remarked that that was the second ship which the Glasgow & Liverpool Royal Steam Packet Company had entrusted to his company, and he hoped that the *Princess Victoria* would give the same satisfaction to the owners as he believed the last vessel had. Mr R E Langlands, with whose name the toast was associated, said that the last vessel built by Messrs W B Thompson & Company had given unbounded satisfaction to the company he represented, and he had no doubt that equal success would attend the *Princess Victoria*. Mr Moir submitted 'The health of the owners', coupling the toast with the name of Mr Nicoll, who replied. Other toasts followed. It is expected that the *Princess Victoria* will leave Dundee about the end of February.

Again full opportunity was used to enhance the good of the company with the launch and christening of the ship being carried out by family members of local merchants. Technical details of the new steamer included some striking dimensions: the poop was 154 feet long, the bridge 16 feet long, and the forecastle 49 feet long. The engines were of the now common triple steam expansion type with cylinders $22^{5}/_{16}$, 35 and 57 inch diameters, and a 39 inch stroke. The operational steam pressure was 160 pounds per square inch, providing 201 nominal horsepower. Steam was generated by single-ended boilers, with six ribbed furnaces, with a grate surface of 105 square feet, and a heating surface of 2,988 square feet. The ship had a cellular double bottom.

The *Aberdeen Evening Express* reported on Friday 30 March 1894:

New steamer for Messrs Langlands & Sons: This well-known firm have added to their already fine fleet of steamers a vessel which, for size and outfit, surpasses any in the ownership of the company. The vessel which is named **Princess Victoria***, was built by a firm in Dundee. She has a registered tonnage of 960, and is fitted with all the newest and most approved machinery. The accommodation for passengers is also very satisfactory. In length and breadth the vessel is considerably larger than either the* **Princess Beatrice** *or* **Princess Louise***, both of which are owned by the same firm. The route of the* **Princess Victoria** *will be by Liverpool, Manchester, Stromness and Aberdeen. She will arrive in Aberdeen tomorrow under the command of Captain McNeil.*

While many deep sea shipping companies were shy of trading to the new port of Manchester, coasting services including Langlands & Sons and G & J Burns had no such qualms and viewed Manchester as a logical extension to their existing services based on Liverpool. During the latter part of 1893 both Langlands and J & G Burns headed their Liverpool sailings advertisements in the *Glasgow Herald* with: 'Until the opening of the Manchester Ship Canal, goods are carried at low through rates for Manchester, Birmingham, Wolverhampton, Nottingham, and all parts of Staffordshire and the Midlands, via Liverpool, in connection with the Ship Canal Company'. The joint Glasgow, Greenock and Liverpool route remained Liverpool-based although additional cargo sailings were arranged to Manchester.

The Manchester Ship Canal was opened to traffic on 1 January 1894 and the official opening was conducted by Queen Victoria in May. The book *Manchester Liners; an extraordinary story* includes a description of some the first traffic on the canal:

One of the first ships into the newly-opened canal was the Belfast Steamship Company's **Dynamic***, offering a return cruise from Belfast and subsequently a passenger and cargo service between Manchester and Belfast. The Lord Mayor and Corporation of both Manchester and Salford headed the procession of ships up the newly-opened canal on New Year's Day. The frustration in the column felt by the* **Dynamic** *and her consorts at the tardy operation of locks and bridges was exacerbated by fears that the banks in some parts had washed in, reducing the navigable width of the waterway. Besides, passengers are quoted as reporting that the countryside for much of the way was uninteresting and 'with very little outlay could be converted into a penal settlement'. And 'the filthy conditions of the water of the canal seemed to those on board as though it received all the rubbish of the seven million or so inhabitants of the new seaport and its surrounding cluster of towns'.*

Nevertheless, Langlands were undeterred and started their Glasgow to Manchester cargo service with the **Princess Helena** leaving Manchester Pomona Docks (Glasgow Wharf) on Wednesday 3 January returning from Glasgow on Saturday 6 January 1894 and arriving back at Manchester on Monday. Thereafter the Saturday departure southbound and Wednesday departure northbound became a regular feature of canal life, the service maintained by the **Princess Helena** supported as required by the **Princess Sophia**. Calls were made at Greenock by inducement. Burns inaugurated a two-ship twice-weekly service with passenger berths available aboard the steamer **Grampus** working alongside the cargo only **Seal**. The inaugural sailing was advertised as a grand cruise to view the canal. Langlands also started to run selected services from Leith to

Liverpool into Manchester early in 1894. These carried passengers and cargo, the passengers being conveyed at the Liverpool rate.

The **Princess Beatrice** was first to come up to Manchester from Leith. On 12 March, for example, the **Princess Helena** arrived at Pomona Docks, Manchester from Glasgow, direct, with general cargo, and the **Princess Beatrice**, with a small number of passengers and a cargo of general merchandise, arrived from Leith.

The main demand was cargo shipments and a firm commitment by Langlands to Manchester came with the announcement in the *Manchester Courier and General Advertiser* on Thursday 5 April 1894 of a specially-built cargo steamer:

Launch of steamer for the canal traffic: Messrs R Napier & Sons launched yesterday from their Govan [Glasgow] shipbuilding yard, a new steamer for the Glasgow & Liverpool Royal Steam Packet Company of which M Langlands & Sons of Glasgow, Liverpool and Manchester, are the managing owners. The new steamer, which was named the **Princess Mary,** *is 200 feet by 30 feet by 14 feet, with engines capable of driving her about 13 knots, and is intended for the company's general coasting trade between Liverpool and Manchester and the various Scotch ports to which the steamers trade.*

The **Princess Mary** (1894) was small enough to enter the lesser ports and called regularly at Inverness and elsewhere. She also worked on the round-Britain service on which duty she is seen approaching Bristol.

From the beginning of September 1894 the **Princess Irene** became second ship on the Manchester to Glasgow service. Almost immediately the **Princess Louise** took over from her, to work alongside the **Princess Helena** in competition with, rather than collaboratively with, G & J Burns. This allowed departures from each port on alternate Tuesdays, Thursdays and Saturdays. The **Princess Louise** worked alongside **Princess Helena** for the remainder of the winter and throughout 1895. As a consequence the relief for the **Princess Royal** during her winter refit early the following year was provided by the **Princess Beatrice**.

Sailings from Leith to Liverpool were on Tuesdays and to Liverpool and Manchester on Thursdays by **Princess Victoria** and **Princess Beatrice**. Departures from Liverpool to Aberdeen, Leith and Dundee were every Wednesday and Saturday. The Manchester service to Leith was consolidated with an acceleration of port handling and passage up the Manchester Ship Canal as reported in a delightfully negative way in the *Manchester Courier & Lancashire Advertiser* on Wednesday 13 March 1895:

Accelerated service between Dundee and Manchester: the steamers **Princess Victoria** *and* **Princess Beatrice***, belonging to Messrs M Langlands & Sons, are keeping up a quick service between Dundee etc and Manchester. For some months past the steamers referred to have left Dundee on Friday night and reached Manchester [after calling at Liverpool] on the following Tuesday morning, goods being delivered in Manchester* *the same day. The* **Princess Beatrice**, *which arrived here yesterday, left Dundee on Friday night last, and reached the Mersey at 7.00am Monday, docked at Liverpool at noon, and left there for Manchester at midnight, arriving here (after 6 hours delay in the fog) at 2.00pm.*

The **Princess Louise** (1888) at No. 2 Dock, Manchester (Pomona Docks) while working the Manchester to Glasgow service in the winter of 1894/1895.

Progress in developing the new destination was rapid, but competition for the trade also developed quickly. The *Manchester Guardian*, Thursday 4 April 1895, reported:

Manchester and the east coast of Scotland: During the past few months this trade, which was formerly of comparatively small dimensions (averaging 150 tons per week inwards [to Manchester], and less than one third that weight outwards), has developed in a very gratifying manner, and large quantities of goods which formerly found their way to and from Manchester through Hull, or by rail all the way, are now being carried by the direct steamers sailing from the Ship Canal. The service was inaugurated early last year by Messrs M Langlands & Sons of Glasgow. Encouraged by the success of the firm, Messrs P M Duncan & Son, Dundee, the owners of the 'Gem Line' of steamers, started an opposition service, also sailing once a week, on the same day as Messrs Langlands & Sons' steamer. Both lines have since maintained regular sailings, and contrary to expectation, each has received a fair share of support, although at a slightly reduced rate of freight. As there appears to be sufficient traffic to support two steamers weekly, it would be greatly to the advantage of all concerned if the rival lines were to adopt different days for their sailings - say Tuesdays and Fridays. By this means a large amount of cargo would be secured as by the steamers between Manchester and Glasgow, which is maintained in a spirit of cooperation by Messrs Langlands and Messrs Burns; it is an example of the success which would in all likelihood attend such an arrangement.

Meanwhile, the faithful **Princess Royal** was plying her trade between Glasgow, Greenock and Liverpool. The hype of the tour guide provides an element of glamour to an otherwise routine trip:

Tour No 3 between Liverpool and Glasgow, calling at Greenock: This service is presently performed by the splendid and fast steamer **Princess Royal**... *a great favourite with passengers. The voyage between Liverpool and Greenock usually occupies about 16 hours, and the steamers pass in close vicinity to the Isle of Man, the Mull of Galloway, the solitary sugarloaf shaped rock of Ailsa Craig, and the islands of Arran, Bute and Cumbrae. The sail up the Firth of Clyde to Greenock is exceedingly fine, especially in the early summer morning. Between Greenock and Glasgow there are numerous railway trains, making the run in about an hour, of which, at a trivial expense, passengers can avail themselves, if they wish to avoid the delay of sailing up or down the River Clyde. Cabin fare single 12/6, return 20/-, steerage 6/-.*

CHAPTER 10

MANCHESTER, RATE WARS, AGREEMENT AND PROGRESS

Following many decades of collaboration with the other operators on the Liverpool to Glasgow route, all service and cargo sharing agreements ceased from the end of December 1895. The rate war that followed was ruinous to the shipowner but attractive to the shipper. The routine advertisement in the *Glasgow Herald* on 25 January 1896 revealed a 50% reduction in passenger fares:

Langlands sailings reduced fares: Cabin single 6/- return (two months) 10/-, steerage single 3/-. M Langlands & Sons, Manchester, Liverpool, Leith, Greenock and Glasgow.

Freight rates were also slashed and the low economic margins of the service were reduced to the bone. Any ideas by the Langlands board of placing an order for a new ***Princess Royal*** were not worth considering, and the only beneficiary was the iron-hulled, compound-engined vessel herself which received a new and unexpected tenure of life.

The problem stemmed from the various new cargo services operated by the Liverpool to Glasgow Conference members which were now running into Manchester. G & J Burns and the Glasgow & Liverpool Royal Steam Packet Company had collaborated closely since the first price war was resolved between them in the early 1840s. In later years, C MacIver & Company, Henry Lamont & Company and R Gilchrist & Company had all joined the club with agreed sailing schedules and rates across the five companies. But once the cargo services commenced between Glasgow and Manchester, the rules no longer applied and commercial pressure meant that each company could take what it may. The consequence was an inevitable division between the five companies so that each reduced its rates to undercut the others. Bulk trades were the preserve of Gilchrist and Lamont in the original agreement but now Langlands and Burns vied with each other to pick up whatever trade was on offer, particularly bulk salt shipments from Runcorn destined for the chemical industry in Glasgow. In hindsight, each company must have quickly realised the need to negotiate with the others, but the damage was done and the negotiating table seemed far away.

Nevertheless, the Liverpool to Leith and the round-Britain services remained in profit. London still remained taboo because of agreements with other shipping companies which now included Fisher, Renwick at Manchester. Langlands & Sons was now well established as a summer tourist attraction, as recalled by James Graham in a letter to *Sea Breezes*, May 1949:

*I was interested to read the article on the 'World's largest coaster fleet' in the February issue of Sea Breezes, and especially to see the picture of Langlands' **Princess Victoria**, as in June 1895 I sailed in that steamer from Liverpool around Scotland to*

Fisher, Renwick Manchester-London Steamers along with others at Liverpool pretty much kept Langlands out of the Thames. Typical of the Fisher, Renwick fleet was the ***Lancer*** (1909), which was sold in 1937 to the Stanhope Steam Shipping Company and sunk by enemy torpedo on 19 November 1939.

Leith, calling at Oban, Stornoway, Stromness, Aberdeen and Dundee, returning by the same route. This enjoyable trip lasted ten days, and the cabin fare, including excellent food, was £5/5/-...

In February 1896 Langlands had the ***Princess Royal*** running into Liverpool, and the ***Princess Helena*** and ***Princess Louise*** into Manchester. G & J Burns operated the ***Spaniel*** and ***Mastiff*** into Liverpool, with a new steamer building, and a two-ship cargo service into Manchester; D & C MacIver had the ***Owl***, ***Bear*** and ***Ferric*** serving Liverpool and Manchester; the ***Fire King*** and ***Fire Queen*** were sailing into Liverpool and Birkenhead for Henry Lamont, while Gilchrist had their steamers also occupied on the Clyde to Mersey trades.

This commercially damaging rate war persisted through 1896 and 1897. It slowly drained the resources of each company. No new ships were commissioned by Langlands who strove to maintain its three core services, to Greenock and Glasgow, to Leith, and round-Britain, with the assets it had available. Apparently, at this time, it was customary aboard Langlands ships to tie a copy of the sailing bill to the patent log before it was lowered over the stern on clearing harbour. Not only did the log measure the miles run but the sailing bill also spurred the voyage on to completion according to schedule.

Langlands continued to advertise its passenger services in a slow dawning that the passenger revenue might be increased if the tours were made more attractive under the banner 'West Highland Cruises'. The limit, however, was the number of passenger berths that were available on the steamers in the peak summer season of June, July and August. A typical advertisement for the services appeared in the *Sheffield Daily Telegraph* on Wednesday 26 August 1896, which stated: 'Summer cruises to the West Highlands and north and east coasts of Scotland weekly. Round the UK fortnightly'. Two years later an advertisement in the *Glasgow Herald* 4 July 1898 read:

*Holiday tours round North of Scotland by the **Princess Victoria** and **Princess Beatrice** from Leith etc to Oban and Liverpool. Every Tuesday during July calling at Stromness, Aberdeen and Leith. Fares (exclusive of meals) between Leith and Liverpool 40/-, Leith and Oban 30/-. M Langlands & Sons, 123 Hope Street, Glasgow.*

Thus the **Princess Victoria** and **Princess Beatrice** maintained the Leith service supported by the **Princess Mary** while the **Princess Royal**, under Captain Alex Reid, still served Glasgow and the **Princess Louise** or the **Princess Helena** maintained the Glasgow to Manchester route while the fortnightly round-Britain route was the province of the **Princess Irene** and **Princess Sophia**.

The **Princess Victoria** (1894) was a key provider of the summer 'Holiday Tours' programme.

In October 1896 the **Princess Helena** was transferred to relief duties leaving Manchester with only a weekly service to Glasgow.

Fares to Glasgow had crept back up with G & J Burns withdrawing from the Liverpool to Glasgow passenger and cargo trade and ceding the goodwill of the service and two elderly Burns steamers, the **Owl** and **Bear**, to C MacIver & Company, who at least now had a collaborative agreement with Langlands over the service from Liverpool:

*Glasgow to Manchester every Friday at 4.00pm; from Manchester every Wednesday 7.00pm. Cabin single 11/-, return 17/-; steerage single 6/-, return 2/6. Returns valid on Messrs MacIver's **Owl** and **Bear**. Liverpool sailings now from Prince's Landing Stage same fares as Manchester with through tickets available via Cheshire Line Stations.*

It was not long before the end of the rate war was announced. On Friday 29 July 1898 the *Journal of Commerce* reported:

The rate war which has been in existence for the past three years between Messrs M Langlands & Sons, Messrs R Gilchrist & Company, Messrs C MacIver & Company and Messrs G & J Burns, is terminated, and on the 1st proximo a new and revised rate of freight comes into operation. This has been to the shipowners of a mischievous character, and satisfaction will be expressed that the companies have arrived at an amicable settlement, thus terminating the suicidal, throat cutting process. It may be safely assumed that the rates existing three years ago will not again be reached, for the steamship companies will not be disposed to allow the trade induced through the competitive rates ruling during the latter period to pass out of their hands, so that while the shippers are practically secure from any radical change in rate, they may be sure that their interests will be carefully studied in the future as in the past.

Some of the detail of the agreement is described by Charles Waine in his book *Coastal and Short Sea Liners*:

It set out the number of sailings per week each was to offer and even the time of sailing, while the bulk salt trade was reserved for Gilchrist's and Lamont's steamers. In addition it was agreed that special rates might have to be offered on large consignments of 100 tons or more to stop the trade being lost to 'stray steamers'. In general all inducements to traders were to be agreed and cargo was to be classified using the General Railway Classification of Goods. Rates were to be quoted quay-to-quay inclusive of dues and a minimum charge for small parcels agreed (28 lbs or less). Heavy items of over three tons and 30 feet in length would have an additional craneage charge. Where cargo was moved from one port to another for export, the exemption from dues was to be passed on to the customer. It was also agreed not to call at Renfrew, Bowling or Port Glasgow for less than 10 tons of cargo. Similarly Birkenhead was not to be called at for less than 50 tons. There were also agreements with cartage companies so that a door-to-door service on a through bill of lading was possible.

On 25 March 1898 a new cargo steamer was launched from the Caledon Shipbuilding & Engineering Company at Dundee and given the name **Princess Ena**. She had a small number of cabin class berths but was essentially a cargo steamer designed principally for the Manchester and Glasgow trade. Her order had been placed at a contract price of £14,900 in anticipation of agreement over the Glasgow rate war, and her commissioning in May was poised to take advantage of the new agreements then being put in place.

The **Princess Ena** (1898) working cargo at Manchester ready for her next sailing to Glasgow.

With business returned to a more sound financial formula a second-hand cargo steamer was acquired from William Robertson of Glasgow early in 1899. This was the part single-deck steamer **Citrine**, dating from 1894, which had a capacity of 602 tons gross and was destined to support the round-Britain service with the new Langlands name **Princess Thyra**. She was equipped with derricks that served her two hatches but unlike her new counterparts she had no steam cranes.

The **Princess Thyra** (1894), seen at Leith, was built as the **Citrine** for William Robertson of Glasgow.

At Liverpool a 'main gang' system of dockers was started by Langlands whereby the company directly employed a gang of about 50 men on a full-time basis. This was innovative for the time and provided the shipowner with a guaranteed reliable workforce rather than the pot luck of the existing day-to-day system of hiring dock labour.

Later in the year alarm spread with the report that the elderly **Princess Helena** had run aground, as reported in the *Evening Telegraph* (Angus) on Friday 7 July 1899:

*The **Princess Helena**, owned by Mathew Langlands of Liverpool, struck at the Point of Ayr Lighthouse at 4.00pm 7 July 1899 during a dense fog. The vessel will probably be got off without harm when the tide rises. The **Princess Helena** is a regular trader between Lancashire and Scottish ports. The fog has been very dense on the coast for the last 15 hours.*

She was indeed refloated and was quickly returned to duty. Nevertheless she was back in the news again on Wednesday 15 November 1899 when the *Aberdeen Journal* reported:

*Peterhead steam liner in collision: On Friday forenoon, the steamer **Princess Helena**, belonging to Messrs M Langlands & Sons, was backing out from the pier at Stromness when the Peterhead steam liner **Active** bore down upon her at right angles and struck the **Princess Helena** opposite the fore hatch, cutting through the belting and driving a hole into her side. The **Princess'** was immediately run aground, and steps were taken to prevent the cargo being damaged by the water, and it is expected that she will proceed after being patched up. The liner was uninjured.*

The **Active** was a cargo ship of 288 tons gross built at Dundee in 1898 and trading on the east coast of Scotland and the Orkney Islands. The **Princess Helena** was patched up and raised on a later tide, and dispatched south under her own steam for permanent repairs to be put in place. Nevertheless the days of the old ship were numbered and an order was placed for her successor early in the New Year. This new ship was the **Princess Olga**, and her launch was reported in *The Evening Post* on Wednesday 26 December 1900:

*Launch of a finely equipped steamer: There was launched yesterday by the Clyde Shipbuilding & Engineering Company, from their Castle Shipbuilding Yard, Port Glasgow, a new steamer for M Langlands & Sons of Glasgow and Liverpool. As the vessel left the ways she was named **Princess Olga**. The **Princess Olga** has been specially designed for Messrs Langlands coasting services. Her dimensions are: length between perpendiculars 235 feet; breadth (moulded) 32 feet; depth 16 feet 7 inches to main deck.*

The **Princess Olga** (1901) was designed for the Liverpool to East Coast cargo service.

Special features of the vessel are the extra large hatches, with winches and cranes, for the rapid handling of cargo. A complete installation of electric light has been fitted on board. The engines, also supplied by the builders, are of the triple expansion type, with large boiler power.

The **Princess Olga** was commissioned early in 1901, but it was decided to retain the **Princess Helena** through one more survey as she had now become entrenched as the regular Manchester to Glasgow steamer running in collaboration with MacIver & Company, departing Glasgow at 6.00pm Fridays and Manchester 1.00pm on Wednesdays. As usual the **Princess Louise** stood in for the **Princess Royal** for her normal February refit at the beginning of the year, but this time it was on a permanent basis. Sadly the ever faithful **Princess Royal** finally stood down from duty and was sold for further service under the Italian flag. The **Princess Royal** took with her the last iron hull and compound engine from the Langlands fleet. The **Princess Louise** worked initially alongside MacIver's **Owl**, although the **Princess Beatrice** stood in for the **Princess Louise** in April. Lamont's **Fire King** and **Fire Queen** also operated a cargo-only service to Liverpool and Birkenhead.

Interestingly the year 1901 was the start of the round-Britain yachting cruises that were operated by the North of Scotland Orkney & Shetland Steam Packet Company before and after its Norwegian cruise season. Gordon Donaldson recalls in his book *Northwards by Sea*:

…it was almost customary, after the season for northern cruises was over, (principally to the Norwegian fjords) to arrange a cruise around Great Britain. This was done for the first time, it seems, in August-September 1901, and probably in each year following – certainly in 1901, 1903, 1905, 1906, 1907 and 1908; in the last of these years there were two cruises round Britain. The itinerary of the 1903 cruise was from Leith to Tilbury, Torquay, Dartmouth, Isle of Man, Greenock, Rothesay, Oban, Skye, Stromness, Aberdeen, Leith and back to Tilbury; it lasted from 15 August to 1 September and the fares ranged down from £20. The 1907 cruise went from Leith to Gravesend, Torquay, Falmouth, Dublin, Isle of Man, Greenock, Oban, Stornoway, Stromness, Aberdeen, Leith and Gravesend.

The success of the inaugural round-Britain cruises, from 1901 onwards, did not go unnoticed by the Langlands board which endeavoured to place one of their larger passenger steamers on the route as soon as suitable tonnage was available. This vision was enhanced by the launch of the **Princess Maud** late in 1901 as reported in the *Glasgow Herald*, 15 November 1901:

A *Langlands steamer at Yoker: Messrs Napier & Miller Limited, Yoker, launched yesterday a steel screw steamer named* **Princess Maud**, *built to the order of Messrs M Langlands & Sons for the Glasgow and Liverpool Royal Steam Packet Company. The principal dimensions are length 255 feet 6 inches between perpendiculars; breadth 36 feet 6 inches moulded; and depth 17 feet 1½ inches, having a gross tonnage of about 1,450 tons. The vessel is fitted up in a handsome manner for summer passenger trade from Liverpool round the north of Scotland to Leith, touching at Oban, Stornoway and the Orkney Islands on the way. The fittings are all made portable, so that in winter months they can be taken down, thus giving additional capacity for carrying goods.*

S.S. "Princess Maud" in Oban Bay.

M. Langlands & Sons' Sea Tours.

S.S. Princess

Official company postcard of the **Princess Maud** (1902) as built in black livery dressed overall in Oban Bay.

Official company postcard of the **Princess Maud** (1902) in the more attractive white livery.

(Linda Gowans collection)

The dining saloon is fitted up in solid oak, carved in an artistic manner, for the accommodation of about 100 first class passengers, and there is also sleeping accommodation for 140 in two and four berth state rooms. The whole accommodation is well ventilated, and the vessel throughout is lighted by electricity, and a complete installation of electric bells is fitted in the passenger accommodation.

The dining saloon aboard the **Princess Maud** (1902). Note the electric lighting and the emergency oil lamps.

The forward wells on the main deck are fitted up for cattle and under the crane deck boxes are constructed for carrying horses. The working of cargo has also been well thought out, there being three winches and four steam cranes. The vessel has large tanks for water ballast, when light or for carrying fresh water. The double bottom is almost the full length of the ship, while the fore and after peaks are also constructed as tanks. Messrs Dunsmore & Jackson are supplying the machinery, which is of large power, and a good rate of speed is expected. Both hull and machinery are built to the highest standard of the British Corporation Register of Shipping [founded in 1890 by Clyde shipbuilders and shipowners as a competitor to Lloyd's Register of Shipping - the two subsequently merged in 1948] and have been under the superintendence of Mr Alex Bowie, the company's consulting engineer. The naming ceremony was performed by Miss F W Langlands in the presence of a large company of ladies and gentlemen.

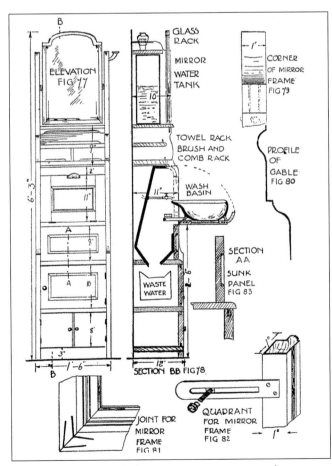

The portable wash basin from a contemporary manual.

(Ian Ramsay collection)

At long last the company realised that the 'tween decks could be used for cattle in winter and cabin class passengers in summer, a conversion which gave rise to the expression 'cattle class' among the ship's stewards. Portable cabins were designed that could be erected in the 'tween decks during the summer and stored away at Liverpool at the end of each season. The access to and layout of the cabins was carefully designed and each was fitted with a folding wash basin which was supplied with hot and cold water by the stewards carrying large spouted cans. The waste water was collected in tanks below the folding wash basins for subsequent emptying by the stewards. A passenger, therefore, could be lulled into thinking that he was not in the cargo hold at all.

Again the new steamer was shown off at selected ports to gain favour with local shippers as reported in *The Evening Post* Friday 28 February 1902:

*New Dundee trader: On the invitation of Messrs M Langlands & Sons, Glasgow, and Mr R K Christie, their local agent, a number of Dundee gentlemen visited the company's new steamer **Princess Maud**, at the Western Wharf today. The vessel has been built in order to cope with the coasting traffic between Dundee and Liverpool, and in her construction special attention has been paid to her passenger accommodation. The steamer is also fitted with the latest appliances for the rapid handling of cargo. Captain John McNeill, an experienced commander in the company's service, is master of the vessel. At the luncheon, the toast of the firm of Messrs Langlands & Sons was proposed by Mr W B Thompson and replied by Mr A M Langlands, Glasgow. Mr Eadie, Newport, proposed the health of the Captain.*

On 24 June 1902 the **Princess Maud** was taken out of service and, equipped with her full set of portable cabins, sailed for Greenwich. Her passengers had two nights aboard ship on the Thames which should have allowed them full opportunity to witness the Coronation celebrations before returning to Liverpool. In the event the celebrations were postponed because the Coronation could not take place as planned as King Edward was diagnosed with appendicitis on 24 June. News of the postponement arrived in Liverpool after the **Princess Maud** had sailed from Liverpool. What alternative revelry was found for her passengers at Greenwich is unrecorded; the trip was not repeated in August when the Coronation finally took place.

Thus in August 1902 the **Princess Maud** and **Princess Victoria** were advertised to sail from Leith, Dundee and Aberdeen on Tuesdays, Wednesdays and Thursdays respectively, to Stromness, Stornoway, Oban and Liverpool, and from Liverpool and Oban every Tuesday and Friday respectively to Stromness, Aberdeen and Leith. In addition, the **Princess Beatrice** sailed from Leith on Thursdays, Dundee Fridays and Aberdeen Saturdays on the direct service to Liverpool and Manchester, returning the following week.

The **Princess Maud** (1902) heading down the Manchester Ship Canal above Barton.

Meanwhile the elderly **Princess Helena** had been withdrawn at the end of 1901 and sold in January 1902 to a Spanish shipowner. She was replaced on the weekly Manchester and Glasgow passenger and cargo service by the **Princess Ena**. The **Princess Ena** still worked the Friday departure from Glasgow at 4.00pm, and Wednesday 7.00pm from Manchester. The **Princess Louise** maintained the Liverpool to Glasgow service while the round-Britain route was in the hands of the **Princess Sophia** and **Princess Irene**. The **Princess Mary** still ran to Manchester from Leith and the **Princess Thyra** and **Princess Olga** supported the Leith and round-Britain services as required, so that occasional extra round-Britain trips could be made the wrong way round, or anticlockwise, to suit cargo arrangements. But the success of the North Company end of season round-Britain yachting cruises weighed heavily in the boardroom at Liverpool and plans were put in hand to have more passenger capacity available for the next summer season.

Charles Waine points out some of the distinctive features of the Langlands' ships in his book *Coastal and Short Sea Liners*:

A feature of the ships was the deep well deck between the foremast and the bridge. This well deck had hinged steel doors which were opened in port on the working side to facilitate discharge and loading of cargo. The doors were kept closed at sea by heavy bolts in board and additionally by extremely heavy angled stanchions which fitted into a steel deck-housing sufficient to stand any weather. The well was used for cargo such as hides, furniture vans, barrels of herring and occasionally sheep and even horses which were housed in stalls, or anything of a bulky nature which could safely be exposed to the weather. This well deck was about six feet deep in the **Princess Beatrice**... *Though in theory they could fill with water in heavy seas, they did not do so.*

An example of the deep forward well deck: this illustration is of the Clyde Shipping Company's steamer **Tuskar** (1890) working cargo through the hull doors of the deep forward well deck at London before the Great War.

The ships were smartly kept with black hulls and red boot topping and in the passenger ships there was a rope scroll around the name and port of registry on the counter stern painted gold. The ship's names, both fore and aft, were in brass letters and kept polished at all times 'or else!'.

...Another feature of Langlands' vessels was the belting, a heavy wooden band running along the line of the 'tween or shelter deck, faced with steel about 9 inches deep and one inch thick. The belting was nearly the whole length of the vessel from the forecastle head to almost 30 feet from the stern, the quarters carried further belting in line with the quarter deck, also sheathed. This feature was customary on Liverpool-based coastal ships. It was a very necessary addition against the heavy blows the vessels had to contend with when docking there in strong west and north-west winds. Normal fenders were of little use and indeed could cause dents in the hulls and the blows could be so severe that crew members were sometimes knocked off their feet.

THE YACHTING CRUISE

Black's Guide for 1903 and 1904 summed up the tourist opportunities offered by Langlands:

Princess Maud, **Princess Victoria**, **Princess Beatrice** or **Princess Louise**. *All have cabins amidships, electric light and cold water baths, etc. Besides the above there are others of smaller tonnage.*

Services: Glasgow, Greenock to Liverpool about four times per fortnight from each end, for dates and hours see Bills and Liverpool and Glasgow daily newspapers. Liverpool to North of Scotland, departures every week. Calls are made at Oban, Kyle, Stornoway, Stromness, Aberdeen, Leith (for Edinburgh) and Dundee. Returning to Liverpool by same route. The steamers sail among the islands of the West Highlands. Round Great Britain (without change of steamer). This tour is run fortnightly and occupies twelve days, steamer starts at Liverpool and calls at Stromness, Aberdeen, Newcastle, Hull, Southampton, Plymouth etc and then up to Liverpool.

But more important for Langlands was the announcement of its first yachting cruise, a dedicated cruise that was not part of the ordinary liner services. This was carried out by the **Princess Maud**, complete with her 'tween decks 'cattle class' cabins. The collapsible and portable cabins were stored in a warehouse in Liverpool during the winter months, dusted down and fitted into the 'tween decks in spring ready for the yachting cruise season. Presumably a lot of cleaning and washing down took place in readiness for the installation of the cabins, as livestock were stowed in stalls on the 'tween decks for many of the southbound voyages in the autumn.

The **Princess Maud** (1902) leaving Oban.

Typical of the Langlands advertisements at the time was that in the *Sheffield Daily Telegraph* on Saturday 23 May 1903:

*Messrs M Langlands & Sons, Liverpool, announce for the coming season a variety of cruises from Liverpool by their well-known steamers **Princess Maud**, **Princess Victoria** and **Princess Beatrice**. There will be a ten-day yachting cruise, starting on 9 June, to the West Highlands and west coast of Scotland in sheltered waters, then from 30 May to 27 June there will be a sailing each Saturday at specially low fares and regular weekly sailings during July and August between Liverpool, Oban, Skye, Orkney, Aberdeen and Leith. Also during these months there are fortnightly sailings from Liverpool round Great Britain without change of steamer. The fares on all these trips are very moderate.*

An impressive view of the **Princess Victoria** (1894) heading up river to Princess Landing Stage at Liverpool to embark passengers.

The **Princess Beatrice** (1893) was a favourite on the Liverpool to Leith service.

Langlands issued a new tour pamphlet in 1904 and this was reviewed in the *Dundee Courier* on Saturday 21 May 1904:

Summer tours on the briny: Messrs Langlands & Sons, Dundee, have just issued their guidebook in connection with the summer tours which they conduct around the coast of Scotland and England. The fleet of steamers employed by this firm is well appointed, and as the fares are moderate, the trips, all of which are to interesting parts, ought to be taken full advantage of by all classes. Many of the trips from Dundee are those to Stromness, Kyle and Oban, Stornoway and Liverpool, and as an instance of the low fares charged, it may be stated that the trip to Stornoway and back only costs £2/2/-. To those wishing to spend the summer holidays on the briny no better mode can be devised than that of a tour round Great Britain, which can be done at a comparatively low figure.

The cover of the 1904 tour guide.

The yachting cruises by the **Princess Maud** were again advertised for 1905, for example, in the *Manchester Courier & Lancashire General Advertiser* on Tuesday 16 May 1905:

*Summer yachting cruises: Messrs M Langlands & Sons, of 10 Rumford Place, Liverpool, have this year placed at the disposal of holiday makers and tourists a delightful little cruise from Liverpool to some of the most beautiful parts of the west coast of Scotland. The steamer **Princess Maud**, which has been fitted out in a manner which is almost luxurious, has been reserved for the service. A great feature of the cruises will be the liberty of the captain to alter the visiting places at times, should he think it advisable in the interests of the majority of the passengers, so that all the advantages of a private yacht will be enjoyed on the voyage. Some of the berths for a nine-day cruise can be obtained for less than £6.*

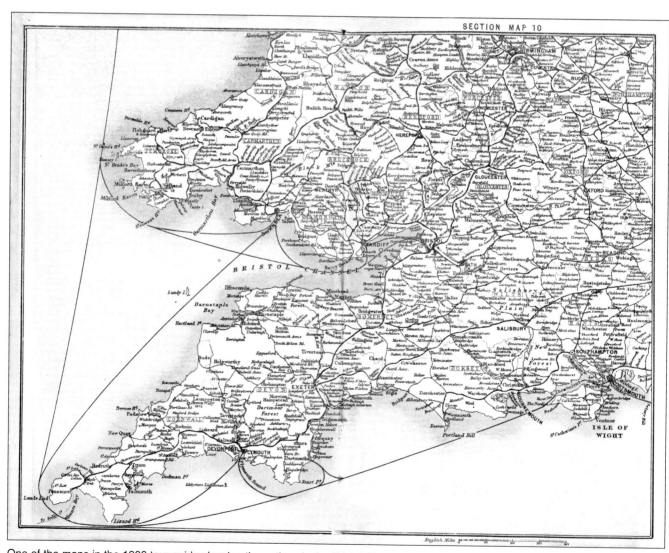

One of the maps in the 1906 tour guide showing the options in the Bristol Channel area.

But the big event of the year was the launch from the Caledon yard at Dundee on 17 October 1905 of the new 'Queen of the Yachting Cruises', the magnificent passenger steamer **Princess Alberta**. Her triple steam expansion engine had cylinders of 20, 32$\frac{1}{2}$, and 52$\frac{1}{2}$ inch diameters and a 36 inch stroke to provide sufficient power to maintain a cruising speed of 12 knots. She was far and away the largest steamer in the fleet being some 1,252 tons gross and 271 feet long with a beam of 36 feet. The agreed contract price for the new steamer was £33,800. On her delivery in May 1906 she was heralded as the ultimate yachting steamer, complete with a grey hull to distinguish her from the ordinary service steamers in the Langlands fleet.

The *Manchester Courier & Lancashire General Advertiser* described the new ship on Wednesday 23 May 1906:

New yachting steamer: A further attraction has been added to the popular route between Liverpool and Scottish ports by the introduction of the new steamer **Princess Alberta** *to the service conducted by M Langlands & Sons. She is a handsome boat of over 1,500 tons, replete with every comfort and convenience. Her dining saloon seats one hundred and thirty-two persons, ladies and smoke rooms are provided to match, while the berths are roomier than those in Atlantic steamers, and beautifully furnished. No finer or grander scenery is to be witnessed around the British coast than on the course through which the steamers pass. They call at Stornoway, and touch at the Orkneys in the Pentland Firth.*

The first master of the **Princess Alberta** was Captain John McNeill, previously master of the Princesses **Victoria**, **Maud** and **Louise**, who had earlier introduced the summer yachting cruises aboard the **Princess Maud**. The master of the **Princess Victoria** from 1906 onwards was Captain W Collister. The **Princess Maud** was commanded by Captain Johnstone and the **Princess Louise** by Captain Cubbin.

The **Princess Alberta** (1905) was given a grey livery to identify her as the company cruise ship.

Captain McNeill had ample experience of serving on both the Liverpool to Glasgow route aboard the **Princess Louise** and the Liverpool to Leith service. The new steamer was delivered with her portable accommodation erected in the forward 'tween deck ready to take up cruise duties from Liverpool, calling first at Ardrossan for the Scottish-based tourists. Her route generally took her through the Kyles of Bute, then out of the Clyde to the Sound of Jura, calling at Oban with an overnight off Tobermory, then through Kyle Rhea and Kyle Akin to Portree and Stornoway. Most nights she anchored in some peaceful haven, providing a tour that lasted about ten days from Liverpool to Liverpool. J T McNeill of Dunfermline wrote about Captain McNeill and the **Princess Alberta** in *Sea Breezes*, August 1949:

On one occasion when he came round the 'corner' of Bute, he found the straight north channel [or Narrows] blocked to him by a sailing yacht and took her through the crooked south channel. There was not sufficient room for a vessel of her size, and her port bilge grazed a rounded toe of rock sticking out from one of the islands, as she cleared the channel. Scarcely anyone on board knew that she had touched and she was undamaged...

Captain McNeill on another trip had an excellent view of a surprising and possibly unique performance. He sighted a large steam yacht heading into the Gulf of Corryvrechan. At the time there was a strong westerly wind driving a heavy sea into the Gulf from the Atlantic and the tide was running out against the sea at anything up to 9 knots. He signalled the yacht, but she took no notice and stood on. When she got into the full force of the tide in the Gulf her rudder had no control over her. She was carried along, mostly broadside, but at times moved neither ahead or astern. She was swept and pounded by heavy water from all angles, but was still afloat, when the tide deposited her – minus boats, bulwarks, ventilators, etc – on the other side of the maelstrom. It was heard afterwards that she had seen the signals but that her owner had instructed the master to take her through 'to see what it was like'.

Captain McNeill was once very highly delighted over a rescue he carried out. He sent away a boat in Portree harbour to rescue a sheriff who was giving his wife a refresher of Portree harbour ozone at 6 pence per hour in a rowing boat on a balmy summer evening. The plug came out of the boat's drain hole, and… all the sheriff could do about it was to make vigorous distress signals in a thin high-pitched voice…

However, before the new **Princess Alberta** was completed, Mr Mathew Langlands, son of the founder of M Langlands & Sons, and current head of the company, died on 22 February 1906 at his residence at Hoylake in the Wirral; he was 70 years old. One of the last actions he had taken was to sanction the preparation of a new comprehensive tour guide and commission Mr George Eyre-Todd to rewrite the text completely. The volume was reviewed in the *Hull Daily Mail* on Wednesday 20 June 1906:

Round the coast of Britain: This is the title of a new guide book issued by M Langlands & Sons, whose steamers with their black funnels with two white bands, are well-known at Hull. The book has been written by Mr George Eyre-Todd, the well-known Scottish author, and it has been tastefully got up and is freely dispersed with views, it forms a most readable and attractive production. The maps by Messrs Bartholomew & Company are on what is called the pull-out principle. Along with the guide book we have received a pamphlet showing the company's sailings, which should prove very attractive to the holiday maker.

There are yachting tours to the Highlands occupying about ten days, during which the steamer calls at the more out-of-the-way places, then there are tours round the north of Scotland from Liverpool to Oban, Stromness, Aberdeen and Leith, returning via Dundee, Aberdeen, Stromness, Stornoway, Oban and Liverpool.

We notice that during the months of June and July, special fares are offered which certainly appear to be drawn up on a most moderate basis, being only £5/5/- for the ten-day tour over 1,500 miles, and this includes, although one might be excused for doubting it, a very liberal table, the whole ten days, whether the steamer is in port or at sea.

Last but not least there is a twelve-day tour round-Great Britain, without change of steamer. The tours commence at Liverpool, proceed north to Oban, then via the extreme north coast of Scotland to Inverness, Aberdeen, Newcastle, Hull, Portsmouth and back to Liverpool.

*The steamers have accommodation, largely in two-berthed rooms, for from 120 to 130 passengers, the latter being the number carried by the latest addition to the fleet, the **Princess Alberta**, a steamer of 1,600 tons, and having what is most unusual for a coasting steamer, a saloon capable of dining the full complement of passengers at one time.*

While the cruise ships were attracting the attention and providing the glamour, Langlands' 'bread and butter' services continued to operate as normal. The launch of the cargo steamer **Princess Patricia** took place from the yard of the Caledon Shipbuilding & Engineering Company at Dundee on 3 November 1903. Ordered only in April, she was built to the Langlands cargo steamer 'template' and delivered to her owners in December at a contract price of £19,850. She was designed to support the round-Britain service and to serve on other routes as required.

The **Princess Patricia** (1903) was designed for the East Coast trade from Liverpool and offered some passenger accommodation.

The **Princess Patricia** was a two-masted fore-and-aft schooner rigged steamship. She was built of steel and was 225 feet long, 32 feet breadth, and the moulded or depth of the hold from the top of the beam amidships to the top of the keel was nearly 17 feet. She was fitted with four watertight bulkheads and six water ballast tanks, and their capacity was 211 tons. Her gross tonnage was 837 tons, and her registered tonnage was 275 tons. She was fitted with one triple steam expansion engine, which gave her a speed of twelve knots. The diameters of the cylinders were 20 inches, $32\frac{1}{2}$ inches, and $52\frac{1}{2}$ inches respectively, and the length of stroke was 3 feet. She had two steel boilers with a working pressure of 170 lbs per square inch. The engines and boilers were constructed by the builders.

The round-Britain steamers inaugurated a summer season call at Torquay with Messrs Renwick, Wilton & Company appointed as the local agents. This became more significant from the following year onwards when the Liverpool to Glasgow passenger steamer **Princess Louise** ran on the round-Britain service for the three summer months.

Another significant change in 1903 was to the Liverpool, Greenock and Glasgow service. With effect from 1 June this became a joint service with C MacIver & Company, with sailings on Tuesdays, Thursdays and Saturdays from each port. The inaugural sailings by Langlands and MacIver were by MacIver's chartered cargo steamer **The Duchess** from Glasgow and the **Princess Louise** from Liverpool on Thursday 2 July. **The Duchess** was chartered from J Hay of Glasgow to inaugurate the service. The **Leona** replaced **The Duchess** in the third week of July but she too did not carry passengers until berths were renovated and her passenger capacity in the meantime was described as 'very limited'. The passenger accommodation was slowly refurbished and the number of berths expanded during the autumn, eventually bringing the steamer up to a standard that matched that of the **Princess Louise**.

The **Leona** was chartered from the Humber Steamship Company. She had two hatches, and her compound engine was aft. The passenger accommodation was around the after hatch and astern of it and when built there were 74 cabin class berths and room for 72 steerage class passengers. She had been very well appointed, but she had not been used for passenger carrying for some years. The **Leona** was designed to load and discharge on the port side, where her cranes were positioned. Cargo and animals came aboard through the bulwark doors in the forward well deck.

In mid-April the following year the charter of the **Leona** was terminated when she was sold to Ralph Hudson of Sunderland to become the **General Havelock** for service between Sunderland and London for the Havelock Line (see Tyne-Tees Steam Shipping Company history). She was replaced by the steamer **Thistle** with an inaugural sailing from Liverpool on Saturday 16 April 1904. The **Thistle** was chartered by MacIver from A A Laird & Company, and remained on the service until the end of June working alongside the **Princess Louise**.

The **Princess Louise** was sent to the Clyde Shipbuilding & Engineering Company at Port Glasgow early in 1904 to receive a new engine and boilers. The opportunity was taken to refurbish some of the passenger accommodation and to install electric lighting throughout the ship.

From 1 July 1904 onwards the **Thistle** was replaced on charter to MacIvers for the joint Liverpool and Glasgow service by the **Merrick**. She was owned by Rowan & Bain (Ayr Steamship Company) and had been built in 1878 as the iron-hulled **Amsterdam** for James Rankine & Sons to inaugurate their Grangemouth to Amsterdam service. At the end of the month the **Princess Irene** stood in for the **Princess Louise** allowing her to take up summer duties on the round-Britain tour, offering a reasonable number of passenger berths to this increasingly popular passenger service. The **Princess Louise** returned to the Glasgow route at the end of September, when MacIver switched the **Merrick** for the venerable steamer **Alexander Pirie**, chartered from the Aberdeen, Newcastle and Hull Steam Company. Sadly this charter was terminated by the owners at the end of December and MacIver had to pull out of the partnership. Langlands covered the missing sailings for the first two weeks of January using one of its cargo steamers and then reverted to the **Princess Louise** running alone on her original two and a half sailings per week roster. Throughout all this chopping and changing on the Liverpool service, the **Princess Ena** steadfastly maintained her weekly round trip between Manchester Pomona Docks and Glasgow, calling at Greenock.

Langlands caused a stir on the Irish Sea when it announced that a new service would operate from Newcastle via the south coast and Bristol Channel ports to Dublin and Liverpool with an inaugural sailing from Newcastle on 28 September 1904. In the event the existing Irish Sea Conferences to Bristol and Liverpool cold shouldered the newcomer and no further sailings across the Irish Sea were advertised. It remained in Langlands' interests to keep friends with these operators as transhipment of goods to and from Ireland continued to be an important source of revenue at both Liverpool and Bristol.

Another cargo steamer was ordered from the Caledon Shipbuilding & Engineering Company at Dundee in November 1904, again intended for service on the round-Britain and Leith to Liverpool routes. This vessel was built, for the contract price of £26,000, in the remarkably rapid time of little over three months and was ready for launch in March as reported by The Evening Post on Friday 17 March 1905:

Smart work by Dundee shipbuilder. Large steamer built in three months: The Caledon Shipbuilding & Engineering Company, have performed a very smart piece of work in the construction of the steamer **Princess Helena**, *the launch of which is expected to take place from the Caledon Yard on Monday afternoon.*

The order was placed by Messrs M Langlands & Sons with the Caledon company at the end of November last, and as some little time elapsed before a start could be made to the work the vessel has been constructed in little over three months time.

The **Princess Helena** *is a vessel of fair dimension, her tonnage being 1,000, and she is practically a duplicate of the steamer* **Princess Patricia**, *built by the Caledon Company two years ago. The new steamer will take part in the summer passenger and goods trade on the coast.*

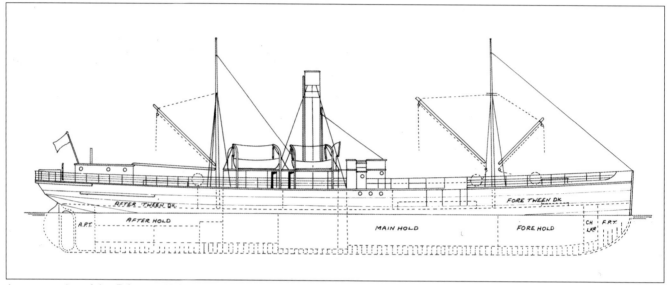

A cross-section of the **Princess Helena** (1906) showing her main cargo carrying and deck handling arrangements.

Commissioning of the **Princess Helena** in April allowed the **Princess Thyra** to be sold. **Princess Thyra** had at best been an interim acquisition for the company; purchased second-hand in 1899, she suffered from inadequate cargo handling gear and was a part single-decker.

Against all these new developments there was a fairly significant setback for the company. Whilst on a routine voyage from Aberdeen to the Bristol Channel for the round-Britain circuit, the steamer **Princess Irene** came to grief in thick fog off Pembrokeshire, as reported in the *Aberdeen Journal* on Thursday 23 August 1906:

Total loss of Glasgow steamer, on a voyage from Aberdeen: The Glasgow steamer **Princess Irene** *has been wrecked off the south coast of Wales. A telegram received by the owners states that the steamer went on the rocks in a fog off Linney Head, Pembrokeshire, on Monday night, while on a passage from Aberdeen to Bristol. There is little hope of saving the vessel. Her engine room and hold are flooded, and her hull torn in several places. Her Captain also regrets that the vessel's back is broken, and there is little hope of doing anything for her. The cargo is being washed away. All the crew are reported to be safe. The* **Princess Irene** *was built by Messrs W B Thompson & Company, Dundee and is 760 tons register. She is owned by M Langlands & Sons of Liverpool and Glasgow.*

Captain Donald McColl was held to blame for the stranding at the subsequent Board of Trade Inquiry. The incident serves as a reminder of the perilous conditions in which the Langlands steamers continually sailed, despite the stranding taking place in still, but foggy, conditions on a mid-summer evening.

The *Princess Irene* Inquiry

In the matter of a formal investigation held at the Magistrates' Room, Liverpool, on the 12th and 13th days of September, 1906, before W J Stewart, Esq, assisted by Captain Barnett Bigley, and Captain Erskine, into the circumstances attending the stranding of the British ss **Princess Irene***, of Glasgow, near Linney Head, Pembrokeshire, on August 20th, 1906, whereby she became a total loss.*

The Court, having carefully inquired into the circumstances attending the above-mentioned shipping casualty, finds, for the reasons stated in the Annex thereto, that the stranding and loss of the said vessel were caused by the default of the master, Mr Donald McColl, but, under the special circumstances set out in the answers below, the Court contents itself with severely reprimanding him.

Dated this 13th day of September, 1906, signed W J Stewart.

The inquiry into the stranding and subsequent loss of the British Steamship **Princess Irene***, of Glasgow, was held in the Magistrates' Room, Dale Street, Liverpool, on the 12th and 13th days of September, 1906, before W J Stewart, Esq, Stipendiary Magistrate, assisted by Captains Wm Barnett Bigley and Wm Erskine, Nautical Assessors. Mr Paxton appeared on behalf of the Board of Trade, Mr Clayton for the master, and Mr Roberts (Hill, Dickinson & Company) for the owners. The first and second officers were made parties to the inquiry, but were not professionally represented.*

The **Princess Irene***, official number 98602, was a British steel screw steamship built by Messrs W B Thompson & Co, Ltd, of Dundee, in 1891, and was of the following dimensions: length, 209 feet; breadth, 30.15 feet; and depth of hold 14 feet. She was fitted with triple expansion engines (by the builders), which were calculated to give her a speed of about 10 knots, and her amended tonnage was 762.88 tons gross, and 352.05 tons net. Mr Mathew Langlands, of 10, Rumford Place, Liverpool, was designated managing owner. She carried four boats in all, two of which were lifeboats, and was supplied with all life-saving appliances required by the Board of Trade. She had two compasses, viz: a standard compass on the bridge by which the courses were set and steered, and another compass aft.*

She sailed from Aberdeen at 10.00pm on 17 August 1906, bound for the Bristol Channel, with a part cargo of about 400 tons, under the command of Mr Donald McColl, who holds a certificate of competency in the home trade No 102790. She carried a crew of 20 hands all told, and one passenger. Her draught of water was 10 feet forward and 13.5 feet aft.

On leaving Aberdeen courses were shaped to pass round the north of Scotland, and all went well till on 20th August, at 9.20am, the vessel was abeam of the Codling Light vessel, at an estimated distance of about 2½ miles. A course was then set S by W by compass with a view to make the Bishop's Light ahead. At 12.30pm a dense fog came on, and continued more or less until the vessel stranded. The course S by W was continued until 5.00pm when the patent log registered 70 miles. The course was then altered to SSW to clear the Bishop's and pass outside the Smalls. At 6.30pm the fog signal on the Smalls was heard, bearing about SSW by compass, and the vessel was gradually brought round on to a SSW course. The fog signal on the Smalls was again heard on the port bow, and afterwards on the port beam, and the patent log showed 80½ miles. After the Smalls signal was heard abeam, the vessel continued on a SSW course for 15 minutes until the sound was well on the port quarter. The master then altered the course to S ¾ E which was continued for 10 minutes, by which time he judged that he was 2½ to 3 miles south of the Smalls. He then altered the course to SE¾ E, expecting to make that course good and to pass the Crow Rock off Linney Head at a distance of from 2½ to 3 miles. He was aware that the tide would set him to the north, but considered that he had made sufficient allowance for it. At 9.00pm the fog signals on St. Ann's Head were faintly heard. The vessel had then run 18 miles from the Smalls. The course was altered to SE to give Linney Head a wider berth. After rounding, the engines were put at full speed until 9.15pm, when the fog became denser and the engines were put to dead slow. The speed was altered from time to time according to the state of the weather, but never more than half speed. At 9.55pm they saw the black loom of land ahead, and the engines which were then going dead slow were put full speed astern and the helm hard a ported, but before these measures had any effect the vessel struck on the north west corner of Linney Head, where she remained fast. Distress signals were sent up and the crew were all rescued by the rocket apparatus of the coastguard. The vessel became a total loss.

At the conclusion of the evidence, Mr Paxton, for the Board of Trade, submitted the following questions for the opinion of the Court:

(1)   What number of compasses had the vessel? Were they in good order and sufficient for the safe navigation of the vessel, and when and by whom were they last adjusted?

(2)   Did the master ascertain the deviation of his compasses by observation from time to time, were the errors correctly ascertained and the proper corrections to the courses applied?

(3)   Was the vessel supplied with proper and sufficient charts and sailing directions?

(4)   Was the course set and steered after rounding the Smalls a safe and proper course having regard to all the circumstances, and was due and proper allowance made for tide and currents?

(5)   Having regard to the state of the weather after 00.30pm of the 20th August last:
(a) Was the vessel navigated at too great a rate of speed?
(b) Was the lead used with sufficient frequency and accuracy?

(6)   Was a good and proper lookout kept?

(7)   What was the cause of the stranding and loss of the vessel?

(8)   Was the vessel navigated with proper and seamanlike care?

(9)   Was the loss of the **Princess Irene** caused by the wrongful act or default of the master?

Mr Clayton having addressed the Court on behalf of the master, the Court gave judgment as above and returned the following answers to the questions of the Board of Trade:

(1)   The vessel had two compasses, one on the bridge by which she was navigated, and the other aft. They were in good order and sufficient for the safe navigation of the vessel, and were last adjusted by Messrs Chadburn, of Liverpool, on 27 January 1903.

(2)   The master stated that he did ascertain the deviation of his compasses from time to time by running courses between the headlands and lights; the errors were correctly ascertained and the proper corrections to the courses applied.

(3)   The vessel was supplied with proper and sufficient charts and sailing directions.

(4)   The course set and steered after rounding the Smalls was not safe or proper having regard to all the circumstances. Due and proper allowance was not made for tide or current.

(5)   Having regard to the state of the weather after 00.30 pm of the 20th August last:
(a) The vessel was not navigated at too great a rate of speed.
(b) The lead was not used with sufficient frequency.

(6)   A good and proper lookout was kept.

(7)   The stranding and loss of the vessel was due to the fact that the master, after rounding the Smalls, steered too fine a course to clear Linney Head, during thick weather.

(8)   After rounding the Smalls the vessel was not navigated with proper and seamanlike care.

(9)   The loss of the **Princess Irene** was caused by the default of the master, but the Court, taking into consideration his long services in the one Company and the straightforward way in which he gave his evidence and admitted his error, contents itself with passing severe censure upon him.

W J Stewart, Judge.
WM Barnett Bigley, William Erskine, Assessors.
Liverpool, 13th September, 1906.

SUMMER HEYDAYS AND LONG WINTER NIGHTS

Services carried on much as before through 1906 and 1907 although Cromarty was now a regular call on the Liverpool to Leith service. The **Princess Maud** and **Princess Victoria** were the mainstay of the Liverpool to Leith service, the **Princess Irene** was the main passenger unit on the round-Britain route and the **Princess Louise** maintained the less glamorous Liverpool to Greenock and Glasgow service. The **Princess Alberta**, of course, was deployed for much of the summer season on the seasonal yachting cruises from Liverpool and Ardrossan, with a ten-day cruise including all meals being priced at £6/15/-. The **Princess Beatrice** supported the Leith service running into Manchester and then transferred in both summer 1906 and 1907 to the round-Britain route alongside **Princess Irene**, at last offering a substantial number of passenger berths to this increasingly important tourist route. The **Princess Beatrice** ran anticlockwise from Leith calling at Dundee, Aberdeen, Bristol, Cardiff, Swansea, Southampton and Hull taking 13 days to return to Leith and offering all-inclusive cabin class accommodation at £13/5/-.

The Bristol and South Wales to Liverpool services were put under serious competition from other operators, notably F H Powell & Company of Liverpool. In 1906 Powell commissioned a large cargo steamer, the **Faithful**, specifically for the weekly round trip from Liverpool. Langlands' attitude, as always, was to face the competition head-on and it does seem that there was enough cargo on offer at that time to satisfy both companies. Indeed the order for the **Princess Dagmar** may well have been prompted partly by competition from Powell. This new cargo steamer was launched from the yard of Napier & Miller at Old Kilpatrick on 28 March 1907 and delivered to Langlands in April. She was designed for the round-Britain service, had a speed of 12 knots and was equipped with a comprehensive array of cargo handling equipment. She offered berths for over 25 cabin class passengers.

F H Powell & Company's new cargo steamer the **Faithful** (1906) operated in direct competition with Langlands on the Liverpool to Bristol service.

The ***Princess Dagmar*** (1907) approaching Bristol on the River Avon.

The Manchester to Glasgow service by the ***Princess Ena*** competed against the Monday, Thursday and Saturday sailings from Pomona Docks to Glasgow by Messrs Burns, whose local office was in Brazennose Street. The Burns' steamers also carried passengers whereas the ***Princess Ena*** had berths for only a few cabin passengers. At the end of May 1907 the ***Princess Ena*** stood down for a fortnight for overhaul and was replaced by one of the cargo steamers and the passenger service was temporarily withdrawn 'until further notice'. In August Langlands were able to charter the cargo steamer ***Glenariff*** from the Antrim Iron Ore Company. She was a single-decker and had been used to carry iron ore from Belfast round the north of Scotland to Stockton-on-Tees, returning largely in ballast. The ***Glenariff*** had been built at Belfast in 1892. She was placed on the Manchester service, so that passengers were again not accepted. The ***Glenariff*** was renamed ***Princess Ena*** early the following year when her former namesake was sold out of the fleet. The original ***Princess Ena*** was a two deck vessel whose passenger accommodation was little used throughout much of the year, whereas the 'new' ***Princess Ena*** offered only cargo-carrying capacity which was in demand, and allowed a better distribution of costs from her tonnage-based dues charged by the Manchester Ship Canal Company.

The ***Princess Ena*** (1892) was acquired from the Antrim Iron Ore Company in 1908. She is seen here as the ***Fife Coast*** after adopting Coast Lines nomenclature and livery in 1920.

On 14 January 1908 both the *London Gazette* and *Edinburgh Gazette* announced:

The firm of M Langlands & Sons, carrying on business as shipowners and shipping agents in Glasgow, Liverpool, and elsewhere, was of consent DISSOLVED as at 30 September 1907, by the retirement therefrom of William Lewis Nicol, one of the partners.

The business will continue to be carried on by the other Partners, being the subscribers other than the Curator Bonis of the said William Lewis Nicol, on their own account and under the same name of M Langlands & Sons. Signed: Ralph Erskine Langlands, Archibald Robert Cameron, Harry Campbell Richardson Sievwright, Alex Wingate Langlands, Mathew Herbert Langlands, and Alexander Stewart Nicol.

The big news in 1908, however, was the loss of the **Princess Mary**. This was reported tersely in the morning edition of the *Glasgow Herald* on Monday 1 June 1908:

*During a dense fog the steamer **Princess Mary**, of Glasgow, went ashore on Saturday forenoon on the rocks near Peterhead. The rocket apparatus was called into requisition, and the lifeboat proceeded to lend assistance. The sea was perfectly calm, however, and the crew resolved to remain on their vessel, which was badly holed. Operations were commenced to take the cargo onshore. The steamer was on a voyage from Liverpool to Aberdeen with general cargo.*

More detail was available in the report provided by the *Evening Telegraph* (Angus) also on Monday 1 June 1908, but in an evening edition:

*Lost on Aberdeen coast, Dundee trader becomes total wreck: Messrs Langlands & Sons steamer the **Princess Mary** that went ashore on Saturday at Peterhead is likely to be a total wreck. The **Princess Mary** belongs to Messrs M Langlands & Sons, Glasgow and Liverpool, and is engaged in the coasting trade. On the east coast of Scotland she regularly calls at Leith, Dundee and Aberdeen, and it is while making her way to the Granite City that she ran ashore about 200 yards west of the Coastguard Station, Peterhead. She struck a reef of rocks about a quarter of a mile from the beach, and remained fast. When it was seen by those on board that the vessel could not be got off by her own steam, signals of distress were made. These were heard by the Coastguardsman on duty, and he immediately summoned the rocket brigade and the crew of the lifeboat. The steamer could not be seen from the shore, and thinking that the vessel was on Craigewen shore, the members of the brigade made for Scotston Head. No vessel was seen, however, and the brigade returned, the fog lifting shortly afterwards and disclosing the vessel as she lay a little over a quarter of a mile from the station. The lifeboat had by this time been alongside the steamer, but, the seas being very calm, her services were not required. Not long after her position was discovered, the steamer was surrounded by small boats from Peterhead, and a start was made to lighten the ship by taking part of the cargo ashore. This was continued throughout the day, the drifter **City of Glasgow**, of Peterhead, and the puffer **Gael**, of Glasgow, being engaged in the work.*

An accident of a more minor nature had occurred during the previous year. On 20 June 1907 a Mersey ferry rammed the **Princess Beatrice** at Prince's Landing Stage, Liverpool. Damage was slight to both vessels although the incident alarmed passengers on the ferry.

Despite these unwanted episodes, the business of the company had to continue unabated, and of course, the summer heydays were once again ready to be enjoyed. The *Manchester Courier and Lancashire General Advertiser* for Saturday 13 June 1908 summed up just what was available to the tourist wanting to spend holidays afloat:

*Cruises in Scottish waters: This fine weather now prevailing is causing everyone to think of summer holidays. One of the most popular, health giving, and reasonable methods of spending a holiday is provided by the steamers of M Langlands & Sons comprising tours to the unrivalled scenery of the lochs and sounds of the West Highlands of Scotland by the **Princess Alberta**, the holiday tours to the West Highlands and Scottish coast ports by the steamers **Princess Maud** and **Princess Beatrice**, and the tours round Great Britain by the steamer **Princess Victoria**.*

*Special attention is drawn to the cruises of the **Princess Alberta** during the summer months of June, July and August. This vessel leaves the Prince's Landing Stage at Liverpool on nine cruises to different parts of the West Highlands of Scotland, the fares, which are exceptionally low, being inclusive of all victualing and usual expenses, and the trip extending over a period of ten days. These cruises are planned to provide a healthful* holiday among some of the finest scenery which Scotland can offer the tourist. Most of the nights of the cruise will be spent at anchor in some quiet loch far from the busy life of the town and city, and almost every day an opportunity is afforded for some time on shore. The **Princess Alberta** is fitted with electric light, salt water baths, hot and cold, and all modern conveniences, while the passengers are accommodated in state rooms containing two or four berths. The fares for the cruise range from £7 to £13 each passenger, and special features are provided for a party of four.

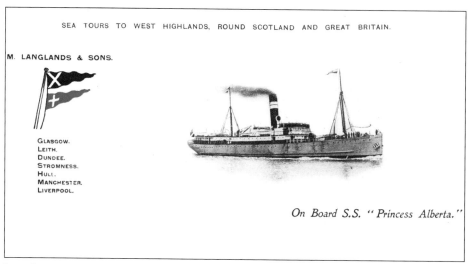

SEA TOURS TO WEST HIGHLANDS, ROUND SCOTLAND AND GREAT BRITAIN.

M. LANGLANDS & SONS.

GLASGOW.
LEITH.
DUNDEE.
STROMNESS.
HULL.
MANCHESTER.
LIVERPOOL.

On Board S.S. " Princess Alberta."

Letterhead available in the lounge for passenger use from the **Princess Alberta** (1905).

The cruises of the **Princess Maud** and **Princess Beatrice** afford a splendid opportunity to visit the Scottish National Exhibition at Edinburgh.

A further delight of the cruising season was described in the *Dundee Courier* on Tuesday 27 September 1910. It depicted part of the end of season Liverpool to Leith 'cruise':

*The cruising steamship **Princess Maud** (Messrs M Langlands & Sons, Liverpool) concluded for the season one of their finest popular motor touring drives when at Dundee last Wednesday, the route being to Coupar Angus, the famous Beech Hedge at Meikleour, and Perth. The drives have proved very interesting for the English visitors, who have in great numbers availed themselves of the opportunity of viewing the city's surroundings. The passengers each trip were conducted and lunched at the Royal Hotel, Couper Angus, under the personal supervision of Mr & Mrs Robertson and staff of servants. At Perth a stay was made to view various places of interest, after which afternoon tea was served, and the journey resumed by the banks of the silvery Tay and Carse of Gowrie to steamer again. The special touring cars were provided by the Dundee Motor Company.*

The new **Princess Thyra** (1909) undergoing trials on the Clyde.

A new cargo steamer named the **Princess Thyra** was launched by Russell & Company at Port Glasgow on 24 December 1908 and delivered to Langlands in the New Year. She was of a totally new and innovative design with her triple steam expansion engine placed aft and bridge amidships, a design that was so successful it was repeated for a number of subsequent orders by Langlands although Caledon were still to produce two more of their traditional engines and accommodation amidships vessels for Langlands, the **Princess Caroline** and **Princess Melita**. The **Princess Thyra** was principally designed for the Leith to Liverpool route but could be deployed on any of the cargo services. She operated at the now standard 12 knots adopted for the fleet.

The business of the company carried on much as before through 1909. A new port of call was announced in the *Evening Telegraph* (Angus) on Friday 22 October 1909:

Messrs Langlands & Sons, Glasgow, propose to establish a steamship line between Kirkcaldy and Liverpool and Manchester. In a letter to the Harbour Committee of Kirkcaldy Town Council, they mentioned that to work the class of traffic they have to deal with it is essential that they should have a suitable covered shed to discharge and load at. The matter was remitted to a committee for consideration.

On 14 December the Caledon Shipbuilding & Engineering Company launched the new cargo steamer **Princess Caroline**. She was designed for the round-Britain route and entered service in January 1910. She was of the traditional Caledon engines amidships design and was similar to the **Princess Dagmar**.

A hugely public and embarrassing mishap occurred to the **Princess Beatrice** as reported in the *Evening Telegraph* (Angus) on Tuesday 28 June 1910:

*Accident to a Langlands steamer, stranded and refloated near Oban: The steamer **Princess Beatrice**, of the Langlands Line, while on a trip round the British Isles from Liverpool, stranded on a submerged rock in the Sound of Luing [on 27 June]. There is strong tide through the Sound of Luing, and the vessel appears to have been caught by the ebb tide along the shore of Scarba Isle. Information of the mishap was sent to Oban, and the same company's steamer **Princess Victoria**, which called there on a southward trip, went to the assistance of the **Princess Beatrice**, but was unable to haul her off. About midnight the **Princess Victoria** put back to Oban for further assistance and the Northern Lighthouse steamer **Pharos** (Captain Ewing) and the local (excursion) steamer **Princess Louise** (Captain Paterson) returned with the **Princess Victoria**, but all efforts to haul off the stranded steamer failed.*

The **Princess Victoria** (1894) at Oban.

(Linda Gowans collection)

*The passengers, of whom there were about ninety for the trip round Britain, were transferred to the **Princess Victoria**, and conveyed back to Liverpool.*

*The **Princess Beatrice** floated off yesterday evening at half past seven o'clock, after having had the bulk of her cargo discharged into lighters, and proceeded under her own steam to Oban, where she arrived at half past nine o'clock, and moored alongside the Railway Quay. She does not appear to have suffered much damage, but will probably be surveyed before proceeding.*

Langlands recovered its dignity the following month by announcing an order placed at Caledon for a new, bigger and better yachting steamer as described in the *Dundee Courier* on Friday 8 July 1910:

Handsome passenger steamer, a tribute to Dundee shipbuilding: The Caledon Shipbuilding & Engineering Company, Dundee, has booked another substantial order from a firm which has tested the merits of Caledon work on former occasions.

The order comes from Messrs M Langlands & Sons, Glasgow and Liverpool, the owners of the well-known Princess Line.

*The new steamer will be somewhat similar in pattern, but larger than the **Princess Alberta**, a high-class vessel of the yacht-type, which was built in the Tayside yard some years ago. She will be 300 feet long, 48 feet beam, and about 17 feet deep, her gross tonnage being about 1,800. She will carry about 160 first class passengers. Her engines will develop from 12 to 13 knots, and they will be constructed at Lilybank Foundry, Dundee...*

The year 1911 was marred by the loss of the steamer **Princess Patricia**. The accident is described in the report of the Formal Investigation of her stranding near Dippin Head, Island of Arran, Firth of Clyde, on 19 October 1911, which was held at Glasgow on 18 and 20 December 1911. The owners of the vessel were

Mr Alexander Wingate Langlands, Mr Mathew Herbert Langlands, and Mr Arthur Wingate joint owners, with Mr Mathew Herbert Langlands, of Hope Street, Glasgow, designated managing owner:

The **Princess Patricia** sailed from Manchester at about 9.00pm on the 18th October last, bound for Glasgow, under the command of Mr Neil McNicol, who held a certificate as master, No 102582. She had a crew of eighteen hands all told, and no passengers, and was loaded with a general cargo of about 800 tons, and her draught was 10 feet 5 inches forward and 13 feet 8 inches aft. The weather on leaving was calm and hazy. At 2.50am on the 19th October the vessel arrived at Eastham Lock, and had to await the tide. At 6.15am the vessel left Eastham, and at 8.27am passed the Bar Buoy. The course was set N by W 1/2 W, and the patent log was streamed, the weather being hazy with drizzling rain and a light SE wind. Various courses were steered, as each headland was abeam, and the readings of the patent log were duly noted in the log book. During the afternoon the wind increased from the ESE with rain. At 5.44pm Black Head was abeam, distance one mile by four-point bearing. Fifteen minutes later, or at 5.59pm, the course was altered to N by E 1/2 E. At 6.00pm the second officer relieved the chief officer, and it may be mentioned here that when before the Court there was a difference in the statements of these officers as to the course given at this time by the chief officer to the second. The former states that the course given by him was N by E 1/2 E. The latter denies this, and states that the course he got and afterwards steered was N by E, and this statement is supported by the entry in the scrap log book (produced) written by the chief officer, and though this officer stated that he was aware of the entry he had made, he later changed his mind as to the course, but neglected to alter the entry.

At 6.45pm Corsewall Point was abeam, distant 1 1/2 miles. This distance is about quarter of a mile inside the position at this time, according to the chief officer, and is three-quarters of a mile inside the position which the vessel should have been in if the course, according to the second officer, was correct. Considering these facts, and not having the evidence of the helmsman to assist them, the Court is of opinion that, notwithstanding the entry in the scrap log, the evidence as to this course given by the chief officer is the more correct of the two.

From the position 1 3/4 miles (accepting the chief officer's reckoning as correct) off Corsewall Point at 6.45pm, the course was set NE by N 1/2 N, and at 8.00pm Ailsa Craig was abeam, distance three-quarters of a mile. At this time the change of the watch took place and both officers were on deck, and were agreed as to the distance off.

After 8.00pm the weather was thick with haze and rain, but lights could be seen at a safe distance. Pladda Light was sighted about three miles away, the vessel having made her course from off Corsewall Point quite correctly. Pladda was abeam at 8.57pm, distant 1 1/2 miles. The course was altered to NE by N, and continued until 9.50, when, owing to the increasing darkness of the night, the chief officer altered course to NE 1/2 N, and five minutes later to NE. The vessel, however, had hardly been steadied on this last course before she ran, still going full speed, on the rocks about Dippin Point.

The engines were stopped, but no attempt was made to back the vessel off owing to the fear of her foundering. The forward holds, when sounded, showed eight or nine feet of water, and though the pumps were put on they were unable to cope with the leak. The boats were put out, and at 11.00pm all hands left the vessel and got safely on shore just as the coastguards arrived, in response to their distress signals, to their assistance with the rocket apparatus.

The vessel, when left, had a heavy and increasing list to port. The crew reached a farm house close to the scene of the casualty, whence next morning they returned to the vessel, and later on in the day a salvage tug and lighters with salvage pumps and gear arrived, but could do nothing owing to the state of the weather.

On the 22nd October, the weather having moderated, salvage operations were begun and continued, unless interrupted by bad weather, until the 4th November, when, the vessel having broken up, she was finally abandoned.

There was also the issue of AB Abernethy and his newly purchased electric torch; the report continued:

During the hearing of this case there have been two points specially before the Court (first) the difference between the chief and second officers as to the course steered for a short time before reaching Corsewall Point, which has already been dealt with, and (second) the incident of the metal electric lamp.

This lamp had been bought by its owner, Abernethy, AB, while the vessel was at Manchester, and the officers were not aware of its existence. Abernethy stated that when he was sent from the bridge to read the patent log when Pladda Light was abeam, he had not the lamp with him, but had to fetch it from his quarters forward before he could carry out the order. After reporting to the chief officer, he returned to his station on the lookout on the port side of the bridge with the lamp in the right-hand pocket of his jacket. In his evidence he stated that he was standing from two to four feet from the compass, but in answer to a question from the Court he could not say whether he might have been at times leaning against the binnacle or not.

Regarding the amount of attraction which might be exerted at various distances by this lamp on the compass, the chief officer informed the Court that he had tried it himself on the day after the stranding, and found that outside the distance of one foot from the compass the attraction was only slight.

Mr A D Wylie, agent for the first mate and owners, stated that at his suggestion a similar experiment had been carried out on the wreck by the salvage officer, with the result that he found the amount of attraction ranged from eight degrees close to the compass to nothing at the distance of four feet.

The experiments of the chief officer and the salvage officer are, however, of very doubtful value considering that when they were carried out the vessel was a wreck lying on the rocks with a very heavy list.

The Superintendent of the Line, Mr Peter Johnstone [formerly master of the **Princess Maud**], spoke to having made experiments with an electric lamp upon a similar compass, and found that when the lamp was held close to the compass the needle was deflected eight degrees, and at two feet distance the deflection was reduced to half this amount.

The Court is unable to accept the result of these experiments as conclusive, considering how and when they were made, and by whom, but in the absence of any other apparent cause must conclude that the compass of the **Princess Patricia** was in fact deflected by the proximity of this lamp, thus causing the casualty.

The chief officer was not held in any way to blame for the stranding and the effect of the lamp on the compass illustrated how little was understood about magnetism and electricity at that time. The Court of Inquiry concluded that:

The cause of the stranding and loss of the vessel so soon after an accurate fix had been obtained for position, and a safe course set therefrom, would be difficult to explain were it not that during the hearing it became known to the Court that an AB named Abernethy, who was on the look-out on the bridge, admitted in evidence that when he was sent to read the patent log off Pladda he used for the purpose an electric lamp of his own, and returned to his position on the port side of the bridge within a foot or two of the compass, having the lamp in his pocket, which, if near enough, would deflect the compass needle towards him, and is, in the opinion of the Court, a sufficient cause in itself to account for the stranding of the vessel.

The wreck of the **Princess Patricia** was sold to Clyde shipbreakers the following July and demolished as she lay.

The new yachting steamer was finally ready to be launched on 6 February 1912. She was launched by family member Miss Langlands, while a Miss Flora McPherson christened the vessel **Princess Royal** as the new ship left the ways, bringing back into the fleet the iconic name that had not been in use since 1901. The new **Princess Royal** could accommodate 164 first class, 39 second class, 715 steerage, and required a crew of 70. The contract price for the order was £36,990, just over £3,000 more than the cost of building the **Princess Alberta** seven years earlier. The *Dundee Courier* reported on Friday 10 May 1912:

New Dundee steamer's trial trip: Under favourable weather conditions the steamer **Princess Royal**, the latest addition to the Langlands Line, left on a trial trip yesterday. The steamer was built by the Caledon Shipbuilding & Engineering Company and is intended for the tourist traffic in the Western Highlands.

Charles Waine described the **Princess Royal** in his book *Coastal and Short Sea Liners*:

The fleet reached its peak prior to the First World War at around 14 steamers. The Commodore's vessel and flagship of the company was the **Princess Royal** which was a passenger cargo vessel in the winter and was converted for cruising in the summer months, to the Western Isles. She carried about 170 passengers and could accommodate them all at one sitting in the large midships saloon which was converted from what was the main 'tween deck cargo hold in winter. The whole of the fittings for the dining saloon were portable and for the winter were placed in the company's store in Porter Street, Liverpool. They were assembled and placed on board by the company's own staff, the tables and swivel chairs being bolted to the deck. The extra cabins were set up similarly.

All the woodwork was polished mahogany with comfortable padded seats, appropriate for the high class of passengers carried both in the cruising vessel and the passenger cargo vessels. Aft of the saloon was the passengers' galley, followed by the smoke room and bar beneath No. 4 hatchway which was covered by a teak skylight when cruising. Two to four berth cabins were placed along the wings of the 'tween and promenade decks. Cold water was available in the cabins but hot water was brought to the cabins in metal cans by the stewards for use in the wash basins which had a cupboard with a mirror mounted above it. When the basin was folded away it tipped the contents into a waste water container below. The fortnightly cruise was from Liverpool to the Scottish lochs and sounds, anchoring every day in a fresh area and remaining at anchor each night at places such as Oban and Tobermory. At some of the calls transport was arranged for short runs to beauty spots. When no berth was available, passengers were ferried ashore by the ship's lifeboats which were boarded from a large gangway lowered down the ship's side and in charge of the master at arms.

The **Princess Royal** (1912) illustrated in an official company postcard.

(Linda Gowans collection)

The **Princess Royal** was commissioned by Commodore John McNeill, who was succeeded aboard the **Princess Alberta** by Captain Alex Reid (then aged 70). Three months after the launch of the **Princess Royal**, on 1 August 1912, Ramage & Fergusson of Leith launched another new cargo steamer for Langlands. She was christened **Princess Melita**. She was a big ship with a gross tonnage of 1,094 and could maintain the company standard of 12 knots. Engines and accommodation were of the traditional amidships design but she was the last ship of this sort to be ordered by Langlands, as all subsequent new ships were of the engines aft type. The **Princess Melita** was delivered in October and took up service on the round-Britain route under Captain McNicol, former captain of the stranded **Princess Patricia**.

Charles Waine again:

Quality of the crews matched the ships and was on a generous scale as were all fittings and stores. All deck crew, who were mostly Scottish or Manxmen, were in the appropriate uniform and the masters in frock coats. Many of these men from the West Highlands spent most of the year passing within sight of their houses along the coast, in villages they returned to once a year to work on their crofts in season and to a spell of lobster fishing. The engineer officers, chief steward/purser and second steward all wore double breasted uniforms. The engineers were also Scottish, but the seamen, firemen and stewards were from Liverpool. This all applied to the passenger cargo vessels on their regular fortnightly sailings too, but in the cargo vessels just the officers were in uniform. These latter ships had steam cranes which were able to swivel in a complete circle and were worked by two crane men carried in each ship. The **Princess Royal** also carried two apprentices indentured to the coasting trade.

The **Princess Melita** (1912) was delivered three months after the **Princess Royal**. She is shown here as the **Highland Coast**, in full Coast Lines livery and with an enclosed bridge as she appeared from 1920 onwards.

(B & A Feilden)

M Langlands & Sons, as managing owner of the Glasgow & Liverpool Royal Steam Packet Company, was now well placed to face the future. It operated a modern fleet of ships and had a sound client base from cargo shippers, and both coastal passengers and yachting cruise clientele. The company had a long history of development and expansion (see below) which had served its purposes very well, and the coming years up until the Great War would prove to be the most successful in the company's history.

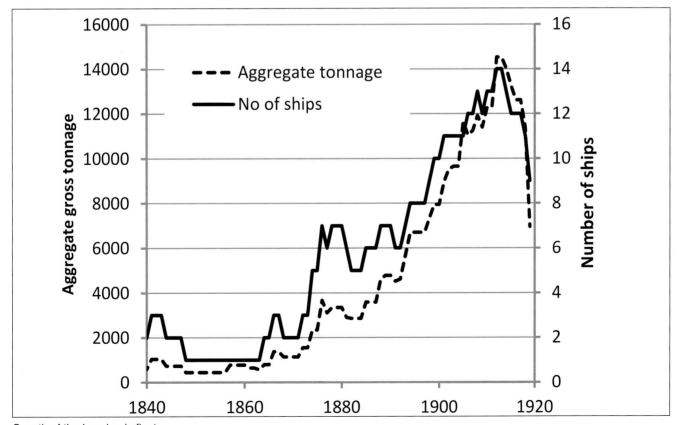

Growth of the Langlands fleet.

SELECTED SHIPPING REPORTS LISTED IN THE *DUNDEE COURIER*

3 July 1905	*Princess Mary* (Capt. McIsaac) loading for Newcastle
3 August 1905	*Princess Maud* (Capt. McNeill) loading for Leith
2 September 1905	*Princess Louise* (Capt. Cubbin) loading for Leith
5 April 1906	*Princess Olga* (Capt. McNicol) working cargo
23 April 1906	*Princess Mary* (Capt. Cubbin) loading for Aberdeen
20 May 1906	*Princess Mary* (Capt. McIsaac) loading for Aberdeen
9 June 1906	*Princess Patricia* (Capt. McIsaac) working cargo
13 October 1906	*Princess Maud* (Capt. Johnstone) working cargo
4 May 1907	*Princess Alberta* (Capt. McNeill) loading for Leith
20 July 1907	*Princess Dagmar* (Capt. McKenzie) loading for Bristol
29 July 1907	*Princess Patricia* (Capt. McIsaac) working cargo;
	Princess Olga (Capt. McNicol) working cargo
29 August 1907	*Princess Maud* (Capt. Johnstone) working cargo
9 November 1907	*Princess Patricia* (Capt. McIsaac) loading for Leith
10 February 1908	*Princess Olga* (Capt. McNicol) loading for Leith
22 February 1908	*Princess Alberta* (Capt. McNeill) loading for Leith
21 March 1908	*Princess Olga* (Capt. McIsaac) loading for Bristol
15 August 1908	*Princess Helena* (Capt. Collister) loading for Leith;
	Princess Beatrice (Capt. McIsaac) arrived from Leith
13 October 1908	*Princess Alberta* (Capt. McNeill) working cargo
22 October 1908	*Princess Victoria* (Capt. Collister) loading for Leith
1 May 1909	*Princess Alberta* (Capt. McNeill) working cargo
18 June 1910	*Princess Helena* (Capt. Kinley) loading for Kirkcaldy
31 October 1910	*Princess Olga* (Capt. McIsaac) working cargo
7 November 1910	*Princess Patricia* (Capt. McNicol) loading for Kirkcaldy
14 November 1910	*Princess Alberta* (Capt. McNeill) loading for Leith
25 March 1911	*Princess Patricia* (Capt. McNicol) working cargo;
	Princess Caroline (Capt. Cubbin) working cargo
27 April 1911	*Princess Caroline* (Capt. Cubbin) loading for Bristol
5 June 1911	*Princess Caroline* (Capt. Watterson) loading for Leith;
	Princess Patricia (Capt. McNicol) loading for Kirkcaldy
14 June 1911	*Princess Beatrice* (Capt. Cubbin) working cargo
14 July 1911	*Princess Patricia* (Capt. McNicol) loading for Leith
25 August 1911	*Princess Caroline* (Capt. Watterson) loading for Leith;
	Princess Victoria (Capt. Crebbin) working cargo
6 January 1912	*Princess Royal* (Capt. Cubbin) loading for Liverpool;
	Princess Dagmar (Capt. Corlett) loading for Bristol
9 May 1912	*Princess Beatrice* (Capt. Cubbin) working cargo
3 June 1912	*Princess Beatrice* (Capt. Taylor) loading for Liverpool
14 September 1912	*Princess Maud* (Capt. McKenzie) loading for Manchester
27 September 1912	*Princess Melita* (Capt. McNicol) working cargo
28 September 1912	*Princess Melita* (Capt. McNicol) working cargo
2 May 1913	*Princess Olga* (Capt. McLauchlin) loading for Kirkcaldy
19 May 1913	*Princess Olga* (Capt. McLauchlin) loading for Liverpool
12 June 1913	*Princess Alberta* (Capt. Cubbin) loading for Manchester
28 June 1913	*Princess Olga* (Capt. McLauchlin) from Liverpool;
	Princess Melita loading for Bristol
16 October 1913	*Princess Maud* (Capt. McKenzie) working cargo
17 November 1913	*Princess Royal* (Capt. Rendell) loading for Leith
13 December 1913	*Princess Dagmar* (Capt. Corlett) working cargo
27 December 1913	*Princess Olga* (Capt. Corlett) and *Princess Maud* (Capt. McKenzie) working cargo
29 December 1913	*Princess Olga* (Capt. Corlett) loading for Liverpool
2 March 1914	*Princess Caroline* (Capt. Gill) loading for Leith
23 May 1914	*Princess Caroline* (Capt. Gill) sailed to Bristol
13 July 1914	*Princess Olga* (Capt. MacLauchlin) loading for Liverpool

CHAPTER 13

THE STORNOWAY CONNECTION

The very first call at Stornoway by a Langlands steamer was by the *Tuskar* on 19 June 1872, only a year after they had introduced sailings from Liverpool to the east coast Scottish ports; it made sense to add the trade to and from the island of Lewis. This was shortly after she had gone aground on one of the Orkney Islands on passage from Dundee to Liverpool; clearly she had been little damaged. A second call was made on 2 August, again with Dundee being recorded as her previous port of call. Thereafter the *Tuskar* made weekly calls throughout the rest of the year, calling either on the outward voyage from Liverpool or on her return from Dundee. The people of Stornoway quickly became used to the sight of the ships with their black funnels with two white bands lying alongside the quay.

The *Tuskar* was the regular steamer, but in January 1873 the *Princess Royal*, considered to be the 'flagship' of the fleet, made a single trip from Liverpool to Stornoway and round to Dundee allowing the former ship to be overhauled. This pattern was repeated the following year when the *Princess Royal* again stood in for the *Tuskar*, sailing from Liverpool on 15 January. In 1875 the *Tuskar* called regularly between June and December, while the *Princess Royal* made her annual visit on 24 March. There were also four calls made by the *Fairy Queen* in July and two in September. On 1 September her last port of call was recorded as Thurso. On the same date the *Ferret*, the Dingwall and Skye Railway Company's Strome Ferry-Stornoway steamer, and David Hutcheson & Company's *Clansman*, normally sailing between Glasgow and Stornoway, also arrived at Stornoway from Thurso. The fact that these ships were diverted from their normal services, and that the *Fairy Queen*'s cargo was recorded as 'passengers' implies that these runs were for the purpose of bringing home fishermen and fisher girls who were returning to Lewis at the end of the fishing season. A fourth Langlands' ship to call at Stornoway that year was the *Princess Beatrice*, arriving from Liverpool on 9 July.

A similar pattern ensued in 1876. The *Tuskar* was the regular steamer, the *Princess Royal* called once on 10 February from Liverpool, and there were eleven calls made by the *Fairy Queen* between 4 May and 12 December, having sailed either outward from Liverpool or on the return journey from Dundee, Aberdeen, or Leith. The *Princess Alice* made a solitary visit, arriving from Aberdeen on 15 September.

Stornoway from an engraving in the official company tour guide.

The pattern of sailings in 1877 is described in Chapter 7. The following three years followed similar arrangements, with the *Princess Alice* making two, three, or four calls each month, mostly on the outward sailing, while the new and fifth *Princess Royal* followed her predecessor in making a single visit. A September sailing was again made from Thurso by the *Princess Alice*, presumably once more carrying returning fish workers. The *Tuskar* and the *Princess Alice* were the only vessels to call in 1881 and 1882, while the following year the latter was relieved during most of August and September by the *Princess Royal*.

Announcement of special sailings to and from Stornoway for the fishing season issued on 11 May 1893.

The records of arrivals at Stornoway between 1884 and 1899 have been lost. It can only be surmised that similar calls were made during these years, with new ships replacing those which were no longer members of the Langlands fleet. During December 1899 there were three calls by three different ships; these were the *Princess Helena*, the *Princess Victoria* and the *Princess Beatrice*. They were joined by the *Princess Ena*, the *Princess Mary*, the *Princess Louise* and the *Princess Irene* the following year.

The importance of Langlands' ships to the people of Stornoway is indicated by the brief item which appeared in the *Highland News* on 12 December 1903, indicating that, 'On Saturday Messrs Langlands & Sons' new cargo steamer, the ***Princess Patricia***, made her first call to Stornoway'.

This use of a variety of ships continued for the next few years, the table below showing the pattern for 1908.

Princess:	J	F	M	A	M	J	J	A	S	O	N	D
Beatrice	X	X	X				X	X	X			
Victoria	X	X	X							X	X	X
Maud	X			X	X	X	X	X	X	X	X	
Alberta	X		X	X						X	X	
Dagmar			X	X	X	X	X	X	X	X	X	X
Patricia						X						

The last visit of the ***Princess Royal*** was in 1913; the other ships that year were the Princesses ***Beatrice***, ***Victoria***, ***Maud***, ***Alberta***, ***Olga***, ***Dagmar*** and ***Caroline***. 1914 was the last year of Langlands' service to Stornoway. With exception of the ***Princess Caroline***, and the addition of one call by the ***Princess Melita***, the same ships called as in the previous year. However, the onset of the First World War saw the cessation of Langlands' service to Stornoway. An indirect connection continued for a short time after this. As described in Chapter 14, the Aberdeen, Leith & Moray Firth Steam Shipping Company had then been bought by Langlands. Two of their ships operated between Stornoway and Scottish east coast ports for just over a year after the last departure of the ***Princess Beatrice***. The ***Earnholm*** called at Stornoway in December 1914, January 1915, and made five visits later in that year, the last being on 8 October. The ***James Crombie*** made monthly calls between April and June in 1915. The ***Earnholm*** also made one trip to Glasgow in February 1916, immediately before she was transferred to the Stornoway Shipping Company, in exchange for their ***Lady Tennant***.

Stornoway Steamship Company's ***Lady Tennant*** alongside at Stornoway with a Langlands steamer beyond.

While some of these services had been cargo only, others carried passengers, and became part of Langlands' cruising programme. The company's brochure in the 1890s advertised a number of different options, including No 6, from Liverpool to Oban, Stornoway and back, with a fare of £2/5/-. In 1911 a ten-day cruise to the west of Scotland, including a visit to Stornoway, cost from £5/5/-, including meals.

The ***Lady Tennant*** (1904) seen at Goole in 1918 in full Langlands livery.

The seasonal alteration of the ships for cruising, with the insertion of extra passenger accommodation in the 'tween decks, increased their gross tonnage. This led to questions at the Stornoway Harbour Commission meetings in 1904, asking 'if it was true that there was a preference given to Messrs Langlands' steamers over those of other firms'. The explanation given by the Chairman, ex-provost Smith, and Mr Peter Macleod was:

That Messrs Langlands' large cargo steamers were converted into passenger boats during the summer months, which materially increased their tonnage, and this would, of course, increase their harbour dues, which are charged on their tonnage. Messrs Langlands asked the Commission to permit their steamers to call in during the summer months at the same rate as during the winter months, and stated that unless they agreed to do so, the large steamers would not call at Stornoway at all, but smaller cargo boats would be sent instead. The Commission thought it was an advantage to have the large boats with their passengers calling, and accordingly agreed to charge them on their winter tonnage.

At the next meeting of the Harbour Commission the matter arose again and this time the report stated:

It was unanimously agreed, on the motion of Provost Anderson, seconded by Mr Peter Macleod, to continue the arrangement which had been in force for the last two years whereby the Langlands' large passenger steamers are allowed to call during the summer months on payment of dues calculated on their winter tonnage.

The arrival of tourists on Langlands' steamers did not pass unnoticed in Stornoway, as the following items from the *Highland News* indicate. In May 1893 it was noted that 'the **Princess Louise**, from Liverpool to Leith, which called here on Tuesday, had about ninety tourists on board', while in July, a 'large number of holiday-makers arrived at Stornoway on the Liverpool steamers'. In 1908 the newspaper reported that 'Messrs Langlands magnificently appointed steamer, the **Princess Maud**, put into Stornoway on Friday last, and lay at the quay for several hours. She had a very large party of tourists on board, and, the day being fine, they enjoyed their short stay in town, visiting the castle grounds and other places of interest.'

Ten years before that, in the *Highland News* of 13 August 1898, in an item entitled 'Lewis Hospital', the secretary of the hospital thanked the passengers of the **Princess Victoria** for a donation of £17. It then stated that:

*In connection with the last we are asked to insert the following: On the evening of the 5th inst. The passengers on board Messrs Langlands' steamer, the **Princess Victoria**, commanded by that popular officer, Captain Macneill, held a most successful concert in aid of the funds of the Lewis Hospital. Mr Marchanton, Moss-side, Manchester; Mr Richard Bramley, Leeds; Mr Thomas Johnson, Broomsgrove, Worcestershire; Mr Park JP, Ashton-under-Lyme; and Mr Black, Erdington, Birmingham; together with Captain Macneill, were the chief promoters. The Right Honourable the Earl of Temple occupied the chair. The programme, which, we regret, we are unable to publish, was interesting and varied. It displayed an amount of talent rarely met with among a number of individuals drawn together merely by chance circumstances.*

Just before the boat left Stornoway on the morning of the 6th, Dr Mackenzie and Mr J M Morrison, Messrs Langlands' Stornoway agent, went on board and were introduced to a number of passengers. Mr Marchanton presented the last-named gentleman with the proceeds of the concert, which amounted to £17. The passengers to the number of about 100 thereafter assembled on the quarter-deck and were addressed by Mr Morrison and Dr Mackenzie, both of whom referred to the good work done by the Hospital, not only among the inhabitants of Lewis, but also among strangers from all parts frequenting the port of Stornoway. An extract from last year's report of the Hospital was read, and

The **Princess Victoria** (1894) depicted on the official company postcard.

was loudly applauded. The passengers were very heartily thanked for their sympathy as expressed by their much-appreciated contribution to so good a cause. The cordial manner in which the donation was made, and the enthusiasm with which the Hospital Committee were received, brought into prominence the very pleasing feature that even when on pleasure bent the British public can reserve a place in their hearts and pockets for the cause of the suffering and distressed.

There were a number of other incidents involving the company and its ships at Stornoway which reached the pages of the *Highland News*. In December 1892, it reported that 'the Liverpool steamer, **Princess Louise**, discharged, on Monday evening, twenty-four large greenheart logs for the new harbour works'. In 1899 the **Princess Ena** had the distinction of carrying the first car to Lewis. It was unloaded on 26 August, and driven round the principal streets of the town carrying a few prominent citizens and causing no little attention. Mr W K Miller, who had taken a lease of the Soval Shootings that year, had brought the car to the island. A third unusual cargo to be carried was a new lifeboat for Stornoway. The issue of 2 November 1901 mentioned that 'the new craft (35 feet keel) (was) expected by the **Princess Olga** in the course of a few days.'

That the steamers had to cope with the winter storms and gales which the Minch could experience is shown by a local newspaper report dated 29 February 1908 about the attempted departure from Stornoway of the **Princess Beatrice**:

*There had been a succession of northerly gales which had raised 'mountainous seas' off the coast of Lewis... The Langlands' steamer **Princess Beatrice** left Stornoway at 1.00am... and after battling unsuccessfully with the sea for some hours (having taken three hours to steam nine miles) she put back and anchored in Branahuie Bay to see if the weather would moderate, and as it showed no signs of doing so she came into [Stornoway] harbour at 6.00pm and landed a pair of horses and two cows which were in danger of being seriously injured through the excessive pitching of the vessel.*

The **Princess Beatrice** (1893), seen at Aberdeen, was a regular visitor to Stornoway.

There was no mention of the condition of any passengers. The severity of the storm can be gauged by the fact that the Stornoway mail steamer, the **Sheila**, which was reckoned to cross the Minch in all but the worst conditions, was anchored overnight by her redoubtable Captain Cameron in Applecross Bay, finally arriving over twelve hours late about noon the following day.

There was a report of a 'theft from a steamer'. In the Sheriff Court 'Peter Macdonald, labourer, Benside, was charged with stealing a quantity of pears from the hold of the steamer **Princess Irene**, on 18 October 1901. He denied the charge, but was convicted on evidence, and a fine of £1 or 14 days imprisonment was imposed. His Lordship commented on the practice of tearing open the corners of parcels either from curiosity or with motives of theft. He himself, he said, as well as others, had frequently complained of the condition in which they sometimes received their parcels by steamer.'

A report of a sadder nature appeared in March the following year:

*On arrival at Stornoway... of Messrs Langlands' steamer **Princess Olga,** the captain reported that Donald Macdonald, ship carpenter, Sandwick, returning to Stornoway as a passenger was accidentally drowned at sea by falling overboard from the forecastle head. The accident happened on Friday morning when the steamer was ten to fifteen miles off the Mull of Galloway. Macdonald was attempting to climb over the breakwater on the forecastle head when he over-balanced, and fell into the sea. The second officer, who was on the bridge,* *immediately stopped the engines in case Macdonald might be caught in the propeller. When she passed him the engines were again started, and the steamer brought round, a small boat being launched in the meantime. The steamer, however, reached the spot first, and the Chief Engineer, Mr William Maclennan, very gallantly, at the risk to his life, went over the side with a rope, and made it fast to the unfortunate man, but unfortunately life was extinct. Mr Maclennan, the gallant rescuer, who is a native of Inverness, was picked up in a very exhausted condition. Macdonald was thirty-five years of age, and leaves a widow and three children. A representation is being made to the Humane Society on Mr Maclennan's behalf with a view to his being awarded the Society's medal for saving life.*

In 1893 a Notice to Shippers informed that Messrs Langlands' steamers would sail during the fishing season to Liverpool and Leith to suit the requirements of the trade, carrying fresh fish and kippers to Liverpool at very moderate rates, and cured herrings via Leith to Hamburg, Stettin, and Petersburg, at low through rates of freight. The importance of the fish trade, both to the shippers and to Stornoway, can be seen by the fact that Langlands would go to the extent of chartering a ship solely for the purpose of carrying fish. In June 1906 it was reported that 'The steamer **Cape Clear**, chartered by Messrs Langlands & Sons, sailed for Leith with cured herrings'. The **Cape Clear** had been built in 1900 for the Cape Steam Shipping Company of Glasgow. The year 1898 saw correspondence between the Harbour Commission and Messrs Langlands regarding damage done to No 1 Wharf to be repaired as economically as possible. The following year tenders were issued for proposed addition to Langlands' stores, the tender going to Messrs Crichton and MacIver.

The *Highland News* of 1 September 1901 reported a collision involving one of Langlands' ships:

*The steamer **Princess Irene**… bound with goods and passengers from Liverpool to Leith, via outlying ports, on arrival at Stornoway on Monday reported having been in collision on Sunday morning with the steamer **Confidence**, of Londonderry. The circumstances under which the collision occurred are somewhat extraordinary. It seems that at about 3.15am on Sunday, during clear weather, the **Princess Irene** was steaming northwards, and approaching the Mull of Kintyre, when a green light was sighted off the port bow. The stranger, it is stated, crossed the **Irene**'s bow about half a mile off, then suddenly altering her course swung round and bore down on the **Irene**, striking her amidships on the starboard side. The passengers, awakened by the crash, rushed on deck in great excitement, but their fears were soon allayed by the boldness and promptitude of the captain and officers, who had taken the precaution to swing the boats out. It is reported that the offending craft, though repeatedly hailed, made no reply; and did not disclose her identity. The captain of the **Irene** having ascertained that his ship was making no water, decided to give chase, and, putting about, steamed southward in pursuit. It is stated that the stranger doubled twice during the chase in order, if possible, to avoid capture or detention, but about 4.00m the **Irene** got sufficiently close to read her name as the **Confidence**. Fortunately the **Confidence** was light at the time, and standing well out of the water forwards she struck the **Irene** above the water line. The damage was also made less serious on account of the fact that a heavy belting round the **Irene** bore the weight of the stroke. As it was, however, part of the belting was cut, two plates broken, five or six plates bent and waterways and decks started.*

After all this excitement, the article rather limply concluded:

*After discharging and loading cargo at Stornoway, the **Irene** proceeded on her voyage.*

The following year the local agent for Messrs Langlands & Sons received a request for a cruise of a different nature to their 'yachting holidays'. It was the custom for an excursion to be organised for the inhabitants of Stornoway on their annual summer holiday. This took the form of a trip to either Ullapool, Gairloch, Portree or Tarbert (Harris), the destination varying from year to year. Normally this service was provided by one of David MacBrayne's Glasgow to Stornoway steamers, usually either the **Clansman** or the **Claymore**, which would otherwise be lying in Stornoway for that day. In 1902, however, MacBrayne 'declined to entertain the proposal'. Langlands were then approached, and 'they expressed themselves as willing to oblige but for the fact that their steamer due on (that) Monday is a cargo boat'. The newspaper report continued, 'As they make their sailing arrangements a month ahead it was, they stated, impracticable to alter them on so short a notice'. The newspaper concluded, 'Those intending to go out of town for the day will therefore have to hire – or walk!'

In 1904 some of the survivors of a greater disaster, the sinking of the Norwegian emigrant ship **Norge**, who had been rescued and landed at Stornoway, left the island for America. They departed on board the **Princess Victoria**, travelling via Liverpool and thence to New York by the Cunard Company. The *Highland News* reported:

They were accompanied to the steamer by many of the leading citizens and ladies [of Stornoway] who had been taking an interest in their unhappy lot. Major Matheson also saw them on board, and took a very warm interest in their welfare. They were very kindly accommodated on board, being treated as first-class passengers so far as purveying was concerned, and all was provided for them at the lowest cost price. There were over 100 cabin passengers, all of whom were greatly interested in the emigrants. They frequently interviewed them as to the sad story of their sufferings, and quite a friendly feeling sprang up between them.

When the steamer was approaching the end of the voyage in the Mersey a concert was organised amongst the passengers for the benefit of the sufferers. Alderman Sharrocks of Darwar presided. The concert was a most enjoyable one, and was attended by the whole of the passengers. The sum of £8/2/6 was collected, and the Chairman, after thanking the various artistes for their kind sympathy, distributed the sum of 12/6d to each of the emigrants, who were quite overcome at the great kindness bestowed upon them during their stay at Stornoway and on their passage to their new home. One of their number in broken English expressed their feelings in a few touching remarks. The concert was organised by Mr Quayle of Wallasey, Cheshire, to whose untiring energy much of the success attending it was due.

Among the distinguished passengers on board were Mr Justice Parry of Manchester, and Mrs and Miss Parry. Captain Collister of the **Princess Victoria** proposed a vote of thanks to the Chairman, and in the course of his remarks referred in feeling terms to the painful circumstances which had called forth their practical assistance and expressed his great pleasure at the handsome sum which the concert had realised. The voyage throughout was sailed in magnificent weather, and all on board were delighted with their experiences of scenery and comfort while on board the good ship **Princess Victoria**, every effort having been put forth by the Captain and officers to make their voyage a pleasant one. The games on deck under the supervision of the genial purser, Mr Smith, were not the least enjoyable part of the programme on this very pleasant voyage.

In 1913 a long letter, signed 'Two Englanders', described in most effusive terms a trip to Lewis by steamer. They ended their letter:

During our three weeks' stay we have enjoyed every minute of the time, and very much regret having to leave tomorrow. However, you can't beat Langlands' steamers for comfort, and if ss **Princess Maud** takes us back to Liverpool as well as she brought us, it's just two days pleasurable sailing... Three cheers and good luck!

The **Princess Maud** (1902) sailing from Aberdeen Harbour on passage for Stromness, Stornoway and Liverpool.

In another piece of reminiscence, W H Macdonald of Stornoway (known locally as 'Willie Spuds') wrote:

The Princess steamers of Messrs Langlands (later incorporated in Coast Lines Ltd, whose cargo boats came here until recently) brought us English tourists. Stornoway lovers of sailing often took advantage of one of those steamers to travel south on business or pleasure. I must have been quite young, but I remember clearly standing with the captain on the bridge of the **Princess Beatrice** as we proceeded slowly through the Manchester Ship Canal.

Clearly Langlands' ships were held in high esteem by both visitors to Stornoway and the locals.

The happy days of cruising and the regular services of Messrs Langlands were not to last long. With the onset of the hostilities of World War One it was not long before things changed. In August 1914 Langlands announced that 'all sailings to and from the port of Inverness are temporarily suspended.' However, this initial panic must have eased, for in October the company was advertising a 'restricted service' between Liverpool, Leith and Aberdeen, but no calls were to be made at Stornoway. There was also the proviso that 'these sailings are, owing to present conditions, subject to alteration.' The last sailing from Stornoway was on 18 September 1914 when the **Princess Beatrice** sailed for east coast ports and the **Princess** names never again appeared in the Stornoway Harbour Authority's arrivals book.

This was not quite the end of Messrs Langlands' connection with Stornoway for in 1914 they bought the ships of the Aberdeen, Leith & Moray Firth Shipping Company, and two of these, the **James Crombie** and the **Earnholm**, called at Stornoway. The former called on a monthly basis from the east coast between April and June of 1915, while the latter vessel made five visits between July and 8 October, after which it would appear that Langlands' connection with Stornoway came to an end. There was little in the press about the end of the connection, merely an item in the *Highland News* under the monthly report of the Harbour Commission:

There was correspondence from Messrs Langlands and Sons regarding the provision of accommodation for them in lieu of their store and offices, which have been taken over by the Admiralty... The company's agent had left instructions that when their boat calls this week all the plant belonging to the firm is to be shipped away by her, as they are to discontinue calling at the port.

Provost Mackenzie responded by saying:

This was a very serious matter for the fishing industry, which was very dependent on the steamer connection with the East Coast for supplies of staves, hoops, chips, boxwood, and empty barrels. It was also a serious matter for the traders, who got most of their oatmeal from the East Coast, and it was also a serious business matter for the harbour that they were going to lose Messrs Langlands, who paid annually from £500 to £600 of dues on their steamers. The Langlands' steamers had been trading regularly to the port for the past thirty or forty years, and they should not let that connection be broken without making an effort to meet them.

The passenger cargo steamer **James Crombie** (1904) was one of three steamers acquired by Langlands when it took over the Aberdeen, Leith and Moray Firth Steam Shipping Company in 1914.

The ships which had served both the company and Stornoway did not fare well during the war; almost none of the ships which had served the islands survived the hostilities. The ships of M Langlands & Sons had quietly disappeared from the quays of Stornoway. The black funnels with the two white hoops would not be seen again, but Messrs Langlands and Sons were absorbed into the Coast Lines group in 1919 and this latter company resurrected the service in the 1920s. Their ships continued to serve Stornoway until the 1960s.

THE GREAT WAR, COAST LINES AND THE LANGLANDS LEGACY

The year 1913 proved to be one of the most profitable the company had ever enjoyed. The three core routes, Liverpool to Glasgow, Liverpool to Leith and Leith round-Britain, clockwise and anticlockwise, were supplemented in summer by the **Princess Royal** and her yachting cruises. The start of one such cruise caused alarm to her passengers and upset to a proposed Royal visit to Liverpool as reported in the *Dundee Courier* on Saturday 21 June 1913:

*Vessel collides with bridge at Liverpool: The overhead bridge near the upper end of the Prince's Landing Stage, Liverpool, sustained a severe accidental knock from the Langlands cruising steamer **Princess Royal**.*

It appears that the vessel, having embarked her passengers, proceeded to leave the landing-stage on her intended pleasure cruise, and for that purpose was in process of being towed off the stage by a tug, bow foremost. A north west wind was blowing very strongly at the time, and to that circumstance is ascribed the fact that instead of clearing the overhead bridge, the stern of the vessel was driven heavily against the structure.

The crash of the impact was described by eye witnesses as something terrific as regards the intensity of the sound. As a result of the collision it was found that one of the wheels of the bridge was broken off, and that several of the girders were bent, the structure taking such a decided inward list that it was considered judicious to place an embargo on passenger traffic along the stage at that part. Fortunately, as far as can be ascertained, no one was injured by the collision.

The loud sounding crash and its destructive results necessarily occasioned considerable commotion and not a little consternation, both on board the departing vessel and on the stage.

The overhead bridge was found to require considerable repair and adjustment, and perforce this has had to be carried out by night-shift lamp lit work. The bridge had just been repainted as part of the scheme of decorations in connection with the forthcoming Royal visit.

The passenger bridge at Liverpool Prince's Landing Stage that the **Princess Royal** (1912) took an attraction to, seen here with the Isle of Man boat **Peel Castle** (1894) off the stage.

The success of the company was such that in the autumn Langlands granted its officers aboard its fleet of fourteen ships a pay rise with extra provision for the supply of uniform and an increase in annual leave.

The **Princess Sophia** was sold to the Clydeside Shipping Company and renamed **Clydebrae**. For the greater part of her career she worked under this name for Hugh Craig & Company of Belfast as a collier. She was eventually sold for scrap in 1958 at the ripe old age of 67.

The **Princess Sophia** (1891) spent the greater part of her career working for Hugh Craig & Company as the **Clydebrae**.

The round-Britain service was increased to weekly clockwise and weekly anticlockwise in January 1914. Calls were made at Liverpool and Manchester, Bristol, Cardiff, Swansea, Plymouth, Southampton, Portsmouth, Hull and Newcastle then up to Leith and Aberdeen. Langlands had its own agency at Newcastle at 79 Quayside.

All was not plain sailing, however. At Dundee there developed a curious dispute between the dock workers and the shipowner as reported in the *Glasgow Herald* on Tuesday 19 May 1914:

Fresh troubles have arisen in Dundee Harbour labour circles. Important issues are at stake.

The Dundee Shipowners' and Shipbrokers' Association are holding a meeting today, and the dispute between the Dundee Branch of the Scottish Union of Dock Labourers and Messrs M Langlands & Sons, steamship owner, Dundee, will probably be discussed.

The dispute revolves around the question of minimum wage for overtime. A week ago a number of the members of the Dundee Branch of the Scottish Dock Labourer's Union were called out at 9 o'clock at night to be in attendance of the arrival of one of the Princess Line of Glasgow. The vessel did not put in an appearance, and an hour afterward the labourers went home. Messrs Langlands offered the men 'waiting money' which is at the rate of 1/- per hour.

Some of the men accepted the offer, but the Union claims that under an agreement signed by the parties and countersigned by Sir George Askwith, Chief Industrial Commissioner, the men on being called out were entitled to receive a minimum wage of 3/-, as they were called out between 9 o'clock at night and 4 o'clock in the morning.

Messrs Langlands contention is that the men were entitled to only 'waiting money' under an agreement made in 1900, but in the agreement under which the dock labourers put forward their claim, the 'waiting money' clause is deleted, reading, in their opinion, that whether the men work or not, the fact could not be got over that they were called out, and therefore were entitled to receive their minimum wage of 3/-.

The dockers state that should Messrs Langlands refuse to pay the minimum wage they will not discharge any vessel of the Princess Line that comes into the port.

The dispute was later resolved but not without a lot of ill feeling and support from Clyde dock workers.

In the early summer of 1914 an order was placed with Sir Raylton Dixon & Company of Middlesbrough for an engines aft type cargo steamer. Although construction work started almost immediately on the new steamer it was suspended in August due to urgent commitments to the Admiralty, following Britain's declaration of war against Germany on 4 August. The steamer was eventually launched as the **Princess Irma** on 13 February 1915 and entered service in March, having taken nearly two years to build. She was a three-masted shelter deck steamer, whereby her 'tween decks were ostensibly drained by large wash ports which in the event were bolted shut and watertight. By nominating the vessel as a shelter decker rather than a spar decker considerable savings could be made in tonnage tax even though the shelter deck was to all intents and purposes used as a 'tween deck cargo space. In 1916 a licence was granted to build a sister to the **Princess Irma** and although a firm order was then placed with Sir Raylton Dixon & Company the launch did not take place until well after the war had ended.

In September 1914 it was still firmly believed by many that 'the war would be over by Christmas'. Nevertheless, all passenger carrying was suspended at the end of the year other than on the Glasgow, Liverpool and Manchester sailings, although berths on other routes were still available to military personnel. Immediately hostilities commenced, it was announced that 'all sailings to and from the port of Inverness are meantime temporarily suspended', while in October the company was advertising a 'restricted service' between Liverpool, Leith and Aberdeen, with the proviso that 'these sailings are, owing to present conditions, subject to alterations'.

Langlands was able to take the initiative in the belief of peace by the end of the year and bought control of the Aberdeen, Leith and Moray Firth Steam Shipping Company, James Crombie, managing owner (see *Coastal Passenger Liners of the British Isles* for company history). It had acted as agents for the company at Leith for many years while James Crombie had been the Aberdeen agents for Langlands and both companies had long maintained close ties to encourage transhipment of goods into and out of the Moray Firth ports, Peterhead and Wick via Aberdeen. The Aberdeen company had run into financial difficulties due to severe competition from overland routes. It owned three steamers, the **Earnholm** which dated from 1874, the **James Crombie** completed for the company in 1904 and the **Silver City**, a smaller steamer which had been built in 1901.

The **Earnholm** originally had berths for 31 first class and 14 steerage class passengers, and was employed on the coastal service between Leith and Lossiemouth calling at Aberdeen, Buckie, Cromarty, Invergordon and Inverness. She had originally traded weekly from Glasgow to Limerick, calling at Galway once every alternative week. She was advertised in the *Glasgow Herald* as 'carrying passengers and goods (with liberty to tow vessels and to sail with or without pilots)', and with fares, 'including stewards fee', of 17/6d (cabin) single (return available for one month 25/-) or deck 8/-. She was described as having 'a good larder and a capital steward'.

The company operated a service from Leith to ports along the east coast of Scotland. At the end of the nineteenth century and until 1911 it was operated by two ships. The **Earnholm** and the **James Crombie** sailed from Leith on Mondays and Tuesdays. The ships also undertook special sailings. In 1895 the **Earnholm** was advertised to provide a 'spring holiday special sea excursion' on 10 April from Thornbush Pier, Inverness, to Invergordon and Cromarty; she made a special Queen's Birthday sailing ('unless prevented by any unforeseen occurrence') on 22 May to the same destinations; while on 2 July she sailed to Invergordon under the heading of 'Volunteers' Camp'. For the Inverness Summer Holiday of 1911 a 'Grand Sea Cruise' was advertised with the **James Crombie** scheduled to sail from Kessock Ferry for Lossiemouth, calling at Cromarty on both the outward and inward journeys. Fares for Lossiemouth were 3/6d (cabin) and 2/- (second cabin). The value of a passage by sea was emphasised in a letter to *The Bugler* (a journal for the Lossiemouth and Elgin neighbourhood) written in 1894 stated:

*Dear Mr Editor, I am surprised that the **Earnholm** does not call at Lossiemouth on her way back to Aberdeen. There can be no doubt that many, in these months of fine weather, would prefer to go south by sea rather than by rail. Is Mr Crombie [the company manager] not letting slip an opportunity by adding to the revenue of his company? It might be worthwhile, at any rate, making the experiment.*

By 1914 the service was operated by one ship, advertised as the 'Swift Screw Steamer, **James Crombie**', which was scheduled to 'sail as under, weather permitting', from Leith to Inverness on Mondays calling at Aberdeen, Buckie, Lossiemouth, Cromarty and Invergordon, returning from Inverness on Thursdays, with calls at Cromarty and Invergordon. The advertisement mentioned that 'the Steamers have superior accommodation for Passengers, and for Sheep, Cattle and other Live Stock'.

The *Earnholm* did not have an unblemished career. Although not of a particularly serious nature, in February 1898 she was delayed for some time in Buckie harbour because of severe north westerly gales. In 1909, on a south-bound voyage with a number of female herring workers on board, she struck rocks near Duncansby Head. Her rudder was damaged and she became unmanageable; she was picked up in fog by Stroma fishermen who towed her to Gills Bay, where she was anchored. After the fog cleared she was piloted by the Stroma fishermen to Wick, with temporary steering gear. On 29 October 1912, the *Earnholm* sank in a collision at Invergordon. She was lifted, repaired and put back in service but downgraded to cargo only, although the passenger berths and public

The *Earnholm* (1874) lying on the bottom after being sunk in collision at Invergordon in 1912.

rooms remained intact. The newer *James Crombie* could accommodate 40 first class passengers and was licensed to carry up to 310 deck passengers, while the smaller *Silver City* had accommodation for only a limited number of deck passengers, but in autumn 1914 was downgraded to cargo only.

The three ships were allowed to maintain their identity under Langlands' ownership, with black topped yellow funnels and black hulls with red boot topping. The business of the company carried on much as before, although on a greatly reduced scale and with wartime grey soon overcoming the company colours. The smallest of the steamers, the *Silver City*, was more than able to contend with the business on hand, while the other two ships were put to trading further afield. However, the small cargo deadweight capacity of the *James Crombie* and *Earnholm* relative to the Langlands cargo steamers limited their profitability and in June 1915 Langlands was able to sell the *James Crombie* to the Laird Line (George MacLellan, Thomas McIntyre and Sir Archibald Shaw), who were keen to replace wartime requisitions, and who renamed her *Broom*. She later became the *Dynamic* of the Belfast Steam Shipping Company, then the City of Cork Steam Packet Company's *Lismore*, before being re-acquired by the Belfast company in 1931, who renamed her *Ulster Star*. By a coincidence she sailed to Stornoway, one of Langlands' regular ports of call, when chartered by David MacBrayne during the Second World War.

In 1916 the passenger and cargo steamer *Earnholm* was 'swapped' for the cargo-only *Lady Tennant* owned by the Stornoway Steamship Company. This seemingly unlikely exchange suited both companies, giving the Stornoway company some passenger berths, albeit in need of refurbishment, to assist in the movement of military personnel on the Minches and supplying Langlands with a small cargo steamer to attend to the business of the Western Isles, so providing a means of shipping valuable cargoes to Liverpool for export. The *Lady Tennant* was registered in Glasgow under the ownership of Langlands & Sons, Liverpool and Glasgow. The *Broom*, *Earnholm*, *Silver City* and *Lady Tennant* all safely survived the war. The *Lady Tennant* operated away from the Scottish west coast under the direction of the Ministry of Shipping for a while in 1917. The *Earnholm* was finally lost on 5 January 1919, on voyage from Vaag to Aberdeen with a cargo of salted fish, when she foundered 17 miles south of the Faroe Islands. It was reported that the crew swam ashore to a rocky shore below cliffs; while the rest of the crew huddled there the second engineer managed to climb the cliffs and, in spite of a badly damaged knee, crawled about a mile toward a light and a house for help. The *Silver City* was sold in 1920 to Cullen, Allen & Company of Belfast; in 1928 she was sailing from Newfoundland and in 1947 sold to Venezuelan buyers before being deleted from Lloyd's Register in 1951.

Only six other ships in the Langlands fleet survived the war: *Princess Louise*, *Princess Beatrice*, *Princess Helena*, *Princess Ena*, *Princess Thyra* and *Princess Melita*. The remaining seven steamers, including all the main passenger units except the *Princess Louise* and *Princess Beatrice*, were lost (Table 1). The first casualty was the *Princess Olga* which was mined off Scarborough at 7.30pm on 16 December 1914. The mines were laid two days previously under cover of two German cruisers shelling the town of Scarborough. The 19 crew members of the *Princess Olga* had time to evacuate safely in the two ship's boats and stood by the vessel until she sank two hours after hitting the mine. The mate's boat arrived at Scarborough early the next morning while the men in the captain's boat had been picked up by the small steamer *Glen Rose* and landed at Scarborough later in the morning.

TABLE 1: Langlands steamers lost in the Great War

	Date of loss	Cause of loss	Voyage
Princess Olga	16 December 1914	Sunk by mine off Scarborough	Liverpool south about to Aberdeen
Princess Victoria	9 March 1915	Sunk by torpedo in Liverpool Bay	Aberdeen to Liverpool
Princess Caroline	13 August 1915	Sunk by mine off Kinnaird Head	Liverpool to Aberdeen
Princess Alberta	21 February 1917	Sunk by mine in Mudros Bay, Aegean Sea	Stavros to Mudros
Princess Dagmar	7 May 1918	Sunk by torpedo in Bristol Channel	Swansea to France
Princess Royal	26 May 1918	Sunk by torpedo off Cornwall	Swansea to Le Havre
Princess Maud	10 June 1918	Sunk by mine off Blyth	London to Leith

M. LANGLANDS & SONS.

ALL SAILINGS TO AND FROM THE PORT OF INVERNESS ARE MEANTIME TEMPORARILY SUSPENDED.

15 Union Street, Inverness,
7th August, 1914.

Emergency service announcements at the start of the Great War:
ABOVE: In the Inverness press on 7 August 1914.
RIGHT: Details for October 1914 in the Aberdeen press.

LANGLANDS' SAILINGS.
(RESTRICTED SERVICE.)

To INVERNESS
From LIVERPOOL............Wednesday, 7th October.
,, LEITH.....................Monday, 5th October.
,, ABERDEEN................Tuesday, 6th October.
Calling at Cromarty and Invergordon (and at Buckie and Lossiemouth.)

From INVERNESS
To ABERDEEN and LEITH......Thursday, 8th Oct.
To LIVERPOOL (via East Coast)—
Saturday, 10th October.

These Sailings are, owing to present conditions, subject to alteration. For full particulars apply to

M. LANGLANDS & SONS,
15 UNION STREET.

On 9 March 1915, at 9.15am, approaching the Liverpool Bar Lighthouse at the end of a voyage from Aberdeen with general cargo, the **Princess Victoria** was sunk by torpedo without warning. The torpedo was fired by U20. All 34 members of her crew were able to abandon ship before she sank and all were landed safely at Liverpool. The sinking of the **Princess Victoria** was graphically described in the *Highland News*:

*Messrs Langlands' steamer **Princess Victoria**, a well-known vessel at Stornoway, last week fell a victim to the German submarine pirates. Mr J D Bell, steward of the **Princess Victoria**, writing to Mr Duncan MacIver, fishcurer, gives the following account of the incident: 'I was in my room when the torpedo struck her. There was a great explosion and the old packet shook terribly fore and aft. I may tell you I was not prepared to get out of her so hurriedly. It was just after breakfast. I had shaved and washed and was just about to put my collar on when the infernal thing struck on the forepart of the bridge. I took off my slippers and donned my boots, vest, jacket and overcoat, and put my watch and chain and other little things which were on my table into my pockets. Then I went on deck and found two of the lifeboats already lowered, so I thought I had better get a move on myself. I went along the deck and up the ladder to the boat deck. The men who were already in the boat swung the lifeline into the ship's side and I swarmed down same into her. It was 9.05am Tuesday when she was struck, and at 9.25am there was nothing of the ship to be seen. One of the Great Yarmouth steam drifters, the **Ocean Harvest** picked us up. She has been patrolling in the vicinity of the Mersey since October last. They landed us at Liverpool landing stage at 2.00pm little the worse for our adventure. Several of the chaps on board lost all their kit, and I had to lend my coat to the first mate who had only his drawers and singlet on'.*

The **Princess Caroline** was the next victim when she hit a mine off Kinnaird Head on 13 August 1915 on passage to Aberdeen, as reported in the *Dundee Courier* on Monday 16 August 1915:

*Dundee trader is sunk, and four of the crew drowned: Information has been received of the sinking of a Dundee trader, the **Princess Caroline**, owned by M Langlands & Sons, Glasgow. The **Princess Caroline** is* *the third vessel of the line to be lost since the commencement of the war. Fifteen of her crew are saved and four are lost.*

While off the Moray Firth she was stopped at 6.00pm by a naval patrol and instructed to pass three miles to the east of her normal route to avoid a newly-laid minefield. Having moved away from the shore she struck a mine at 9.20pm which detonated beneath No 4 hatch blowing the hatch cover and part of the deck away. The **Princess Caroline** was carrying about 300 tons of general cargo and sank within three minutes of the explosion. Four men were believed killed when the mine went off but the others were able to lower the ship's boats and row ashore to the village of Pennan where they arrived at 7.00am the next day.

Operating costs were increasing as the war progressed. Dock labour shortages meant longer times for loading and unloading and coastal convoys required unarmed steamers to wait until a convoy was formed. From 1 May 1915 an increase in passenger fares was announced for the Glasgow and Liverpool service to 13/- cabin and 7/- steerage – there were no return fare packages on offer. In July the service reduced to weekly with departures from Glasgow on Saturday and return from Liverpool on Tuesday. This changed to Tuesday from Glasgow and Thursday from Liverpool in February 1916 but reverted to Saturday and Tuesday in April. Thereafter passengers were not carried and the service was operated as demand required. The same applied to the weekly boat to Manchester which now operated on an ad hoc schedule according to demand. Other services were maintained as best they could, although sailing schedules became haphazard as extended periods were required at each port for cargo handling and routes had to be varied under instruction from the Admiralty.

On 5 May 1916 the **Princess Maud**, then a defensively armed ship, was requisitioned and converted for duties as Fleet Messenger Y4.63. The **Princess Alberta** was also requisitioned in 1916 to become Fleet Messenger No 58. Although many of the Langlands crews stayed with both ships, they were supplemented by naval officers and men and specialists such as gunners and signalmen. It was while working in this role that the HMS **Princess Alberta** was lost in the Aegean Sea carrying a leave party from the 80th Infantry Brigade Regiment from Skyros Island to Mudros Bay. The submarine U23 had laid mines in the area and when HMS **Princess Alberta** arrived off Mudros Bay on Wednesday 21 February 1917 she struck and detonated one of these mines. Only 16 men in the leave party survived; nearly 100 men aboard HMS **Princess Alberta** lost their lives that day, including 35 members of the ship's company from both Merchant and Royal navies and two members of the Royal Marine Light Infantry. The soldiers aboard ship that lost their lives belonged to: Rifle Brigade, King's Royal Rifle Corps, King's Shropshire Light Infantry, Royal Field Artillery, Royal Engineers, The King's (Liverpool Regiment), Royal Army Medical Corps and Army Service Corps.

The **Princess Beatrice** had a run in with the Admiralty when she brushed alongside the anchored torpedo gunboat HMS **Leda**. Neither vessel was seriously damaged but the incident caused some embarrassment aboard the Langlands vessel.

A number of unusual voyages were made during the war. For example, the **Princess Louise** was used briefly on the Penzance to Isles of Scilly ferry run during the mackerel season in 1917, while other vessels visited many ports not normally associated with Langlands.

On 4 February 1918 the Fleet Messenger HMS **Princess Maud** was decommissioned and returned to Langlands management. No more ships were lost for nearly fifteen months, but on 7 May 1918 the big defensively armed cargo steamer **Princess Dagmar** was sunk by torpedo in the Bristol Channel. She had loaded a cargo of coal at Swansea and was destined for a French port when submarine U54 struck without warning. The heavily loaded ship sunk rapidly and the master and 23 of the crew lost their lives.

On 26 May 1918 at 4.15am the **Princess Royal** was torpedoed and sunk in the English Channel 3 miles WNW of St Agnes Head by submarine U101 whilst on a voyage from Swansea to Le Havre with general cargo including a large consignment of heavy steel billets. Although 19 lives were lost, the ship's two apprentices survived to tell the tale and were transferred to the **Princess Louise** to continue their training. Two weeks later, on 10 June 1918, the **Princess Maud** was sunk by torpedo 5 miles NE by N from Blyth, probably by U74. She was on passage from London to Leith with general cargo; 3 lives were lost, 26 saved. Five months later, on the eleventh hour of the eleventh day of the eleventh month, the armistice agreed earlier that day came into effect.

The war had been extremely costly for Langlands. The company had maintained its coastal services with the limited resources it had at hand, as ships were either requisitioned for Admiralty duties or taken up for commercial voyages on instruction from the Ministry of Transport. Langlands & Sons emerged into peace, stunned by its own human and physical losses and now with only half the ships afloat that it had at the start of the war. There was one cargo ship laid down, but not at an advanced stage of construction, on the stocks at Middlesbrough. Financially it was reasonably well resourced, having received lucrative charter fees for the **Princess Alberta** and **Princess Maud** while they were on active duty, and it was in line for extensive compensation payments for ship losses. But there was no way it could resume business at the pre-war scale, nor was there business on offer to warrant this. Resumption of its passenger services was nigh impossible with the loss of four of its five main passenger units including its cherished flagship the **Princess Royal**. It would take time to rebuild business and for the national economy to recover as industry slowly tried to return to civilian duties. Messrs Langlands & Sons would have to bide its time and little by little rebuild its own business.

In the event this did not happen as circumstances were to overtake it, as described in the *Aberdeen Journal* on Thursday 16 October 1919:

Shipping Combine, Messrs Langlands & Sons, Glasgow: The firm of Messrs Langlands & Sons, Glasgow and Liverpool, has passed into the control of Messrs Powell, Bacon & Hough of Liverpool, whose variety of interests in the coastwise shipping trade are grouped under the title of the Coast Lines.

By the combination of forces, most of the better known coasting firms of the UK are merged in one large organisation, which operates practically in every port. The British & Irish Steam Packet Company, which is stated to have acquired the Tedcastle Line, Dublin, and also the Irish coastal interests of the London Maritime Investment Company [a Royal Mail Steam Packet subsidiary which had earlier bought the five ships of the City of Dublin Steam Packet Company], is one of the subsidiary organisations of Messrs Powell, Bacon & Hough, the Chairman of which is Mr Alfred H Read. The City of Dublin Steam Packet Company was acquired recently by him in conjunction with the Coast Line, and the Cork Steam Packet Company and the Limerick Steamship Company passed into the group at earlier dates.

Messrs Langlands began business in 1839 with sailings between the Clyde and the Mersey. Later the scope of their concerns was extended to both the east and west coasts of Scotland and in more recent times to all the large English ports. The value of their coordination with the Coast Lines will be that there will not be a port of any pretensions in the UK not included in the regular sailings which it is hoped to arrange soon as nearly on pre-war lines as possible. The amalgamation will control about four-fifths of the tonnage in the coasting trade.

At first Mr Read allowed the Langlands business to retain its identity and its ships their rightful **Princess** names and livery. The business was very much as before and included a weekly sailing from Liverpool to Leith, weekly round-Britain sailings and an ad hoc service between Liverpool or Manchester and Greenock and Glasgow. Coast Lines sanctioned the order of three engines aft cargo steamers of similar design to the **Princess Irma** although slightly larger in capacity. However, in 1920 there was a change of heart and the Langlands fleet was rebranded and the ships given corporate 'Coast Lines' names, while the only surviving major passenger unit in the group, the **Princess Beatrice**, was sold to the Carron Line of Grangemouth to become the **Avon**. The Carron Company was undecided whether to resume passenger carrying other than on a small scale post-war and it saw the **Avon** as a useful addition to its fleet should passengers again become profitable.

The shelter deck cargo steamer building at Middlesbrough and ordered in the war was finally launched on 23 March 1920 and christened **Princess Olga**. She was delivered in May and promptly renamed **Lancashire Coast** and painted up with the black funnel and white chevron of her new owners. The first two of the triplets ordered through Coast Lines were allocated the names **Princess Dagmar** and **Princess Caroline**, but at their launches from the Harland & Wolff yard at Govan in October and December 1920 they were christened **Gorilla** and **Redbreast** and placed under the management of G & J Burns when delivered in February 1921 and February 1922 respectively. Built as single-deck ships with one hold, they were altered in 1925 to shelter deck ships, the original main deck becoming the shelter deck with the forecastle extending back to the bridge to become the new weather deck. At the same time the large hold was divided into two equal length holds with cargo handling machinery placed between the hatches. The third ship in the trio was launched from the Inglis yard at Pointhouse as G & J Burns' **Lurcher** in September 1922.

The one-time **Princess Caroline** remained under the Red Ensign with the Coast Lines group throughout her career. She was reboilered in 1951 and ended up on the weekly Belfast to Manchester service as **Lairdsbrook** until sold for demolition in 1960. Her sister, complete with her original boiler, was sold for demolition in 1954 as the **Ulster Merchant**.

The shelter deck steamer **Princess Olga** (1920) was ordered during the war as a consort to
Princess Irma (1915) and was renamed **Lancashire Coast** shortly after she was commissioned.
The **Lancashire Coast** is seen lying at Pomona Docks in Manchester.

(J Clarkson)

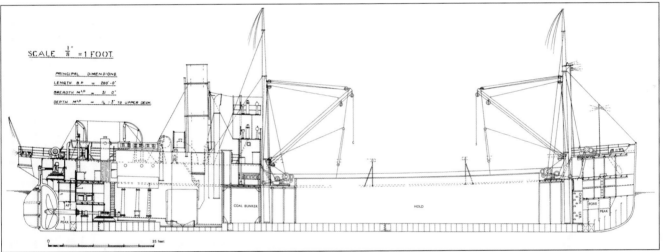

Builder's drawing of the single-deckers intended to be named **Princess Dagmar** and **Princess Caroline**.

The **Princess Dagmar** (1921) was launched as the **Gorilla** and is seen here in the late 1930s as
Coast Lines' **Cambrian Coast**. Note the weather deck and cargo handling gear (see the builder's
drawing above for original design).

(B & A Feilden)

Although the name **Princess Caroline** was allocated to this ship she was launched as the **Redbreast** (1921) for G & J Burns. She was the last former Langlands steamer to fly the Red Ensign when she was finally sent to the scrapyard in 1960 having ended her days as the **Lairdsbrook** as seen here.

Under Coast Lines management the Langlands survivors were put to serve whichever route they best suited and few of them were seen on their design routes after 1920. For example, the Liverpool to Leith service became the province of the **Hampshire Coast**, a big engines aft steamer originally built to serve the Liverpool to London trade of F H Powell & Company and dating from 1911. The Liverpool to Bristol service and the Aberdeen to Bristol service were advertised as Coast Lines (Langlands Service) between the wars although this designation was dropped thereafter.

Coast Lines did recognise the revenue-earning potential of the Langlands' yachting cruises and reinstated the summer ritual of holidays on the briny. It employed a number of its passenger ships on cruise duties both between the wars, when the adopted marketing brand was 'Langlands Yachting Cruises', and again during the early 1950s. From 1922 to 1926 the Burns & Laird Lines' **Tiger** was deployed as the summer cruise yacht, and the new Dublin steamer **Lady Louth** stood in for a couple of her cruises in July 1923 when the Liverpool to Dublin ferry service was strikebound.

The dedicated cruising yacht **Killarney** took over in 1927. She had been built in 1893 as the **Magic** for the Belfast Steamship Company; she was later renamed **Classic** and when transferred to the City of Cork company was given the name **Killarney**. She was based at Liverpool and called at Ardrossan before proceeding to the Western Isles on a ten-day round trip. At the start and end of each season she undertook a round-Britain cruise. When she first arrived on the west coast in June 1927, the *Highland News* was prompted to write:

*The arrival of the **Killarney** .... recalled pleasant memories of pre-war days when Messrs Langlands' splendidly equipped steamers, with their courteous and efficient officers and men called regularly each week and helped materially in the social activities of the town. We were delighted to welcome old friends in Captain Rendall, in charge of the **Killarney**; Mr Mara, superintendent steward of the Coast Line; Mr Bell, chief steward, and Mr Duncan Fletcher, quartermaster, all of the former Langlands, with its traditions for courtesy and the care and comfort of the passengers. These have now been carried into the yachting business of Coast Lines.*

TWIN-SCREW STEAM YACHT "KILLARNEY" 2150 TONS.
(Oil-burning).

CRUISES THROUGH THE WESTERN HIGHLANDS.
(LANGLANDS SERVICES)

COAST LINES LTD., 19 CASTLE STREET, LIVERPOOL

RIGHT: The **Killarney** (1893) advertising cruises under the banner 'Cruises through the Western Highlands (Langlands' Services)' and advising clients that she was an oil burner in an attempt to bring her up to date.

(Linda Gowans collection)

After the Second World War the tradition was continued by another former ferry, the **Lady Killarney**, although the Langlands branding was no longer used. The **Lady Killarney** was the former **Patriotic** dating from 1912. She had a dining saloon that could seat one hundred at a time, a panelled smoke room and a card room. In 1953 she initiated cruises that included visits to National Trust for Scotland gardens. Her final cruise ended at Liverpool on 27 September 1956 and had taken her passengers to Lamlash and Corrie, Tobermory, Ballachulish, Oban and Crinan. Plans for the Coast Lines relief steamer **Irish Coast** to operate the cruises in 1957 fell through but the Langlands legacy did continue a little longer. Between 1958 and 1966 summer cruises to a variety of destinations, including the Western Isles, were offered by British Railways Heysham steamer **Duke of Lancaster**. Various operators from home and abroad have since offered cruises to the Western Isles but the memory of M Langlands & Sons had long been forgotten.

A State Room S/Y "KILLARNEY".

YACHTING CRUISES FROM LIVERPOOL
TO THE SCOTTISH FJORDS.
COAST LINES LTD. (LANGLANDS SAILINGS)
ROYAL LIVER BUILDING, LIVERPOOL.

LEFT: A state room aboard the venerable steam yacht **Killarney** (1893).

BELOW: The **Lady Killarney** (1912) approaching Prince's Landing Stage at Liverpool in 1956 after one of the very last 'yachting cruises'.

(B & A Feilden)

It is a great shame that so little of the Glasgow & Liverpool Royal Steam Packet Company and M Langlands & Sons company records survived. Most of the Langlands company files and records had to be destroyed after rotting in storage in a damp Liverpool warehouse for many decades. Over the years a great deal of fabrication has developed in the telling of the Langlands history, but inspection of newspaper reports and advertisements along with a variety of official public records has allowed a reliable record of

the company to be assembled. Langlands was clearly a very proud business run to the highest possible standards with the highest calibre of staff. It was unable to recover from the devastation of the Great War and welcomed the overtures from Alfred Read to be absorbed into the burgeoning Coast Lines group in 1919. It can only be a matter for conjecture that, had it not been for the War, who knows, Langlands might have been able to give Mr Read a run for his money, and compete against Coast Lines, although the latter had already cosied up to the Royal Mail Group as described in *The Tyne-Tees Steam Shipping Company and its Associates*:

F H Powell & Company, John Bacon Limited and Samuel Hough Limited amalgamated their services, many of which were shared routes, to form Powell, Bacon and Hough Lines in 1913, under the directorship of Chairman Sir Alfred Read (also a Colonel). The company was rebranded Coast Lines in April 1917 when Read, now appointed company Chairman, oversaw the majority shareholding being acquired by the Royal Mail group. Read took Powell, Bacon and Hough into Royal Mail ownership in order to cement the coastal feeder deal for the Royal Mail group's network of deep sea cargo liners, and to draw on the massive resources of the Royal Mail empire to develop the Coast Lines network. Read went on a shopping spree using resources from the Royal Mail group to buy... M Langlands & Sons and British & Irish and the City of Cork company in 1917 and 1918, Belfast Steamship Company in 1919, and Burns and Laird was formed soon afterwards with the purchase of the Laird Line and G & J Burns in 1920. George Bazeley & Sons at Penzance and its three ships were bought out, also in 1920. Sir Alfred Read was invested as a Knight Bachelor in 1919.

And so it was that the vision of the Langlands family went forward under the guidance of Sir Alfred Read. It was remembered as a commercial entity between the wars on the Liverpool to Leith and round-Britain routes operated by Coast Lines and was branded 'Coast Lines (Langlands Service)'. The Langlands dynasty was sadly overlooked thereafter and has been almost completely forgotten by shipping historians. Let it now be remembered as a key part of the Coast Lines empire, and a major contributor to the success of the Coast Lines Group.

THE LANGLANDS FAMILY DYNASTY

Mathew Langlands was born in 1798 in Campbeltown, Argyllshire, the son of Ralph Langlands, a bleacher, and Jean Fleming. Jean's father was Mathew Fleming, and it appears Mathew Langlands took his name. Mathew Langlands married Janet, née Watson, who was born in 1801 also in Campbeltown. They had ten children: Martha Stevenson in Glasgow May 1824, Ralph born in Glasgow 1826, William Watson born in Campbeltown in 1828, Jean and Harriet born in Ireland in 1829 and 1831, John in Glasgow 1834, Janet born in Glasgow in October 1835, James W born in Glasgow and Mathew in Ireland in 1838 and 1839 respectively, and finally Elizabeth born in Glasgow 1841. Janet was assisted at home by a housekeeper and a cook. The family lived at Kent Place, Barony, on the north side of the river in Glasgow, near to where Strathclyde University's Barony Hall now stands, and later moved to a bigger house at 247 St Vincent Street. In the 1841 census Mathew Langlands described himself as 'Steam packet agent'. Martha married Robert Stewart in 1852.

In 1851 Alexander Langlands, from Mathew's family, and born in September 1810 in Campbeltown, took up an appointment as the Stranraer agent for the Glasgow & Stranraer Steam Packet Company. Alexander was watched closely as Mathew (senior) was the company agent in Glasgow. Alexander also had a large family and he and his wife Helen produced ten children.

By 1851 John and William were employed as 'Agents clerks' in the Langlands office in Glasgow, while the other children were still at school. John became a partner with his father in the Glasgow office to form M Langlands & Son, Glasgow, in 1857. In April 1862 William also became a partner in Langlands & Son, which now became Langlands & Sons, when he moved to Liverpool to form the shipping agents MacMillan and Langlands. In due course James and Mathew (junior) also joined the family firm. James also moved south and lived at Tranmere. He later set up in business on his own as a general produce broker.

Mathew died after contracting pneumonia on 28 April 1862, aged 64. John Langlands assumed the role of head of the company.

Jean Langlands married John Wingate in 1862 and confusingly John Langlands married Jane Wingate, born in 1835, at Glasgow in November 1862. John and Jane Langlands lived at 3 Hamilton Drive, Hillhead in Partick, later moving next door to a detached town house at 5 Hamilton Drive. They had five children: Ralph Erskine born 22 January 1865, Alexander Wingate born 18 January 1866, Alice and Florence born respectively in 1868 and 1869, and Mathew Herbert born 22 October 1871. John Langlands, head of Langlands & Sons, lived at 2 Montague Terrace, Kelvinside, and died at Partick in October 1889, aged 56. Mathew, his brother, then took charge of Langlands & Sons at Liverpool. He died in 1906.

John Langlands' three sons all joined Langlands & Sons. Mathew moved to Liverpool, which had become the focus of operations, and Alexander and Ralph stayed in Glasgow but later also moved south. Ralph married Ethel Valentine of Belfast in 1892 and they had a daughter Edith in 1894. Ralph and his family lived at Heswall in Cheshire and he died in 1918 after taking charge of Langlands & Sons in 1906. Mathew later returned to Hillhead and died aged 64 in 1935.

Other families became intertwined with the Langlands through marriage and business. It was a close-knit, proud and hard-working family that strove always for quality and excellence. These were also the hallmarks of M Langlands & Sons and were reflected in the service the company provided and the calibre of the company's staff and even its ships, the latter complete with polished brass lettering at the stern and holystoned decks.

REFERENCES

Much use has been made of the British Library Newspaper Archive.

ARMSTRONG J 1991. *Railways and Coastal Shipping in Britain in the Late Nineteenth Century: co-operation and competition.* In C Wrigley and J Shepherd (Editors) *On the move: essays in labour and transport history presented to Philip Baywell.* The Hambledon Press, London and Ohio.

BAUR K J & ROBERTS S S 1991. *Register of Ships in the US Navy, 1775-1990, major combatants.* Greenwood Publishing Group, Westport Connecticut.

DONALDSON G 1978. *Northwards by Sea.* Paul Harris Publishing, Edinburgh.

DUCKWORTH C L D & LANGMUIR G E 1977. *Clyde and Other Coastal Steamers, 2nd edition.* T Stephenson & Sons, Prescot.

FLETCHER R A 1910. *Steam-Ships, the story of their development to the present day.* Sidgwick & Jackson Ltd, London.

FRASER W H & MARER I (Editors) 1996. *Glasgow 1830-1912.* Manchester University Press.

HEYL E 1953. *Early American Steamers.* Erik Heyl, Buffalo, Erie.

KENNEDY J 1903. *The History of Steam Navigation.* Charles Birchall, Liverpool.

McNEILL D B 1969. *Irish Passenger Steamship Services, Volume 1: North of Ireland.* David & Charles, Newton Abbot.

REID R 1884. *Glasgow Past and Present.* David Robertson & Company.

ROBINS N S 2011. *Manchester Liners - an extraordinary story.* Bernard McCall, Portishead.

ROBINS N S 2011. *Coastal Passenger Liners of the British Isles.* Seaforth Publishing, Barnsley.

ROBINS N S 2014. *The Tyne-Tees Steam Shipping Company and its Associates.* Bernard McCall, Portishead.

WAINE C V 1999. *Coastal and Short Sea Liners.* Waine Research Publications, Wolverhampton.

FLEET LISTS

Aberdeen, Leith & Moray Firth Steam Shipping Company (bought by M Langlands & Sons 1914)

Name	AL&MF service	Gross tons	Comments
Earnholm	1882-1916	418	Built 1874 as *Earnholm* for Hugh McPhail & Co (Clyde & West Scotland Direct Steamers); exchanged 1916 for Stornoway Shipping Co's *Lady Tennant*, which was put into the fleet of M Langland's & Sons (see below)
Silver City	1901-1920	313	Sold to Cullen, Allen & Co, Belfast 1920, no change of name; sold 1924 to Wilson & Reid, Belfast, no change of name; sold 1928 to W A Munn, St John's, Newfoundland, no change of name; sold 1938 to Job Bros & Co, St John's, Newfoundland, no change of name; re-engined 1939; out of register 1951
James Crombie	1904-1915	576	Sold to Laird Line 1915 and renamed *Broom*; transferred 1922 to Belfast Steamship Co and renamed *Dynamic*; transferred to City of Cork Steam Packet Co 1922 and renamed *Lismore*; transferred to Belfast Steamship Co 1931 and renamed *Ulster Star*; scrapped 1949

Pre-1914 fleet member was: *James Hall* (1888-1904)

Galloway Steam Navigation Company (managed by M Langlands from 1843 and bought by M Langlands & Sons 1876 when the company was wound up)

Name	GSN service	Gross tons	Comments
Countess of Galloway	1847-1876	451	Paddle steamer; new engines 1859; sold to M Langlands & Sons

Pre-1876 fleet member was *Countess of Galloway* 1835-1847

Glasgow & Liverpool Royal Steam Packet Company

Name	G&LRSP service	Gross tons	Comments
Royal Sovereign	1839-1843	308	Paddle steamer; sold 1843 to Henry F Denny, Liverpool; resold 1846 to G Kilby and M Edwards, Calcutta and converted to sailing ship (barque); sold 1848 to J Ray, London; June 1848 foundered 35 miles west of Toe Head, Co Cork
Royal George	1839-1847	288	Paddle steamer; chartered for use in the Mediterranean from April 1845 and sold in June 1847
Princess Royal	1841-1856	447	Paddle steamer; new boilers 1856; wrecked on the Scaur of Laggan near Corsewall 26 May 1856
Princess Royal	1857-1860	779	Paddle steamer; sold to General Steam Navigation Co, London, renamed *Berlin*; scrapped 1875

Glasgow & New York Steam Shipping Company (bought by Inman Line (Liverpool & Philadelphia Steamship Company) 1859)

Name	G&NY service	Gross tons	Comments
Edinburgh	1855-1859	2,197	Acquired by Inman Line, Liverpool; chartered 1870 to H E Bates & Co; sold 1872 to Telegraph Construction & Maintenance Co, no change of name; sold 1879 to J W Adamson & T Ronaldson, London, no change of name; transferred 1881 to Stoomvaart Maatshappij 'Insulinde', Amsterdam and renamed *Amsterdam*; returned 1882 to J W Adamson & T Ronaldson, London and renamed *Edinburgh*; sold 1886 to Italian owners and renamed *Eridano*; sold 1907 to Italian naval authorities for use as static supply hulk; 1917 scrapped
Glasgow	1851-1859	1,962	Sold to William Inman, Liverpool; on fire and sank off Nantucket 31 July 1865
New York	1854-1858	2,049	Wrecked on Mull of Kintyre, 13 June 1858, on passage Glasgow to New York

Glasgow & South American Steamship Company

Name	G&SA service	Gross tons	Comments
Andes	1870-1877	1,505	Sold to Steiman & Ludwig (White Cross Line), Antwerp, and renamed *Hermann Ludwig*; foundered in the North Atlantic 28 September 1878
Alps	1871-1873	1,566	Sold to Steiman & Ludwig (White Cross Line), Antwerp, and renamed *C F Funch*; destroyed by fire in Flushing Roads 24 August 1876

Glasgow & Stranraer Steam Packet Company (bought by Langlands 1864)

Name	G&S service	Gross tons	Comments
Albion	1860-1865 1869-1879	307	Paddle steamer; built 1860 for Glasgow & Stranraer Steam Packet Co as *Albion*, registered owner James Reid, Glasgow; sold 1865 to Peter Lindsay Henderson, shipbroker, Liverpool, no change of name, and chartered to Somerset & Dorset Railway Co; sold 1867 to John Pool, Hayle, no change of name; sold 1968 to John S Bickford, Hayle, no change of name; sold 1869 to John Langlands, Glasgow, no change of name; sold 1879 to Mann Redhead, Liverpool; converted to sail 1882
Albion	1873-1868	224	Built 1865 as *Albion* for Glasgow & Stranraer Steam Packet Co; sold to London & Edinburgh Shipping Co, no change of name; sold 1880 to Lloyd Austro Ungarico and renamed *Pan*; sold 1891 to North West Railway Society, Piraeus, Greece and renamed *Caledon*; owners became North West Railway Co in 1918; scrapped 1932

Pre-1864 fleet members were *Maid of Galloway* (1836-1850); *Albion* (1844-1860); *Scotia* (1846-1863); *Briton* (1847-1855); *Caledonia* (1856-1862); *Briton* (1862 only)

Matthew Langlands

Name	ML service	Gross tons	Comments
Princess Royal	1861-1862	652	Registered owner Matthew Langlands, first screw steamer operated by Glasgow & Liverpool Royal Steam Packet Co; sold 1862 to J F Sichel, London as American blockade runner; captured by Federals and sold March 1863 by Philadelphia Prize Court to US Navy Department and commissioned as USS *Princess Royal*; sold 1865 to Samuel C Cook and renamed *General Sherman*; confiscated 1866 by Chinese Government and sold to Meadows & Co, Tientsin and resold to W B Preston, no change of name; beached and on fire near Pyongnang, Korea, 5 September 1866; taken by Korean Navy and refurbished; 1867 returned to Samuel C Cook; sold 1868 to William F Weld Company Boston (Merchants of Boston Steamship Company), no change of name; foundered off Wilmington, North Carolina, 10 January 1874

M Langlands & Sons

Name	ML&S service	Gross tons	Comments
Princess Royal	1863-1876	566	Lengthened by 29 feet and new compound engines 1870; sold and renamed *Juan G Meiks*, Havana
Blanche	1864-1867	234	Built 1863 as *Blanche* for H L Seligman, Glasgow; sold 1864 to Matthew Langlands, no change of name; sold 1867 to Joseph Weatherly, London, no change of name; 1872 to Weatherly, Mead & Hussey, London, no change of name; sold 1875 to Wm Lewis, Cardiff, no change of name; sold 1889 to Furness Withy, no change of name; sold 1892 to Osborn & Wallis, Bristol, no change of name; re-engined 1893; wrecked off Brittany, 15 July 1901
Princess Alice	1866-1890	572	Original registered owner John Langlands; to J & M Langlands 1870, reboilered and re-engined 1883; sold to Sociedad Isleña Maritima, Palma and renamed *Isleño*; sold 1928 to Cia Transmediterranea, Spain, no change of name; sold 1942 to Joachim Velasco Martin, Spain and renamed *Mina Entrago*; sold 1946 to Naviera del Nalon, Spain, no change of name; scrapped 1969

Name	Years	Tonnage	Notes
Tuskar	1872-1891	410	Built 1863 as *Tuskar* for Clyde Shipping Co, (original registered owner A G Kidston); sold 1869 to George A Mill, Dundee, no change of name; sold 1870 to Laing & Co, Montrose, no change of name; sold to John Langlands; new engines and boilers by Lees, Anderson & Co, lengthened by 9 feet 1877; wrecked on Skernaghan Rocks, Islandmagee, Co Antrim on 27 November 1891 on passage from Dundee to Liverpool
Fairy Queen	1874-1877	345	Built 1861 as *Fairy Queen* for R W Jackson, West Hartlepool; sold 1863 to Long & Curtis, West Hartlepool, no change of name; sold 1865 to W S Leng, West Hartlepool; sold 1866 to Wm. H Scott, Newcastle, no change of name; sold 1869 to Chas Mitchell, Newcastle, no change of name; sold 1871 to Louis Merton, London, no change of name; sold 1873 to Alfred Davies, London, no change of name; sold 1874 to Thomas L Boyd, London, no change of name; sold 1874 to Matthew Langlands; ashore near Machrihanish, 19 July 1876; wrecked on Carr Rock, Firth of Forth, 28 December 1877, on passage Leith to Liverpool
Princess Beatrice	1874-1890	448	Original registered owner J & M Langlands; sold to W A Black, Glasgow, no change of name; wrecked on New Harbour Ledge, Isaacs Harbour, Nova Scotia, 17 September 1890
Countess of Galloway	1876-1880	451	Built 1874 for Galloway Steam Navigation Co (see above); scrapped
Princess Royal	1876-1901	876	New boilers 1885; sold 1901 to La Veloce Italiana and renamed *Calabria*; scrapped 1910
Enterprise	1878-1881	42	Built 1865 for John Barclay of Kirkcaldy; sold to Robert McDowall of Alloa 1873; registered owner J & M Langlands
Wasp	1878-1888	550	Built 1874 as *Wasp* for G & J Burns; Jointly owned with G & J Burns in 1878, later wholly-owned by Langlands; sunk following collision with the barque *Hypatia* in the Mersey, 11 July 1888
Princess Maud	1885-1893	732	Sold to V Salinas, Spain, and renamed *Sitges Hermanos*; sold 1902 to Maritime Isleña, Spain, renamed *Balear*; scrapped 1932
Princess Louise	1888-1919	1,029	New engines 1902; acquired by Coast Lines 1919; renamed *Clyde Coast* 1921; transferred to Burns & Laird Lines 1922 and renamed *Setter*; transferred to City of Cork Steam Packet Co and renamed *Macroom*; scrapped 1929
Princess Helena	1889-1902	709	Built 1867 as *Galvanic* for Belfast Steamship Co; 1877 lengthened by 24 feet; sold 1885 to Harland & Wolff; sold 1886 to John H McIlwaine, Belfast and resold to W A Grainger, D Grainger & V Grainger, Belfast, no change of name; 1887 new engines and boilers; to M Langlands & Sons; sold 1902 to Salinas, Shäfer y Ca, J Salinas Sempere, Alicante and Barcelona and renamed *Vincente Salinas*; sold 1916 to Linea de Vapores Tintoré, Barcelona and renamed *Angelia*; sold 1917 to Hijos de Enrique Gironella, Barcelona and renamed *Tirso*; sold 1922 to S A Franco-Española de Navegacion, Barelona, no change of name; sold 1925 to Hijo di Ramon A Ramos, Barcelona and renamed *Manuela C de R*; scrapped 1934
Princess Irene	1891-1906	763	Wrecked off Linney Head, Pembrokeshire, 20 August 1906
Princess Sophia	1892-1913	502	Built as *Topaz* 1891 for William Robertson, Glasgow; bought 1892 by M Langlands & Sons and renamed *Princess Sophia*; sold 1913 to Clydeside Steamship Co, J B Couper manager, Glasgow and renamed *Clydebrae*; registered owner Albert Chester 1916, no change of name; torpedoed 3 miles east of Scarborough on voyage Calais to Middlesbrough, beached and later salvaged and re-engined, as owned by North of England Protecting and Indemnity Association; 1918 sold to J Craig, J S Todd manager, Belfast, no change of name; ownership transferred to Hugh Craig & Co, Belfast 1926; scrapped at Dublin 1958
Princess Beatrice	1893-1920	1,033	Sold to Carron Line, Grangemouth 1920 and renamed *Avon*; scrapped 1928
Princess Mary	1894-1908	657	Wrecked near Peterhead, 30 May 1908
Princess Victoria	1894-1915	1,135	Sunk by torpedo 16 nautical miles, north by north west of Liverpool Bar light vessel, 9 March 1915
Princess Ena	1898-1908	636	Sold to Bosphorus Steam Navigation Co (Chirketri-Heire) and renamed *Mushteri*; wrecked Busheira Reef, on passage Jeddah to Hodeida, Yemen 30 May 1909
Princess Thyra	1899-1905	602	Built 1894 as *Citrine* for William Robertson, Glasgow; bought 1899 by M Langlands & Sons and renamed *Princess Thyra*; sold 1905 to William Robertson, Glasgow and renamed *Bronzite*; sold 1946 to G A Sheves and renamed *Archgrove*; scrapped 1957
Princess Olga	1901-1914	998	Sunk by mine 5 nautical miles east north east of Scarborough, 16 December 1914 on passage Liverpool to Aberdeen
Princess Maud	1902-1918	1,463	Sunk by torpedo 5 nautical miles north east by north of Blyth, Northumberland, 10 June 1918, on passage London to Leith

Princess Patricia	1903-1911	837	Wrecked on Dippin Point, Isle of Arran, 19 October 1911, on passage Manchester to Glasgow
Princess Alberta	1905-1917	1,252	Sunk by mine, 21 February 1917, on passage Stavros to Mudros
Princess Helena	1905-1919	733	Acquired by Coast Lines 1919, no change of name; renamed *Moray Coast* 1920; sold 1935 to J N Vlassopoulos, Ithaca, and renamed *Olga*; sold 1936 to Danube Steamship Trading Co of London and renamed *Olga S*; sold 1937 to Cape Lines, London and renamed *Caper*; sold 1938 to Alcyone Shipping Finance Co, London and renamed *Pacifico*; 1939 requisitioned; scuttled at Dunkirk as a blockship 4 June 1940
Princess Dagmar	1907-1918	968	Sunk by torpedo in the Bristol Channel, 7 May 1918, on passage Swansea to France
Princess Ena	1908-1919	665	Built as *Glenariff* 1892 for Antrim Iron Ore Co; acquired by Coast Lines 1919; renamed *Fife Coast* 1920; sold 1932 to G Rizzo and renamed *Siciliano*; sold 1937 to L Mangiarotti and renamed *Mino*; sold 1939 to L Messina and renamed *Amalia Messina*; scrapped in Italy 1947
Princess Thyra	1909-1919	781	Acquired by Coast Lines 1919; renamed *Orkney Coast* 1921; sold to Oy Wirma, Kulosaari, Finland 1937 and renamed *Wilpas*; sunk by gunfire, off Vasa, 29 December 1939
Princess Caroline	1910-1914	888	Sunk by mine 14 nautical miles north east of Kinnaird Head, 13 August 1915, on passage Liverpool to Aberdeen
Princess Royal	1912-1918	1,981	Sunk by torpedo 3 nautical miles west north west of St Agnes Head, Cornwall, 26 May 1918, on passage Swansea to Le Havre
Princess Melita	1912-1919	1,094	Acquired by Coast Lines 1919, renamed *Highland Coast* 1920; sold 1938 to D Tripcovich & Ci SA di Nav, Rimorchi e Salvataggi, Trieste and renamed *Tripolino*; sunk by torpedo (RAF), 1 November 1942, on passage Benghazi to Tobruk
Princess Irma	1915-1919	1,122	Acquired by Coast Lines 1919; renamed *Cheshire Coast* 1920; sold to Union d'Enterprises Marocaines, Casablanca 1946 and renamed *Caid Allal*; sold to Simon D Attar, Casablanca 1951 and renamed *Rab*; scrapped 1955
Lady Tennant	1916-1919	492	Built 1904 as *Lady Tennant* for Nobel's Explosives Co, Ardeer; sold 1914 to Stornoway Shipping Co, no change of name; sold 1916 to M Langlands & Sons, no change of name; acquired by Coast Lines 1919, no change of name; transferred 1920 to British & Irish Steam Packet Co, no change of name; transferred 1923 to Coast Lines and renamed *Elgin Coast*; renamed *Kilkenny* 1930; sold 1936 to H W B Ohlmeier, Hamburg and renamed *Lisa*; sold 1962 to T O & H T Vavatsioulas of Thessaloniki and renamed *Orestis*; sold 1969 to A Pastrikos & G&D Papageorgiou of Thessaloniki and renamed *Margio*; scrapped 1974
Princess Olga	1920	1,104	Ordered by M Langlands & Sons 1916 as a consort to *Princess Irma* but delivery delayed until May 1920 after the Coast Lines acquisition; renamed *Lancashire Coast* 1920; to Belfast Steamship Co 1947 and renamed *Ulster Hero*; scrapped 1954
Princess Dagmar	1921	758	Launched as *Gorilla* for G & J Burns after Langlands' identity dropped in March 1920; 1925 renamed *Cumberland Coast* for Coast Lines; 1929 renamed *Kinsale* for City of Cork Steam Packet Co; 1933 renamed *Cambrian Coast* for Coast Lines; 1947 renamed *Ulster Merchant* for Belfast Steamship Co; scrapped 1954
Princess Caroline	1921	760	Launched as *Redbreast* for G & J Burns after Langlands' identity dropped in March 1920; 1925 renamed *Sutherland Coast* for Coast Lines; 1930 renamed *Lairdsbrook* for Burns & Laird Lines; scrapped 1960
Name not allocated	1922	774	Launched as *Lurcher* for G & J Burns after Langlands' identity dropped in March 1920; 1925 renamed *Scottish Coast* for Coast Lines; 1938 renamed *Ulster Coast* for Belfast Steamship Co; 1954 sold to Ahern Shipping Co, Montreal and renamed *Ahern Trader*; wrecked 10 January 1960 in Gander Bay, Newfoundland

Tod & McGregor (managed by M Langlands)

Name	T&M service	Gross tons	Comments
City of Glasgow	1850	1,609	Sold to Inman Line (Liverpool & Philadelphia Steamship Co), no change of name; wrecked March 1854 on passage Liverpool to Philadelphia
City of New York	1851	2,360	Sold to William Inman, renamed *City of Manchester*; sold and converted to barque 1871; 1876 wrecked

APPENDIX 2

J & G BURNS AND G & J BURNS STEAMERS BUILT FOR THE CLYDE TO MERSEY SERVICE BETWEEN 1828 AND 1922

After Ernest Reader, 1949, *Sea Breezes, Vol 8*, pp104-129

Ship	Type	Built	Gross tons	Horsepower
Glasgow	Wood-hulled paddle steamer	1828	280	250
Ailsa Craig	Wood-hulled paddle steamer	1829	297	250
Liverpool	Wood-hulled paddle steamer	1830	330	340
City of Glasgow	Wood-hulled paddle steamer	1830	300	300
John Wood	Wood-hulled paddle steamer	1832	370	340
Clyde	Wood-hulled paddle steamer	1832	342	360
Manchester	Wood-hulled paddle steamer	1832	385	400
Gazelle	Wood-hulled paddle steamer	1832	300	250
Vulcan	Wood-hulled paddle steamer	1834	450	450
Colonsay	Wood-hulled paddle steamer	1834	711	560
Eagle	Wood-hulled paddle steamer	1835	640	560
City of Glasgow	Wood-hulled paddle steamer	1835	650	560
Unicorn	Wood-hulled paddle steamer	1836	649	560
Commodore	Wood-hulled paddle steamer	1837	705	820
Actœon	Wood-hulled paddle steamer	1838	685	640
Fire King	Wood-hulled paddle steamer	1838	564	570
Achilles	Wood-hulled paddle steamer	1839	992	1,000
Admiral	Wood-hulled paddle steamer	1840	930	900
Orion	Iron-hulled paddle steamer	1846	899	1,120
Lyra	Iron-hulled paddle steamer	1849	592	260
Camilla	Iron-hulled paddle steamer	1849	529	560
Beaver	Iron-hulled screw steamer	1854	365	320
Zebra	Iron-hulled screw steamer	1855	792	1,020
Otter	Iron-hulled screw steamer	1855	473	470
Panther	Iron-hulled paddle steamer	1856	702	930
Leopard	Iron-hulled paddle steamer	1858	691	930
Harrier	Iron-hulled screw steamer	1858	384	300
Heron	Iron-hulled screw steamer	1860	624	600
Ostrich	Iron-hulled screw steamer	1860	624	600
Penguin	Iron-hulled screw steamer	1864	680	720
Beagle	Iron-hulled screw steamer	1864	454	400
Snipe	Iron-hulled screw steamer	1866	638	650
Raven	Iron-hulled screw steamer	1868	778	650
Bison	Iron-hulled screw steamer	1871	1,015	700
Owl	Iron-hulled screw steamer	1873	923	1,335
Spaniel	Steel-hulled screw steamer	1895	1,174	1,800
Pointer	Steel-hulled screw steamer	1896	1,183	1,800
Lurcher	Steel-hulled screw steamer	1906	993	1,600
Setter	Steel-hulled screw steamer	1906	993	1,600
Setter	Steel-hulled screw steamer	1920	1,216	1,700

INDEX OF SHIP NAMES

The date in brackets is the year each vessel was built.